Java™
Methods AB

Data Structures

Maria Litvin
Phillips Academy, Andover, Massachusetts

Gary Litvin
Skylight Software, Inc.

Skylight Publishing
Andover, Massachusetts

Skylight Publishing
9 Bartlet Street, Suite 70
Andover, MA 01810

web: http://www.skylit.com
e-mail: sales@skylit.com
           support@skylit.com

Library of Congress Control Number: 2002093456

ISBN 0-9654853-1-5

1 2 3 4 5 6 7 8 9   07 06 05 04 03

Printed in the United States of America

To our parents

Brief Contents

---

* AP and Advanced Placement Program are registered trademarks of the College Entrance Examination Board, which was not involved in the production of this book. The use of the College Board's trademarks does not constitute endorsement by the College Board.

Contents

Preface

This book has two purposes. First, it explains standard data structures and algorithms — lists, stacks, queues, trees, priority queues, hashing — and their implementation in Java. Second, it introduces elements of object-oriented software design and illustrates them in many case studies and labs. The book covers the material required for the AB-level Advanced Placement computer science course that is not covered in the A-level course. This is roughly equivalent to a typical Data Structures (CS2) college course.

Java Methods AB: Data Structures continues *Java Methods: An Introduction to Object-Oriented Programming* (Skylight Publishing, 2001: ISBN 0-9654853-7-4). There are obvious similarities in format and style between this book and *Java Methods*, but the material covered here does not directly depend on any specific material in *Java Methods*. We assume that the reader is familiar with Java within the scope covered in Chapters 3-12 and 17 of *Java Methods*: data types; arithmetic; control statements; arrays and strings; classes, constructors, and methods; private, public, or static fields and methods; encapsulation; inheritance and polymorphism. Some knowledge of recursion and the basic sorting algorithms presented in *Java Methods* is helpful, too.

Although we use GUI with Swing in most case studies and labs, we do not expect any knowledge of graphics or Swing — we supply all the necessary GUI classes. At the same time, the case studies present numerous GUI/Swing examples.

Chapter 1 is a thorough review of classes and interfaces, abstraction, encapsulation, inheritance, and polymorphism. A reader familiar with these concepts should read it quickly, see if there are any gaps to be filled, and move on.

Chapters 2-7 deal with lists, stacks and queues, recursion, trees, hashing, and priority queues. Our discussion of these data structures stays within the AP Java subset and follows the AP guidelines for teachers and students: we discuss implementation ideas but do not go into all the technical details, focusing instead on the appropriate use of Java library classes. At the same time, end-of-chapter exercises provide ample opportunities for practice with code and implementation details. Each of these chapters has one or two case studies / labs, which illustrate the use of each data structure in a realistic setting. We believe that OOP projects can be fun and instructive at the same time.

Chapter 8 deals with big-O analysis of algorithms and reviews common sorting algorithms and their big-O properties: Selection Sort, Insertion Sort, Bubble Sort, Mergesort, Quicksort, and Heapsort. This chapter is a theoretical interlude.

Back to practical matters, Chapter 9 is a more extended lab project, *SafeTrade*, which models trading stocks in a stock exchange. This project combines many of the data structures discussed in the previous chapters. We discuss in detail the design of this application, in terms of both the data structures used and the best layout for classes and objects. This case study is suitable for a team project or for individual work.

Finally, Chapter 10 offers an introduction to OO design patterns and briefly discusses six popular patterns: Façade, Strategy, Singleton, Composite, Decorator, and Model-View-Controller. While knowledge of specific design patterns is not a part of the AP CS course, we feel it is important for the student to be aware of design issues in general and to get a glimpse of what lies beyond the classroom.

Without further delay, let us proceed with data structures!

How to Use This Book

The *Java Methods* companion web site —

> http://www.skylit.com/javamethods

— is an integral part of this book. It contains instructions on how to acquire and set up various Java development tools and documentation. It also has a downloadable version of all our student disk files (with the code for case studies, labs, and exercises), as well as appendices, web "footnotes," web links, errata, supplemental papers, and syllabi and technical support information for teachers.

✿   The web symbol indicates a "footnote" that is on the book's web site in the alphabetical list of "footnote" links.

▯   The disk icon marks those programs in the book that are included on the "student disk."

     This icon brings your attention to a lab exercise or a hands-on exploration of an example.

1.■, 2.◆ In exercises, a square marks an "intermediate" question that may require more thought or work than an ordinary question or exercise. A diamond marks an "advanced" question that could be treacherous or lead to unexplored territory — proceed at your own risk.

✓   A checkmark at the end of a question in the exercises means that a solution is included on your student disk. We have included solutions to about half of the exercises. They can be found in the Solutions ▯ folder on your student disk and on the book's web site.✿ABsolutions

A teacher's disk with solutions to all the labs and complete solutions to all the exercises is available free of charge to teachers who use this book as a textbook in their schools.

❖   ❖   ❖

(To a slightly different subject...)

We have provided `EasyReader` and `EasyWriter` classes to supplement Java's stream I/O classes. `EasyReader` lets you read numbers, characters, words, and strings from the console and from a text file. `EasyWriter` lets you write these data elements into a text file (or append data to an existing file). These classes are in the `EasyReader` 💾 folder on your student disk. You can combine these two classes into a `com.skylit.io` package and install it properly, but it may be easier at first to simply add one or both of them to your project. Each of these classes has a simple example in its source file, and a more detailed description is available in Appendix E✳ on the web. You can also generate standard HTML documentation from `EasyReader.java` and `EasyWriter.java` with *javadoc*.

About the Authors

Maria Litvin has taught computer science and mathematics at Phillips Academy in Andover, Massachusetts, since 1987. She is an Advanced Placement Computer Science exam reader and, as a consultant for The College Board, provides Java training for high school computer science teachers. Prior to joining Phillips Academy, Maria taught computer science at Boston University. Maria is co-author of *C++ for You++: An Introduction to Programming and Computer Science* (Skylight Publishing, 1998), one of the leading textbooks for high school computer science courses when C++ was the AP language. She is also the author of *Be Prepared for the AP Computer Science Exam* (Skylight Publishing, 1999) and co-author of *Java Methods* (Skylight Publishing, 2001). Maria is a recipient of the 1999 Siemens Award for Advanced Placement for Mathematics, Science, and Technology for New England.

Gary Litvin has worked in many areas of software development including artificial intelligence, pattern recognition, computer graphics, and neural networks. As founder of Skylight Software, Inc., he developed SKYLIGHTS/GX, one of the first visual programming tools for C and C++ programmers. Gary led in the development of several state-of-the-art software products including interactive touch screen development tools, OCR and handwritten character recognition systems, and credit card fraud detection software. Gary is co-author of *C++ for You++* and *Java Methods*.

public abstract class

ChapterOne

Classes and Interfaces

1.1   Prologue

If you go to a computer museum, you will find pictures of the first computers from the 1950s. Each of them was custom-designed and built, with special electronics for the CPU and memory. What is now inside a small laptop took up a whole room: rows of cabinets filled with vacuum tubes, connected by massive cables; as in a sci-fi movie, you could enter and walk inside. By contrast, modern computers are designed around standard components and built in automated factories. That's what makes it possible to put one on your lap for a reasonable price.

You won't find pictures of computer software in a museum. But if you could enter and walk around software systems, you would find all kinds of things, from rather elegant structures to huge monstrosities, often barely standing, with pieces held together by the software equivalent of string and duct tape. A small change in one place upsets the whole structure; more strings and tape and props become necessary to prevent the contraption from collapsing. Perhaps these specimens do belong in a museum after all! For better or worse, software remains mostly invisible, hidden behind thousands of lines of code. It is mysterious, sometimes even full of surprises (Figure 1-1).

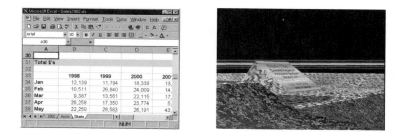

Figure 1-1.   Microsoft's *Office 97* version of *Excel*, a popular spreadsheet program used by millions of people for serious work ranging from financial forecasting to scientific modeling, has a well-hidden toy *Flight Simulator* built into it. Did a mischievous developer put it in? In *Excel 97*, press `Ctrl-G`, type `L97:X97`, press `Enter`, press `Tab`, then click on the "Chart Wizard" icon while holding the `Shift` and `Ctrl` keys down. Expert flying eventually reveals a monolith with the names of the product development team scrolling on it. Press `Esc` to return to the spreadsheet.

When we say that a computer program is "written," like a book or a tune, this implies an individual creative effort with few constraints. The notion of programs as being "written" influenced the way we thought about software for a long time. But a while ago, software researchers and professionals started asking themselves: Can we, instead, assemble computer programs from standard pre-tested software components, just as modern computers are assembled from ready-made hardware components? Object-oriented programming has taken up the task of realizing this dream.

The main goals of OOP are team development, software reusability, and easier program maintenance. The main OOP concepts and tools that serve these goals are abstraction, encapsulation, inheritance, and polymorphism. In this chapter we review these key concepts and their implementation in Java. We take a closer look at how Java uses classes and interfaces, inheritance hierarchies, and polymorphism to achieve the goal of better-engineered programs. Our case study and lab for this chapter is an applet that plays the *Chomp* board game with the user. It demonstrates abstraction, encapsulation, inheritance, and polymorphism.

1.2   Inheritance

As we know, in Java all objects belong to classes. A class defines the features and responsibilities of its objects: their fields (data elements) and methods. In strongly-typed computer languages, like Java, the class determines the data type of its objects.

> **Inheritance allows us to take a class and *extend* it, "inheriting" all the fields and methods of the *base class* in the *derived class*. The derived class can redefine some of the features or add new features.**

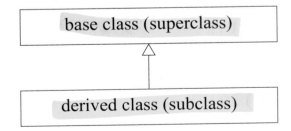

**Figure 1-2. Terminology and notation for inheritance:
base class is extended to make derived class**

The base class is also called the ***superclass***, and the derived class is also called the ***subclass*** (Figure 1-2). In Java, `super` is a reserved word that allows constructors and methods of the subclass to refer to constructors, methods, and fields of the superclass.

Several classes are often derived from the same class. A derived class may in turn become a base class for a new derivation, resulting in a hierarchy of classes. In Java, all classes belong to one big hierarchy derived from the most basic class, called `Object`. This class provides a few features common to all objects; more importantly, it makes sure that any object is an `Object`, an instance of the `Object` class, which is useful for implementing structures that can deal with any type of objects. If we start our own class "from scratch," then our class automatically extends `Object`. For example:

```
public class Player
{
    . . .
}
```

is equivalent to:

```
public class Player extends Object
{
    . . .
}
```

When we derive new classes from `Player`, we start building a class hierarchy for our application or package. For example:

```
public class HumanPlayer extends Player
{
    . . .
}

public class ComputerPlayer extends Player
{
    . . .
}
```

This results in the hierarchy shown in Figure 1-3.

The classes that lie closer to the top of the hierarchy are more general and abstract; the classes closer to the bottom are more specialized. Java allows us to formally define an ***abstract*** class. In an abstract class, some or all methods are declared `abstract` and left without code.

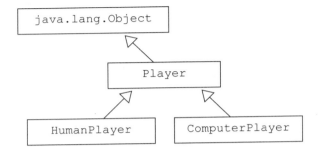

Figure 1-3. Player and two derived classes

> **An `abstract` method has only a heading: a declaration that gives the method's name, return type, and arguments. An `abstract` method has no code.**

For example, consider the definition of `Player` in Figure 1-4. All its methods are abstract. `Player` tells us what methods a player must have but does not tell us exactly how they work.

> **In an `abstract` class, some methods and constructors may be fully defined and have code supplied for them while other methods are `abstract`.**

A class may be declared abstract for other reasons, too. For example, some of the fields in an abstract class may belong to abstract classes.

More specialized subclasses of an abstract class have more and more methods defined. Eventually, down the inheritance line, the code is supplied for all methods.

> **A class where all the methods are fully defined and which has no abstract fields is called a *concrete* class.**

A program can only create objects of concrete classes. An object is called an *instance* of its class. An `abstract` class cannot be *instantiated*.

```
/**
 *  A player in a board game
 */

public abstract class Player
{
  /**
   *    Returns a prompt to be displayed before
   *    the next move of this player
   */
  public abstract String getPrompt();

  /**
   *    Returns a message to be displayed when
   *    this player has won
   */
  public abstract String getWinMessage();

  /**
   *    Called to initiate this player's next move
   */
  public abstract void makeMove();
}
```

Figure 1-4.   The abstract class Player

Different concrete classes in the same hierarchy may define the same method in different ways. For example:

```
public class ComputerPlayer extends Player
{
  ...
  /**
   *    Returns a prompt to be displayed before
   *    the next move of this player
   */
  public String getPrompt()
  {
    return " Hmm... Let me think...";
  }
  ...
}
```

```
public class HumanPlayer extends Player
{
   ...
  /**
   *    Returns a prompt to be displayed before
   *    the next move of this player
   */
  public String getPrompt()
  {
    return " Your turn...";
  }
   ...
}
```

❖   ❖   ❖

Java library packages provide classes for all kinds of things. Classes in your application often extend library classes. This lets you reuse library code and add your own features.

You do not need access to its source code to extend someone else's class or a library class.

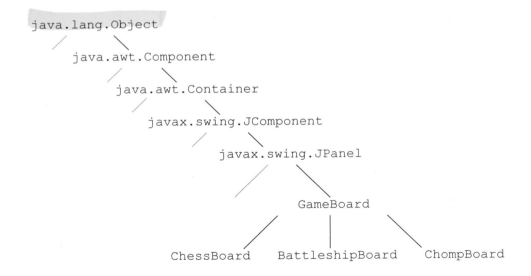

Figure 1-5. A hierarchy of classes (progressing from standard library classes to classes from a hypothetical package for board games)

The class hierarchy shown in Figure 1-5 starts with `Object`. Below it are a few library classes from the standard Java packages AWT and Swing. Under these are classes from a hypothetical package for board games. The `GameBoard` class may be an abstract class, but `ChessBoard`, `BattleshipBoard`, and `ChompBoard` are probably concrete classes.

❖   ❖   ❖

> **In Java, constructors are not inherited, so subclasses of the same superclass may have different constructors with different arguments.**

But the superclass constructors' code does not have to be duplicated in a subclass.

> **A subclass's constructor can explicitly call any constructor of its superclass by using the keyword `super`. If `super(...)` is called, then `super(...)` must be the first statement in the constructor.**

Suppose, for example, that the `Player` class has a constructor that sets the value of the field `myName` to the string passed to it as an argument:

```
public abstract class Player
{
  private string myName;
  ...
  public Player(String name)  // constructor
  {
    myName = name;
  }
  ...
}
```

`HumanPlayer` and `ComputerPlayer` inherit the field `myName`, but they cannot directly access it because `myName` is `private` in `Player`. However, constructors of these classes can call `Player`'s constructor to set `myName`. This is accomplished using Java's reserved word `super`:

```
public class HumanPlayer extends Player
{
  public HumanPlayer(String name)  // constructor
  {
    super(name);
  }
  ...
}
```

Calls the constructor in the Player class bc that's its superclass

Or:

```
public class ComputerPlayer extends Player
{
  public ComputerPlayer()  // constructor
  {
    super("Computer");
  }
  ...
}
```

Recall that if you do not define any constructors for a class, then Java provides one default constructor that takes no arguments and initializes all the fields to their default values: 0 for numbers, `false` for `booleans`, `null` for objects. However, if you provide at least one constructor, then the default constructor is not provided automatically.

> **It is a good idea to define a so-called** *no-args* **constructor (a constructor with no arguments) for your class if you plan to define other constructors.**

❖   ❖   ❖

Derived classes can not only add fields and methods to the base class's fields, they can also redefine a method from the superclass. Sometimes a method of a subclass needs to expand the functionality of the superclass's method. Again, there is no need to duplicate the code from the superclass, no need even to have access to that code. Instead, the subclass's method can explicitly call any method of the superclass using `super`. For example:

```
public class ChompBoard extends JPanel
{
  ...
  public void paintComponent(Graphics g)
  {
    setBackground(Color.orange);
    super.paintComponent(g);    // fills the background

    // Now add your own drawing:
    ...
  }
}
```

When you derive a class from a library class or someone else's class, you have to be careful not to redefine a base class's method inadvertently.

To recap: inheritance allows us to <u>reuse</u> some code from the base class in a derived class, saving development time. It also helps to avoid duplicate code, thus making program maintenance easier: if you need to change the code, the change needs to be made in only one place.

1.3   Polymorphism

With inheritance and class hierarchies, the notion of an object's data type becomes a little blurred. Suppose we create an instance of the ComputerPlayer class. The data type of that object is ComputerPlayer. But a ComputerPlayer is also a kind of Player; if we need to refer to that object in a more generic way, ignoring the specifics of precisely what kind of Player it is, Java allows us to do that. For example:

```
Player p;
p = new ComputerPlayer(...);
...
p.makeMove();
```

There may be several situations where we need to refer to an object using its more generic supertype rather than its most specific type. One such situation is when we want to mix different subtypes of objects in the same collection (array, list, etc.). For example:

```
Player players[] = new Player[2];
players[0] = new HumanPlayer(...);
players[1] = new ComputerPlayer(...);
...
player[currentPlayer].makeMove();
```

This is possible because both HumanPlayer and ComputerPlayer are Players.

Therefore, besides reusing code, inheritance serves a second purpose: it provides a common base data type that lets us refer to objects of specific types through more generic types of references; in particular, we can mix objects of different subtypes in the same collection. This is Java's response to two contradictory demands. On one hand, we want a programming language to strongly enforce the discipline of data types; on the other hand, we want to be able to apply the same algorithms to objects of slightly different data types and to mix different objects in the same collection.

You may be wondering: Once we start referring to objects using variables of more generic types, don't we lose the specific data type information about the object? For example, once we state

```
Player players[] = new Player[2];
players[0] = new HumanPlayer(...);
players[1] = new ComputerPlayer(...);
```

how can we (or the compiler) keep track of exactly what kinds of players `players[0]` and `players[1]` really are? When we write

```
players[currentPlayer].makeMove();
```

how does the compiler know which method to call? Both `HumanPlayer` and `ComputerPlayer` have a `makeMove` method, but these methods do different things.

The answer to this question is ***polymorphism***. When the code is compiled, the decision on which method to call is postponed until the program is executed — a technique called ***late*** or ***dynamic method binding***. When the program is running, each object <u>itself</u> knows exactly what kind of object it is, and it automatically makes sure the correct method is called. Roughly speaking, each object contains a link to a table that holds the entry points of its methods.

> **Polymorphism ensures that the correct method is called for an object of a specific type, even when the object is disguised as a reference to a more generic type.**

Among other things, polymorphism is essential for plugging in your own methods in place of the default calls in library methods. For example, it is common to redefine the `paintComponent` method for the GUI components you have derived from library classes:

```
public class ChompBoard extends JPanel
{
    ...
  public void paintComponent(Graphics g)
  {
      ...
  }
}
```

Java's library code does not know what kind of components you have placed on your application window's content pane — it just repaints all of them in order by calling each one's `paintComponent`. Thanks to polymorphism, your own `paintComponent` methods are called for your components.

Polymorphism is automatic; all you have to do is properly derive your classes from a common base class.

Without polymorphism, the program would have to query objects about their type and then call the appropriate methods. That would look ugly, something like this:

```
String typeOfPlayer = players[currentPlayer].getClass().getName();

if (typeOfPlayer.equals("HumanPlayer"))
  ((HumanPlayer)players[currentPlayer]).makeMove();

else // if (typeOfPlayer.equals("ComputerPlayer"))
  ((ComputerPlayer)players[currentPlayer]).makeMove();
```

Polymorphism streamlines the code by making explicit type checks and conditional branching unnecessary.

1.4   Encapsulation and Abstraction

A well-designed class hides all the details of its implementation from other classes (and from the programmers who work on other classes). In particular, all fields in a class are usually declared `private`, as are "helper methods" used only internally by the class. A class interacts with other classes that use it (its *clients*) through a well-defined set of public constructors and public methods. This principle is called *encapsulation*.

It is useful to think of "privacy" as applied to the programmer who defines the class rather than to individual objects of the class. If a program creates several objects of the same class, methods of one such object can call the public and private methods of another and can access its private fields. For example:

```
public class Fraction
{
  private int num, denom;

  // Constructor:
  public Fraction(int a, int b)
  {
    num = a;
    denom = b;
    reduce();
  }

    ...

  public Fraction multiply(Fraction other)
  {
    return new Fraction(num * other.num, denom * other.denom);
          // this object's method can access and even modify
          // other object's private fields, as long as other
          // belongs to the same class.
  }
    ...

  /*
   * Reduces this fraction
   */
  private void reduce()
  {
    ...
  }
}
```

[handwritten margin note: use the Constructor to Create vs. two statements (like Complex # project)]

But the private fields and private methods of one class are not accessible in other classes. For example:

```
public class MyMath
{
  public static void main(String[] args)
  {
    Fraction f1(1, 2), f2(1,3);

    Fraction product = f1.multiply(f2);
    product.reduce();              // Syntax error -- can't call
                                   //   Fraction's private method
    System.out.println(product.num
          + "/" + product.denom); // Syntax error -- can't access
                                   //   Fraction's private fields
  }
}
```

Encapsulation facilitates team development because it minimizes the required interactions between developers. After several programmers agree on the public interfaces for their classes, each can go his own way to develop and test the code for his class.

Encapsulation also makes sure that any changes to the implementation of the class remain hidden from other classes. You can do whatever you want to your class, and other classes in the project are not affected, as long as the class's interface remains the same. A local change in the code does not propagate through the whole program — a principle called *locality*. This makes software maintenance more manageable.

Finally, encapsulation forces the programmer to focus on the important public features of the class, making the class's definition more abstract. ***Abstraction*** basically means ignoring irrelevant details and emphasizing the relevant ones. Encapsulation forces the programmer to formally define what is relevant. As a result, a class describes well-defined responsibilities of its objects. A more abstract definition makes the class more likely to be reused in other projects.

❖   ❖   ❖

A class does not have to be declared `abstract` to be abstract to some degree. There are different levels of abstraction; more and more details become clarified as your objects become more specific. Still, it is a good idea to maintain some level of abstraction and not to make your classes very specialized too quickly. At the top levels of the inheritance hierarchy, the classes are often `abstract` in the Java reserved-word sense: the code for some of their methods remains undefined (or some of their fields are variables of abstract class types and remain uninitialized). You cannot create objects of such classes, but they do help you formalize the properties and responsibilities of objects.

More abstract often means more reusable.

For example, the `Player` class in Section 1.2 (Figure 1-4 on page 6) defines three public methods:

```
public abstract String getPrompt();
public abstract String getWinMessage();
public abstract void makeMove();
```

Such a "player" can participate in any game for any number of players.

❖   ❖   ❖

An encapsulated class usually provides some public methods called ***accessors*** that return the values of private fields and some ***modifiers*** that set the values of private fields. It is common to start an accessor's name with "get" and a modifier's name with "set." For example:

```
public class Player
{
  private string myName;
  ...
  public String getName()
  {
    return myName;
  }

  public void setName(String name)
  {
    myName = name;
  }
  ...
}
```

If necessary, accessors and modifiers can convert the field's value into a different data type or perform additional transformations or adjustments. A modifier can perform additional checks to make sure that the modified field always gets a valid value. For example:

```
public void setName(String name)
{
  if (name != null)
    myName = name.trim();
}
```

❖   ❖   ❖

The same programmer often works on a whole hierarchy of classes; still, the programmer encapsulates all the classes in the hierarchy, relying on accessors and modifiers for access to private fields. In fact, a programmer may prefer to use accessors and modifiers rather than access the fields directly even within the same class. That increases locality, making the code less dependent on the class's implementation.

Java allows you to declare a field or a method as `protected` rather than `private` or `public`. A protected field is directly accessible in subclasses but acts as private for other classes. You may be tempted to use protected fields in your base class and refer to them directly in your derived class, as opposed to using private fields with accessors and modifiers. However, if you do that and later change the fields in your base class, you might need to change your derived class, too. Bad for locality. Even worse: What if another programmer derives a class from your base class and refers directly to your class's protected fields?   Then you make changes to the implementation of your class in the next release of your package, and the other programmer's class no longer works. That is why it is safer to always make all fields `private`. You may occasionally want to declare a method `protected` rather than `public`. This would indicate that the method is somewhat more technical, like a specialized more intricate tool: perhaps useful in derived classes, but not for general use.

1.5   Interfaces vs. Abstract Classes

Java class hierarchies are great, but the real world is not always quite as neat, and OOP applications may have trouble fitting all the objects into one hierarchy of types. A `HumanPlayer` is a `Player`, but what if we want it to also be a `Person` with such attributes as name, age, e-mail address, and so on? Wouldn't it be nice to be able to combine the features of two or more base classes in one derived class? Something like

```
public class HumanPlayer extends Player, Person // syntax error!
```

Java does <u>not</u> allow such ***multiple inheritance***. The reason is simple: if more than one of the base classes define a method or field with the same name, which one of them is inherited in the derived class? If all of them are inherited, how can we distinguish between them? The compiler (and the programmer) may get confused.

As usual, Java offers a compromise: a class can <u>extend</u> only one base class, but it can ***implement*** several ***interfaces***.

> An *interface* is akin to an `abstract` class: it gives a formal specification for objects by listing all the required methods, but does not provide the actual code.

`implements` and `interface` are Java reserved words. The choice of the word "interface" is perhaps unfortunate: this computer term is already overused (or, as a programmer might say, "overloaded"). We have "hardware interface," "user interface," "class's interface..." It is the latter usage that has inspired Java's keyword `interface`.

> When we state in a class's definition that the class `implements` an `interface`, it means that the class supplies code for all the methods specified in that interface.

An interface simply gives the prototype for each method (its name, return type, and the argument list) but no code. In that respect an interface is very similar to an `abstract` class. The difference is that an `abstract` class can have some fields, constructors, and public or private methods implemented. An interface does not have any constructors and no code is defined for <u>any</u> of its methods. Thus an interface is even more abstract than an `abstract` class!

Writing interfaces is easy. Let us take, for example, the abstract class `Player` from Section 1.2 (Figure 1-4 on page 6). Figure 1-6 shows `Player` rewritten as an interface. Instead of `public class` we write `public interface`. We can also omit the keyword `public` in all the methods because they are assumed to be public by default. (Likewise, if an interface has fields, they are assumed to be `public static final` by default and must be initialized.)

```
/**
 *   A player in a board game
 */

public interface Player
{
  /**
   *    Returns a prompt to be displayed before
   *    the next move of this player
   */
  String getPrompt();

  /**
   *    Returns a message to be displayed when
   *    this player has won
   */
  String getWinMessage();

  /**
   *    Called to initiate this player's next move
   */
  void makeMove();
}
```

public by default so public not needed

Figure 1-6. `Player`, rewritten as an interface

Now, instead of <u>deriving</u> `HumanPlayer` and `ComputerPlayer` from the abstract class `Player`, we can make them <u>implement</u> the interface `Player`:

```
public class HumanPlayer implements Player
{
  ...
}

public class ComputerPlayer implements Player
{
  ...
}
```

We don't have to change anything else.

The abstract class `Player` did not have any code for its methods anyway: all of them were abstract. So we have not lost anything by rewriting it as an interface. But we have gained something: we have freed the "extends" slot previously occupied by `Player`. Now, if necessary, we can derive `HumanPlayer`, `ComputerPlayer`, and other classes that <u>implement</u> `Player` from something else. For example:

```
public class HumanPlayer extends Person
   implements Player
{
  ...
}
```

❖   ❖   ❖

If necessary, the same class can implement multiple interfaces.

For example:

```
public class HumanPlayer
   implements Player, MouseListener
{
  ...
}
```

Or:

```
public class ComputerPlayer
   implements Player, ActionListener
{
  ...
}
```

Interfaces are usually pretty short — it doesn't make much sense to declare too many methods in one interface. If necessary, you can split the methods between several interfaces. Then a class can implement all the interfaces it needs. Recall how the library interface `MouseListener` specifies five methods: `mouseClicked`, `mouseEntered`, `mouseExited`, `mousePressed`, and `mouseReleased`. Another interface, `MouseMotionListener`, specifies two methods, `mouseMoved` and `mouseDragged`. A class can implement one or both of these interfaces.

It is also possible to add methods to an interface by deriving a "subinterface" from it. Something like:

```
public interface ChessPlayer extends Player
{
   String getCheckMessage();
}
```

❖   ❖   ❖

We have already mentioned the dual benefits of inheritance: it helps us reuse code, and it provides a common base data type for polymorphic collections. Java's variety of "multiple inheritance" with interfaces offers nothing for reusability of code because interfaces don't have any code. But interfaces are very helpful for supplying secondary data types to objects and for supporting polymorphism. Just as a real-life object may be used in different ways depending on the situation (e.g., for tossing up in the air, as a container, or to cover one's head), an object in a program may assume different "appearances" for different purposes.

> **If a class implements an interface or several interfaces, an object of that class has the primary data type defined by its class, plus secondary data types defined by all the interfaces that the class implements.**

Consider, for example, a class `HumanPlayer`:

```
public class HumanPlayer
   implements Player, MouseListener
{
   ...
}
```

An object of this class has the data type `HumanPlayer`. For example,

```
    HumanPlayer p = new HumanPlayer("Joe");
```

Once the interface `Player` is introduced, it becomes a legitimate data type. For example, we can create an array of `Player`s:

```
Player players[] = new Player[2];
```

Since `HumanPlayer` implements `Player`, we can put a `HumanPlayer` object into the array `players`, together with objects of other classes that implement the `Player` interface. For example:

```
players[0] = new HumanPlayer(...);
players[1] = new ComputerPlayer(...);
```

`HumanPlayer` also implements the `MouseListener` interface that specifies methods for capturing mouse events (the moves for this player are entered with a click of the mouse). Therefore, a `HumanPlayer` object is a kind of `MouseListener`; `MouseListener` is yet another of its secondary data types. This makes its possible to pass a `HumanPlayer` object as an argument to a method that expects a `MouseListener` and to place a `HumanPlayer` object into a list of `MouseListener`s. For example:

```
ChompBoard board = new ChompBoard(...);
HumanPlayer p = new HumanPlayer(...);
board.addMouseListener(p);
```

Polymorphism ensures that the correct methods are automatically called for an object that implements an interface.

❖   ❖   ❖

A class that implements an interface must supply all the methods specified by that interface.

For example, even though `HumanPlayer` actually uses only one of `MouseListener`'s methods, `mouseReleased`, all five `MouseListener` methods must be defined, even if the code of the unused methods consists only of empty braces (Figure 1-7).

The reverse is not true: even if you implement all the interface's required methods in a class, that class still doesn't "implement" the interface unless you formally state that it does. If, for example, you supply all five `MouseListener` methods in `HumanPlayer` but forget the words `implements MouseListener` in the class's header and then try

```
HumanPlayer p = new HumanPlayer(...);
board.addMouseListener(p);
```

the compiler will report a syntax error and show a somewhat cryptic error message, something like this:

```
addMouseListener(java.awt.event.MouseListener) in java.awt.Component
cannot be applied to (HumanPlayer)
```

That means the data types do not match: HumanPlayer is not a MouseListener.

```
public class HumanPlayer
    implements Player, MouseListener
{
  ...

  /**
   *    Called automatically when the mouse button is released
   */
  public void mouseReleased(MouseEvent e)
  {
    if (!myTurn)
      return;
    ...
  }

  // Not used but required by the MouseListener interface spec:
  public void mouseClicked(MouseEvent e) {}
  public void mousePressed(MouseEvent e) {}
  public void mouseEntered(MouseEvent e) {}
  public void mouseExited(MouseEvent e) {}
}
```

Figure 1-7. HumanPlayer implements MouseListener

❖   ❖   ❖

Inheritance, encapsulation, accessors and modifiers, abstract and concrete classes, interfaces — all of this may seem overwhelming at first. But this is the essence of OOP. It is not sufficient to say that your program consists of interacting objects; you need to know how objects of different types relate to each other. After all, if you are hoping to assemble programs from reusable components, you need to know the general properties of the components and the rules for putting them together.

1.6   *Case Study and Lab:* Chomp

The game of "Chomp" can be played on a rectangular board of any size. The board is divided into squares (let's say the board represents a chocolate bar). The rules are quite simple: the two players alternate taking rectangular "bites" from the board. On each move, the player must take any one of the remaining squares as well as all the squares that lie below and to the right (Figure 1-8). The square in the upper left corner of the board is "poison": whoever takes it loses the game. Run the *Chomp* applet using the compiled Java files on your student disk in the `Ch01\RunChomp` folder to get a feel for this game.

The number of all possible positions in Chomp is finite and the players make steady progress from the initial position to the end, as the total number of remaining "edible" squares on the board decreases with each move. Games of this type always have a winning strategy either for the first or for the second player. But, despite its simple rules, Chomp turns out to be a tricky game: you can prove mathematically that the first player has a winning strategy, but the proof does not tell you what that strategy is.* You know you can win if you go first, but you don't know how! Frustrating...

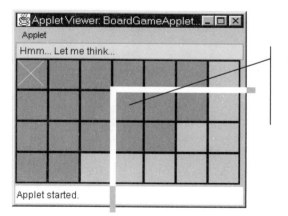

Next move: the five remaining squares inside the angle will be "eaten."

Figure 1-8. The *Chomp* game applet

---

* The proof looks like this. The first player can try to take the lower right corner on the first move. If this is the correct move in a winning strategy, the first player is all set. If it is not, the second player must have a winning move in response. But the first player could "steal" that winning response move and make it his own first move! In the theory of finite games, this argument is called "strategy stealing." Unfortunately, this proof gives no clue as to what the winning strategy might be.

As of now, no one has been able to come up with a formula for the winning Chomp positions (except for the 2 by *n* and *n* by *n* boards). There are computer programs that can backtrack from the final position (where only the "poison" square is left) and generate a list of all the winning positions. Our *Chomp* applet uses such a list, so the computer has an unfair advantage. You could try to "steal" the winning moves from the computer, but the applet's author has foreseen such a possibility and programmed the computer to intentionally make a few random moves before it settles into its winning strategy.

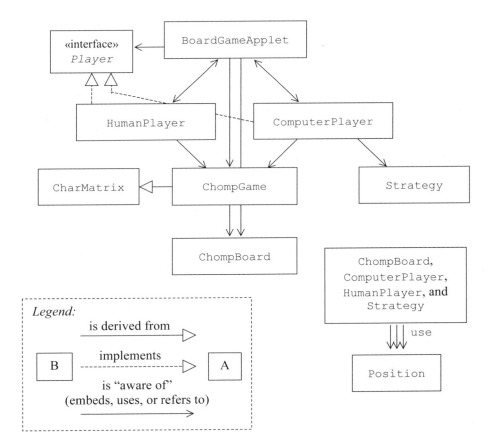

Figure 1-9. The classes in the *Chomp* applet

Luckily, our goal here is not to beat the computer at Chomp, but to learn some principles of object-oriented software design and to practice our Java programming skills. Let us begin by looking at the overall structure of this applet (Figure 1-9). The applet consists of eight classes and one interface, *Player*. An arrow from one class to another indicates that the first class "knows" something about the second one: it uses the second class's constructors or methods. An arrow with a triangular head represents inheritance: it connects the derived class to its base class. A dotted arrow with a triangle from a class to an interface indicates that the class implements that interface.

In OOP, a large number of classes is not considered a problem, as long as they are reasonably short and manageable and clearly define the responsibilities of their objects. In designing this applet we tried to reduce dependencies between classes, called *coupling*. BoardGameApplet, HumanPlayer, and ComputerPlayer, for instance, know very little about ChompBoard. ComputerPlayer is the only class that is aware of Strategy's constructors and methods.

Let us briefly review the responsibilities of each of these classes.

The top class, BoardGameApplet (Figure 1-10), derived from JApplet, represents the applet as a whole. Its init method creates the game object, the board, and the players, and adds a display field and the board to the applet's content pane. Note how general this class is: it doesn't really care what game is played or how the players make their moves, as long as they take turns. The BoardGameApplet's hasMoved method is called by each player when that player completes its current move. This method either displays a winning message if the game is over or else prompts the other player to make the next move. (hasMoved is needed because a player does not complete the move right away when makeMove is called: the "human player" waits for a mouse click and the "computer player" waits until the display stops flashing.)

As discussed in the previous sections, the Player interface, implemented by both the HumanPlayer and ComputerPlayer classes, allows us to place different kinds of "players" into the same array and rely on polymorphism to call their appropriate methods. The HumanPlayer object gets its next move from a mouse click on a particular square. The ComputerPlayer object creates a Strategy object and then consults it for each move.

The ChompGame class is designed to keep track of the board's configuration and implement the moves. But ChompGame does not display the board — that function is left to a separate "view" class. ChompGame only represents the "model" of the game. This class and the Strategy class are really the only classes that "know" and use the rules of Chomp.

```
/**
 *   Implements a board game applet with someone
 *   playing against the computer
 */
import java.awt.*;
import javax.swing.*;

public class BoardGameApplet extends JApplet
{
  private ChompGame game;
  private JTextField display;
  private Player players[];
  private int currentPlayer;

 .public void init()
  {
    Container c = getContentPane();

    display = new JTextField(20);
    display.setBackground(Color.yellow);
    display.setEditable(false);
    c.add(display, BorderLayout.NORTH);

    ChompBoard board = new ChompBoard();
    c.add(board, BorderLayout.CENTER);

    game = new ChompGame(board);

    players = new Player[2];
    players[0] = new HumanPlayer(this, game, board);
    players[1] = new ComputerPlayer(this, game, board);
    currentPlayer = 0;                        // optional -- default

    display.setText(" You go first...");
    players[currentPlayer].makeMove();
  }

  /**
   *   Called by the player when its move is completed
   */
  public void hasMoved()
  {
    currentPlayer = (currentPlayer + 1) % 2;
    Player p = players[currentPlayer];
    ...
  }
}
```

Figure 1-10. `Ch01\Chomp\BoardGameApplet.java` 🖫

The `ChompGame` class extends `CharMatrix`, a general-purpose class that represents a 2-D array of characters. A matrix of characters helps `ChompGame` to represent the current configuration of the board. We could potentially put all the code from `CharMatrix` directly into `ChompGame`. That would make the `ChompGame` class rather large. More importantly, general methods dealing with a character matrix would be mixed together in the same class with much more specific methods that deal with the rules of Chomp. Such a class would become intractable and hardly reusable. By separating the more general functions from the more specific ones, we have created a reusable class `CharMatrix` without any extra effort.

`Strategy` encapsulates the winning Chomp strategy and contains the list of winning positions for a 4 by 7 Chomp board. This class provides two public methods, `findBestMove` and `findRandomMove`. The code for this class is rather cryptic, but we don't really need to know much about it beyond this class's public interface, its constructor, and its two public methods. Whoever wrote and tested this class is responsible for it! This is team development at its best.

`ChompBoard` is the longest class in this project. It implements the "view," the graphics display of the board. The code in this class has to deal with rendering different squares in different colors and to support the "flashing" feedback for computer moves.

Finally, the `Position` class represents a (*row, col*) position on the board. It is a simple class: one constructor, `Position(row, col)`, and two accessors, `getRow()` and `getCol()`. We could have used one of the library classes instead but decided to write our own as an example. Such small auxiliary classes often define objects that carry information between other objects. In the *Chomp* applet, `Position` objects are passed from the strategy object to the computer player and from the board to the human player.

Looking ahead a little, we should mention that this applet's design fits the model-view-controller (MVC) design pattern explained in detail in Chapter 10. The main idea of such a design is to clearly separate the "model" (a more abstract object that describes the situation) from the "controller" (the object that changes the state of the model) and from the "view" (the object that displays the model). The "view" is attached to the model and changes automatically (or almost automatically) when the model changes. This way we can easily attach several different views to the same model if we need to. In the *Chomp* applet, the `ChompGame` class implements the "model." The applet's main class and both "players" together work as the "controller." Finally, the `ChompBoard` object is the "view."

We should also point out an intentional flaw in our design. The strategy object is created by the computer player, which makes it hard to change the strategy (e.g., to support different levels of play). A proper design would have a higher level object (e.g., the applet itself) attach a strategy to the computer player. Strategy would be an interface, which different strategy classes would implement. This improved design would follow the Strategy design pattern. Fixing the *Chomp* applet along these lines is the subject of Question 7 in the exercises.

As an exercise, restore the missing code in two of *Chomp's* classes. All the *Chomp* source files, as well as the HTML file that runs the applet and an audioclip file, are provided in the Ch01\Chomp 🖫 folder on your student disk. Fill in the blanks in the hasMoved method of the BoardGameApplet class, calling as necessary the methods specified by the Player interface. Supply the missing code for all the methods in the CharMatrix class as described in their respective *javadoc* comments. Test your applet.

1.7   Summary

The key OOP concepts — abstraction, encapsulation, inheritance, and polymorphism — aim at better-engineered software, team development, software reusability, and easier program maintenance.

Inheritance allows a programmer to extend a base class (a superclass) into a derived class (a subclass). You can add new fields and methods and redefine some of the base class's methods in the derived class. Constructors are not inherited, but a constructor of a derived class can call any of the superclass's constructors. In Java, all classes with no specific derivation automatically extend the class Object.

Inheritance helps to arrange classes into a hierarchy, with more abstract classes near the top and more specialized classes below. Java allows you to declare a class abstract and declare some of its methods abstract with no code provided. The abstract methods eventually get defined further down the inheritance tree. A class in which all the methods are fully defined and implemented is called a ***concrete*** class.

Inheritance serves a dual purpose: it allows us to reuse the base class's code and avoid duplication of code; it also supplies a common generic data type of the base class to objects of different classes derived from that base class. Objects of different but related types can be mixed together in the same array or list or another collection.

Polymorphism ensures that the correct methods are called for an object of a specific type, even when that object is disguised as a more generic type.

A proper class hides the details of its implementation by making all its fields and some methods private. This concept is known as encapsulation. An encapsulated class is accessible to other classes, its clients, through a well-defined and documented interface consisting of public constructors and public methods. An encapsulated class may provide public accessor methods that return the values of the object's fields and public modifier methods that set the values of the fields. Encapsulation enforces locality: a change in the implementation of the class does not affect the rest of the program. This makes program maintenance more manageable. Encapsulation also makes team development easier: to use someone else's class a programmer needs to know only its public interface. Encapsulation forces programmers to pay more attention to the public features of their classes, leading to more abstract, reusable classes.

An interface in Java is akin to an abstract class: it lists a few methods, giving their names, return types, and argument lists, but does not give any code. The difference is that an abstract class may have its constructors and some of its methods implemented, while an interface does not give any code for its methods, leaving their implementation to a class that implements that interface. `interface` and `implements` are Java reserved words. A class that implements an interface must implement all the methods specified by that interface.

The same class can implement multiple interfaces. Each of the implemented interfaces supplies an additional secondary data type to an object of the class. This allows the program to treat the same object in different situations as an object of different data types. For example, an object can be passed to methods that expect an argument of a particular interface type. An interface can also serve as a common data type for mixing objects of different classes in the same polymorphic collection (array, list, etc.), as long as all the classes implement that interface.

Exercises

1.   (a)   Define an abstract class `WelcomeMessage` with a method

```
String getWelcomeMessage();
```

that returns a welcome message. Define subclasses `WelcomeEnglish`, `WelcomeSpanish`, and `WelcomeFrench` whose `getWelcomeMessage` method returns a welcome message in English, Spanish, and French, respectively. Write a test class that declares an array of three welcome messages (`WelcomeMessage` objects), initializes the elements to three messages in different languages, then displays all three.

   (b)   Modify the project, replacing the `WelcomeMessage` class with the `WelcomeMessage` interface.

   (c)   Explain the advantage of using an interface rather than an abstract class in this project.

2.   Java documentation indicates that the `Character` class implements the `Comparable` interface. Which method(s) are required for this interface? ✓

3.   If class `B` implements interface `I` and class `D` extends `B`, is "implements I" in

```
public class D extends B implements I
```

required, optional, or forbidden? Set up a little test and see what the compiler says.

4.   The class below (Ch01\Exercises\Triangle.java 🖫) has methods for calculating the area, the perimeter, and their ratio. The class works for equilateral triangles and for right isosceles triangles; the type of the triangle is passed in a string to the constructor:

```java
public class Triangle
{
  private String type;
  private double side;

  public Triangle(String aType, double aSide)
  {
    type = aType;
    side = aSide;
  }

  public double getPerimeter()
  {
    if ("equilateral".equals(type))
      return 3 * side;
    else if ("right".equals(type))
      return (2 + Math.sqrt(2.0)) * side;
    else
      throw new RuntimeException("Invalid triangle type");
  }

  public double getArea()
  {
    if ("equilateral".equals(type))
      return Math.sqrt(3) / 4 * side * side;
    else if ("right".equals(type))
      return side * side / 2;
    else
      throw new RuntimeException("Invalid triangle type");
  }

  public double getRatio()
  {
    return getArea()/getPerimeter();
  }

  public static void main(String[] args)
  {
    Triangle equilateralTr = new Triangle("equilateral", 12);
    Triangle rightTr = new Triangle("right", 12);
    System.out.println("Equilateral " +
                       equilateralTr.getRatio());
    System.out.println("Right Isosceles " +
                       rightTr.getRatio());
  }
}
```

Continued ☞

(a)   Restructure the above program in the OOP style. Make the `Triangle` class abstract. Keep the `side` field but eliminate the `type` field. Make the `getArea` and `getPerimeter` methods abstract. Derive the concrete classes `EquilateralTriangle` and `RightTriangle` from `Triangle`. Provide an appropriate constructor for each of the two derived classes and make them call the superclass's constructor. Redefine the abstract methods appropriately in the derived classes. Put `main` in a separate test class and change it appropriately.

(b)   The area of a triangle is equal to one half of its perimeter times the radius of the inscribed circle. If the length of a side of an equilateral triangle is the same as the length of the legs in a right isosceles triangle, which of these triangles can hold a bigger circle inside? ✓

5.   (a)   Modify the *Chomp* applet to make it played by two human players.

    (b)   Change the applet further so that it displays different prompts for the two players (e.g., "Your turn, Player 1" and "Your turn, Player 2"). Implement this change by deriving `HumanPlayer1` and `HumanPlayer2` from `HumanPlayer` and redefining the `getPrompt` method in them.

    (c)   Consider an alternative implementation of different prompts for different human players: instead of using derived classes, accept the name of the player as a parameter in `HumanPlayer`'s constructor; make `getPrompt` return a standard message concatenated with the player's name. Is this implementation more appropriate or less appropriate in an OOP program than the one suggested in Part (b)? Why? ✓

6.   Turn the *Chomp* applet into a game for three players: two human players and one computer player.

7.   In the *Chomp* applet, a `ComputerPlayer` object creates a `Strategy` for itself. Restructure the applet as follows. Rename the `Strategy` class into `ChompStrategy4by7`. Define a new `Strategy` interface with methods from the former `Strategy` class and state that `ChompStrategy4by7` implements `Strategy`. Rather than creating a `Strategy` object in `ComputerPlayer`, make `BoardGameApplet` pass a `Strategy` object (of the `ChompStrategy4by7` type) to the `ComputerPlayer`'s constructor:

```
public ComputerPlayer(BoardGameApplet applet,
            ChompGame game, ChompBoard board, Strategy s)
```

8.   Recall that objects are called ***immutable*** if they cannot be modified after they are created. Explain the relationship between encapsulated classes and classes that define immutable objects. ✓

9.   Examine the Java documentation and tell which of the following library classes define immutable objects:

```
java.lang.Integer _____
java.awt.Point _____
java.awt.Color _____
java.util.Calendar _____
```

10.■   A Java class can be declared `final`, which means that you cannot derive classes from it. For example, `Integer` and `String` are `final` classes. Why? ✓

11.   (a)   Make the *Chomp* applet scalable. Eliminate the `CELLSIZE` constant in the `ChompBoard` class and obtain the cell's width and height from the current dimensions of the panel when necessary.

(b)   Add a constructor to the `ChompBoard` class that sets the row and column dimensions of the board. Make the applet play on a 3 by 6 board. Which properties of the code make this change easy? ✓

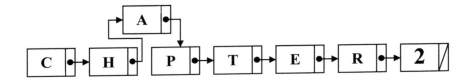

Lists and Iterators

2.1   Prologue

This chapter opens our discussion of a series of data structures that constitute a standard set of tools in software design and development. These include lists, stacks, queues, trees, priority queues, hash tables, and other structures.

> **A data structure combines data organization with methods of accessing and manipulating the data.**

For example, an array becomes a data structure for storing a list of values when we provide methods to find, insert, and remove a value. Similar functionality can be achieved with a ***linked list*** structure, which we will explain shortly. At a very abstract level, we can think of a general "list" object: a list contains a number of values arranged in sequence; we can find a target value in a list, add values to the list, and remove values from the list.

The "List" can be further specialized. We can require, for example, that the values in the list be arranged in ascending (e.g., alphabetic) order and stipulate that the insert function put the new value into the appropriate place in the order. This can be called the "Ordered List."

The data structures that we are going to study are not specific to Java — they can be implemented in any programming language. In Java, a data structure can be described as an interface and implemented as a class or several classes. For example, the Java library interface `java.util.List` describes the "List" data structure. Two Java library classes, `ArrayList` and `LinkedList`, implement this interface.

In this chapter we will discuss the following topics:

- Some of the methods of the `List` interface

- The `ArrayList` and `LinkedList` library implementations of the `List` interface; their advantages and disadvantages in different situations

- Traversing a list using `Iterator` or `ListIterator` objects

We will also learn the basics of implementing our own linked list. Finally we will use the Java library class `LinkedList` in a case study that creates an actor index for a database of movies.

2.2   The `List` Interface

The `List` interface from the `java.util` package gives a formal description of a list. The Java library also provides two classes, `ArrayList` and `LinkedList` that implement the `List` interface. When you use the `List` interface or `ArrayList` or `LinkedList` classes, add

```
import java.util.*;
```

(or

```
import java.util.List;
import java.util.ArrayList;
import java.util.LinkedList;
```

as needed) to your code.

Note: the `java.util.List` interface is not to be confused with the `java.awt.List` class, which represents a GUI component (a list of items displayed on the screen).

The `List` interface stipulates that the elements of a list are objects (i.e., have the `Object` data type). For example:

```
void add(Object obj);   // append obj to the list
Object get(int i);      // return the value of the i-th element
```

Since any class extends `Object`, you can put any kind of object into a list, including arrays and `String`s. The methods that retrieve values from the list, such as `get`, return an `Object`; you have to cast the object back into its type when you retrieve it from the list. For example:

```
List bandNames = new ArrayList();
bandNames.add("ABBA");
...
int i = ...;
String name = (String)bandNames.get(i);
```

With primitive data types (`int`, `double`, `boolean`, etc.), the situation is slightly more complicated because in Java they are not objects. If you want to have a list of `ints` or `doubles`, you have to convert them into objects using the `Integer` or `Double` **wrapper** class (*Java Methods*, p. 268). For example:

```
List list = new ArrayList();
double x = ...;
int m = ...;

list.add(new Double(x));
list.add(new Integer(m));
...

int i = ...;

x = ((Double)list.get(i)).doubleValue();
m = ((Integer)list.get(i+1)).intValue();
...
```

The `List` interface has methods for accessing elements through their integer index (position in the list). The elements are numbered starting from 0, as in Java strings and arrays. There are also methods for searching for a given value in the list. The Java API for the `List` interface specifies over two dozen methods; however, some of them are marked as optional and don't have to be present in every implementation.

```
int size();                      // Returns the number of values
                                 //    currently stored in the list
boolean isEmpty();               // Returns true if the list is empty,
                                 //    otherwise returns false
boolean add(Object obj);         // Appends obj at the end of the list;
                                 //    returns true
void add(int i, Object obj);     // Inserts obj before the i-th element;
                                 //    increments the indices of the
                                 //    subsequent elements by 1
Object set(int i, Object obj);   // Replaces the i-th element
                                 //    with obj; returns the old value
Object get(int i);               // Returns the value of the i-th
                                 //    element
Object remove(int i);            // Removes the i-th element from the
                                 //    list and returns its old value;
                                 //    decrements the indices of the
                                 //    subsequent elements by 1
```

Figure 2-1. Commonly used `List` methods

Like other interfaces, `List` does not tell us anything about constructors. It is up to a class that implements `List` to supply suitable constructors that initialize an empty list, build a list from given items, read a list from a file, and so on.

A few commonly used `List` methods are summarized in Figure 2-1. The `size()` method returns the total number of values currently stored in the list. The `boolean` method `isEmpty()` returns `true` if the list is empty, `false` otherwise. The `add(Object obj)` method appends a given value at the end of the list; the overloaded version with two arguments, `add(int i, Object obj)`, inserts the new value at the given position `i` and increments the indices of the subsequent elements by one. The `get(int i)` method returns the value of the *i*-th element in the list. The `set(int i, Object obj)` replaces the value of the *i*-th element with a new value and returns the old value. The `remove(int i)` method removes the *i*-th element and decrements the indices of all the subsequent elements by one. The `add`, `get`, `set`, and `remove` methods check that the given index `i` is within the legal range, $0 \le i < \texttt{size()}$. If the index is out of range, these methods cause a run-time error, `IndexOutOfBoundsException`.

2.3   Array Implementation of a List

A one-dimensional Java array already provides most of the functionality of a list. When we want to use an array as a list, we create an array that can hold a certain maximum number of values; we then keep track of the actual number of values stored in the array. The array's length becomes its maximum <u>capacity</u> and the number of values currently stored in the array is the size of the list.

However, Java arrays are not resizable. If we want to be able to add values to the list and not worry about exceeding its maximum capacity, we have to use a class with an `add` method, which allocates a bigger array and copies the list values into the new array when the list runs out of space. That's what the `ArrayList` library class does.

Before looking at the library class, let's make our own sketch for an encapsulated class that implements a list as an array (Figure 2-2). Our class defines a field of the `Object[]` type (array of objects) that holds the list's values. Another field keeps track of the current list size (the number of values stored in the array). The no-args constructor creates an array of some default capacity and makes the list empty (sets the count of stored values to 0). Another constructor creates an array of a given capacity, passed to it as a parameter.

Some methods of the Java `List` interface, such as `get` and `set`, translate directly into array operations. Other methods, such as `add` and `remove`, require extra work.

```
public class MyArrayList
{
  private static final int DEFAULT_CAPACITY = 16;    Constant.
  private Object myValues[];
  private int myNumValues;

  public MyArrayList()
  {
    myValues = new Object[DEFAULT_CAPACITY];
    myNumValues = 0;     // optional -- default
  }

  public MyArrayList(int capacity)
  {
    myValues = new Object[capacity];
    myNumValues = 0;     // optional -- default
  }

  public int size()
  {
    return myNumValues;
  }

  public boolean isEmpty()
  {
    return myNumValues == 0;
  }

  public Object get(int i)
  {
    if (i < 0 || i >= myNumValues)
      throw new IndexOutOfBoundsException();
              // report an error by creating and "throwing"
              //   an IndexOutOfBoundsException object
    return myValues[i];
  }

  public void add(Object obj)
  {
    if (myNumValues == myValues.length)
    {
      Object temp[] = new Object[2 * myValues.length];
      for (int i = 0; i < myNumValues; i++)
        temp[i] = myValues[i];
      myValues = temp;
    }
    myValues[myNumValues] = obj;
    myNumValues++;
  }
}
```

Figure 2-2.   A sketch for implementing a list class using an array

In `add` you need to expand the array's capacity when the list runs out of space. We have chosen in that case to double the current capacity: we allocate a new array twice the length of the old one and then copy all the values into the new array. You have to use such an `add` method with caution because copying large arrays may slow down your program. The `remove` method (not shown) may require shifting the remaining elements towards the beginning of the array.

The Java library class `java.util.ArrayList`, which implements the `List` interface, is much more involved, but the basic approach is similar to the sketch above.

> Note that in our **MyArrayList** class, as well as in the **ArrayList** library class, the **add** method does not create a copy of the object when it adds it to the list; **add** adds to the list a reference to the original object.

Therefore, you can modify an object <u>after</u> it has been added to a list; when you extract that object from the list, you will get the modified value.

2.4   Linked Lists

The elements of an array are stored in consecutive locations in computer memory. We can calculate the address of each element from its index in the array. By contrast, the elements of a linked list may be scattered in various locations in memory, but each element contains the memory address of the next element in the list. In Java, referring to addresses of objects is easy because all objects are represented as references, which are essentially their memory addresses. The last element in the list points to nothing, so its reference to the next element is set to `null`.

Metaphorically, we can compare an array to a book: we can read its pages sequentially or we can open it to any page. A linked list is like a magazine article: at the end of the first installment it says, "continued on page 27." We read the second installment on page 27, and at the end it says, "continued on page 36," and so on, until we finally reach the ♦ symbol that marks the end of the article.

> We will refer to the elements of a linked list as "nodes." A node contains some information useful for a specific application and a reference to the next node.

Let us say that the information stored in a node is represented by an object called value and that the reference to the next node is called next. We can encapsulate these fields in a class ListNode with one constructor, two accessors, and two modifiers (Figure 2-3).[*]

```java
public class ListNode
{
  private Object value;
  private ListNode next;

  // Constructor:
  public ListNode(Object initValue, ListNode initNext)
  {
    value = initValue;
    next = initNext;
  }

  public Object getValue()
  {
    return value;
  }

  public ListNode getNext()
  {
    return next;
  }

  public void setValue(Object theNewValue)
  {
    value = theNewValue;
  }

  public void setNext(ListNode theNewNext)
  {
    next = theNewNext;
  }
}
```

Figure 2-3. A class that represents a node in a linked list

(Ch02\ListNode.java 🖪)

---

[*] Adapted from The College Board's *AP Computer Science AB: Implementation Classes and Interfaces.*

Note two things about `ListNode`'s definition. First, "next" is a name chosen by the programmer: it is not required by Java syntax. We could have called it "link" or "nextnode" or whatever name we wanted. The name of the class, "ListNode," is also chosen by the programmer.

Second, the definition is self-referential: it refers to the `ListNode` data type inside the `ListNode` data type definition! The compiler is able to untangle this because `next` is a reference to an object and represents an address. An address takes a fixed number of bytes regardless of the data type, so the compiler can calculate the total size of a `ListNode` without paying much attention to what type of reference `next` is.

As an example, let us consider a list of departing flights on an airport display. The flight information may be represented by an object of the type `Flight`:

```
public class Flight
{
  private int number;          // Flight number
  private String destination;  // Destination city
  ...                          // Other fields and methods
}
```

Suppose a program has to maintain a list of flights departing in the next few hours, and we have decided to implement it as a linked list. We can use the following statements to create a new node that holds information about a given flight:

```
Flight flt = new Flight(...);
...
ListNode node = new ListNode(flt, null);
```

To extract the flight info we need to cast the object returned by `getValue` back into the `Flight` type:

```
flt = (Flight)node.getValue();
```

❖ ❖ ❖

A linked list is accessed through a reference to its first node. When a program creates a linked list, it usually starts with an empty list — the `head` reference is `null`:

```
ListNode head;        // head is set to null by default
```

The first node can be created using the `ListNode` constructor and appended to the list:

```
head = new ListNode(value0, null);
```

This results in a list with one node (Figure 2-4).

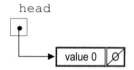

Figure 2-4.   A linked list with only one node

A second node may be appended to the first:

```
ListNode node1 = new ListNode(value1, null);
head.setNext(node1);
```

Or, combining the above two statements into one:

```
head.setNext(new ListNode(value1, null));
```

This statement changes the `next` field in the `head` node from `null` to a reference to the second node. This is illustrated in Figure 2-5. Diagrams like this one help us understand how links in a linked list are reassigned in various operations.

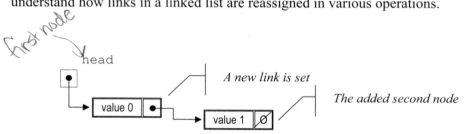

Figure 2-5.   The second node is appended to the list

When we build a list, we can keep track of the last node and append a new node to it:

```
ListNode head = null, tail = null, node;
while (...) // more values to insert
{
  Object value = ... ; // get the next value
  node = new ListNode(value, null);
  if (head == null)
    head = node;
  else
    tail.next = node;
  tail = node;     // update tail
}
```

Figure 2-6 shows the resulting linked list.

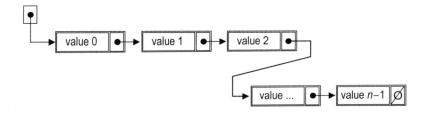

Figure 2-6. A linked list

Alternatively, we can easily attach a new node at the head of the list. For example:

```
ListNode node = new ListNode(value, null);
node.setNext(head);
head = node;
```

Or simply:

```
head = new ListNode(value, head);
```

The above statement creates a new node and sets its `next` field equal to the current head of the list. It then sets `head` to refer to the newly created node (Figure 2-7).

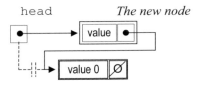

Figure 2-7. A new node inserted at the head of a linked list

2.5   Linked Lists vs. Arrays

As we have seen, a list can be implemented as either an <u>array</u> or a <u>linked list</u> — this is what the Java library classes `ArrayList` and `LinkedList` do. Since these two classes implement the same interface and provide the same methods, a novice might think that they are completely interchangeable. Indeed, either class is likely to work equally well on small lists. However, each of these implementations has its strengths and limitations, and choosing the wrong one may result in dramatic deterioration of performance on large lists.

The array implementation provides direct access to the i-th element of the array. This property, called ***random access***, is important in many algorithms. For example, the Binary Search algorithm requires access to the element directly in the middle between two elements. This is fast with arrays but slow with linked lists.

Arrays have two drawbacks, however. First, it is not easy to insert or remove a value at the beginning or in the middle of an array — a lot of bytes may need to be moved if the array is large. Second, we have to declare an array of a particular size. If the list outgrows the allocated space, we need to allocate a bigger array and copy all the values into it.

Linked lists get around both of these problems. First, a node can be easily inserted or removed from a linked list simply by rearranging the links. This is a crucial property if we have a frequently updated list. Second, the nodes of a linked list are allocated only when new values are added, so no memory is wasted for vacant nodes and a list can grow as large as the total memory permits.

The above considerations directly affect the performance of different methods in `ArrayList` and `LinkedList`. In `ArrayList`, the `get(i)` and `set(i, obj)` method calls are quick and become the primary tools for handling a list. But if we want to get to the i-th element in a linked list, we have to start from the head node and proceed down the list, counting the nodes, until we get to the i-th node. Thus the `get` and `set` operations may become costly. On the other hand, the `add(0, value)` method call may be quite slow for `ArrayList` because all the values must shift to make room for the added first value. In `LinkedList`, this method call just rearranges the links, so it is fast. If a class that implements linked lists keeps track of the list's last node, then appending new values at the end of the list is fast, too. And we can insert a whole linked list in the middle of another linked list or concatenate two linked lists together simply by rearranging a few links, without moving any data.

To make it simple to use linked lists appropriately, the `LinkedList` class provides a few specialized methods that are particularly efficient for linked lists: `addFirst`, `addLast`, `getFirst`, `getLast`, `removeFirst`, and `removeLast` (Figure 2-8).

```
void addFirst(Object obj);  // Appends obj at the beginning of the list
void addLast(Object obj);   // Appends obj at the end of the list
Object getFirst();          // Returns the first element
Object getLast();           // Returns the last element
Object removeFirst();       // Removes the first element from the
                            //   list and returns its old value
Object removeLast();        // Removes the last element from the
                            //   list and returns its old value
```

Figure 2-8. Efficient methods in `java.util.LinkedList`

On the surface,

```
Object obj = list.getLast();
```

and

```
Object obj = list.get(list.size() - 1);
```

may appear interchangeable. But, depending on the `LinkedList` implementation, the former statement may work faster.

2.6   Traversals and Iterators

A procedure that processes in sequence all the values stored in a data structure is called a *traversal*. For an array, traversal is accomplished simply by accessing consecutive elements using a position index and incrementing the index on each iteration. For example, suppose an `ArrayList` contains `Strings`. We can print them all out within a simple loop:

```
List movies = new ArrayList();
// Add values to the list:
...

// Print all the values in the list:
for (int i = 0; i < movies.size(); i++)
  System.out.println((String)movies.get(i));
```

In the last statement, `println(movies.get(i))`, without the cast to `String`, would also work: `println(Object obj)` uses `println(obj.toString())` and polymorphism takes care of calling the correct `toString` method for different types of objects.

❖   ❖   ❖

> **For linked lists, traversals that access elements through their indices are inefficient.**

A loop

```
for (int i = 0; i < list.size(); i++)
{
  value = list.get(i);
  . . .
}
```

does work for a linked list, but, as we discussed in the previous section, it is quite inefficient. If we have access to the head of the list, we can write a more efficient traversal loop for a linked list, which follows the links starting from the head of the list:

```
ListNode head;
// Add values to the list:
. . .

// Print all the values in the list:

ListNode node;
for (node = head; node != null; node = node.getNext())
  System.out.println((String)node.getValue());
```

This works fine as long as `head` is accessible to us. The problems begin when we implement a linked list as an encapsulated class. How can we deal with traversals? If we make the `head` field public in our class or if we provide a method that returns `head`, the whole list becomes exposed and our attempt at encapsulation fails. If we hide `head` inside our class and try to make traversal a class method, how will this method know what we want to do with each node? Traversals will become too specialized.

This dilemma is resolved with the help of ***iterators***. As the term suggests,

> **the purpose of an iterator is to iterate through the list and provide access to the consecutive elements.**

Iterators work both for array lists and linked lists, but they are much more important for linked lists. If your method's argument is a generic `List` object and the method needs to traverse the list, use an iterator just in case you get a linked list.

An iterator is an object associated with the list. When an iterator is created, it points to a specified element in the list, usually the first element. We call the iterator's methods to check whether there are more elements to be visited left in the list and to obtain the next element. In Java, this concept is expressed in the library interface `java.util.Iterator`. Classes that implement the `Iterator` interface are implemented as private *inner* classes in `ArrayList` and `LinkedList` — a topic that is outside the scope of this book. What is important for us is that the list itself provides an iterator when we call its `iterator()` method. For example:

```
LinkedList list = new LinkedList();
// Add values to the list:
...

Iterator iter = list.iterator();
```

An iterator is an object with three methods:

```
Object next();          // Returns the next element in the
                        //   list and advances the iterator's
                        //   "cursor" to the following element
boolean hasNext();      // Returns true if there are more elements
                        //   to visit, false otherwise
void remove();          // Removes the last element returned by next
                        //   from the list
```

Now our list traversal may look as follows:

```
LinkedList list = new LinkedList();
// Add values to the list
...

Iterator iter = list.iterator();
while (iter.hasNext())
  System.out.println(iter.next());
```

The increment for the `while` loop is hidden inside the `next` method. For linked lists, this implementation is much more efficient than the one with `get(i)`.

❖ ❖ ❖

You may be wondering at all this complexity. Why, for example, couldn't the `LinkedList` class itself have provided something like `startIterations`, `next`, and `hasNext` methods? The answer is, it could, as long as you used simple iterations. But when you tried <u>nested</u> iterations, this approach would fall apart.

Suppose, for example, you want to find duplicate titles in a linked list of movies. For that you have to run nested iterations on the same list, comparing every pair. The idea of a list serving as its own iterator would lead to an error, something like this:

```
String movie1, movie2;

movies.startIterations();
while (movies.hasNext())
{
  movie1 = (String)movies.next();
  movies.startIterations();  // Oops, a bug -- the outer loop's
                             //    position is lost
  while (movies.hasNext())
  {
    movie2 = (String)movies.next();
    if (movie1 != movie2 && movie1.equals(movie2))
      System.out.println("Duplicate name: " + movie1);
  }
}
```

What you need is two separate iterators, one for the outer loop and one for the inner loop:

```
String movie1, movie2;
Iterator iter1, iter2;

iter1 = movies.iterator();
while (iter1.hasNext())
{
  movie1 = (String)iter1.next();

  iter2 = movies.iterator();
  while (iter2.hasNext())
  {
    movie2 = (String)iter2.next();
    if (movie1 != movie2 && movie1.equals(movie2))
      System.out.println("Duplicate name: " + movie1);
  }
}
```

You may still notice a problem with the above code: it is inefficient because we always start iterations from the beginning of the list and test the same pair of movies twice. In addition, the same "duplicate name" message will be displayed twice. The Iterator interface turns out to be very limited: an iterator always iterates from the beginning of the list and only in one direction.

Luckily, Java offers a fancier iterator, the java.util.ListIterator interface, which overcomes these limitations. ListIterator extends Iterator (recall that in Java, a "subinterface" can extend a "superinterface").

A `ListIterator` object is returned by `List`'s `listIterator()` method. If you want to start iterations from the *i*-th element, use the overloaded version, `listIterator(i)`, where `i` is the initial position. In addition to the `next`, `hasNext`, and `remove` methods, `ListIterator` supplies the `previous` and `hasPrevious` methods.

> If you obtain a `ListIterator` with the `listIterator(i)` call, then the first value returned by `next` will be the value of the element with the index `i`, and the first value returned by `previous` will be the value of the element with the index `i-1`.

It may be useful to envision a list iterator as a logical "cursor" positioned before the list, after the list, or between two consecutive elements of the list (Figure 2-9). `list.listIterator(0)` positions the cursor before the first element of the list (the element with the index 0). `list.listIterator(list.size())` positions the cursor after the end of the list. `list.listIterator(i)` positions the cursor between the elements with indices `i-1` and `i`. The `next` method returns the element immediately after the cursor position, and the `previous` method returns the element immediately before the cursor position.

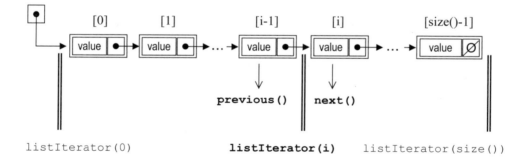

Figure 2-9. Logical "cursor" positioning for a list iterator

To traverse the list from the end backwards, all you have to do is obtain a list iterator that starts past the end of the list, then call `previous`. For example:

```
ListIterator iter = list.listIterator(list.size());
while (iter.hasPrevious())
{
  value = iter.previous();
  . . .
}
```

The ListIterator interface also provides an add method that inserts an element into the list (at the current "cursor" position) and a set method that changes the value of an element. The commonly used ListIterator methods are summarized in Figure 2-10.

```
Object next();          // Returns the next element in the list
boolean hasNext();      // Returns true if the next element in the
                        //   list is available and false otherwise
Object previous();      // Returns the previous element in the list
boolean hasPrevious();  // Returns true if the previous element in the
                        //   list is available and false otherwise
void add(Object obj);   // Inserts a new element obj at the current
                        //   iterator position
void set(Object obj);   // Sets the value of the last element that was
                        //   returned by next or previous to obj
void remove();          // Removes from the list the last element that
                        //   was returned by next or previous
int nextIndex();        // Returns the index of the element that
                        //   will be retrieved by next
int previousIndex();    // Returns the index of the element that
                        //   will be retrieved by previous
```

Figure 2-10. Commonly used `java.util.ListIterator` methods

Now, armed with ListIterators, we can make our nested loop for finding duplicates in a list more efficient, comparing each value only with the subsequent values in the list:

```
String movie1, movie2;
ListIterator iter1, iter2;

iter1 = movies.listIterator();

while (iter1.hasNext())
{
  movie1 = (String)iter1.next();
  if (!iter1.hasNext())  // if this is the last element
    break;

  iter2 = movies.listIterator(iter1.nextIndex());
    // Start the inner loop at the current position
    //   of iter1

  while (iter2.hasNext())
  {
    movie2 = (String)iter2.next();
    if (movie1.equals(movie2))
      System.out.println("Duplicate name: " + movie1);
  }
}
```

2.7   *Lab:* Movie Actors Index

A movie database consists of a movies file and an actors file. The task is to produce a cross-index, listing for each actor or actress all the movies that he or she starred in. Use linked lists in this project.

The movies file lists movies in chronological order by date of release. It is a text file. Each line has the year of release, the movie title, and the list of actors and actresses starring in the movie. Use movies.txt 🖬 in the Ch02\movies folder on your student disk as an example or create your own. The actors file contains names of actors and actresses, one name per line. Use actors.txt 🖬 in the Ch02\movies folder or create your own. The actor cross-index should display the actor's name and the list of movies he or she starred in, <u>starting from the most recent ones</u>.

Follow these steps:

1. Write a class `LinkedListFromFile` derived from `LinkedList`. In addition to the default (no-args) constructor, supply a constructor that takes the file name as an argument, reads lines of text from the file, and adds them to the list (in the same order). Recall that the `EasyReader` class (available at this book's companion web site) provides an easy way to open a text file and read data from it. For example:

```
EasyReader file = new EasyReader(fileName);
if (file.bad())
{
   ... // display an error message and quit
}

String str;
while ((str = file.readLine()) != null)
{
   ...      // Add str to the list
}
```

2. Write a main class that creates two linked lists, one from the `actors.txt` file and the other from the `movies.txt` file. Use your `LinkedListFromFile` class to construct the lists. For each actor or actress in the actors list, scan the list of movies and print out all those in which that person stars. Use a simple iterator to obtain the names of actors from the list. Use a list iterator (a `ListIterator` object) to obtain records from the list of movies. Iterate backwards in the list of movies, starting at the end, to display the more recent movies first.

   Assume that the names of actors start in a fixed position in the movie record. If the record contains additional information (e.g., the movie director's name), assume that it starts at a fixed position after the names of the actors. Search for a matching actor name only in a substring that cuts to the relevant portion of the record.

3. Test your program thoroughly. In particular, make sure that the first and the last elements in each list are handled properly. Redirect the console output to a file or use the `EasyWriter` class to write the output to a file instead of the console window. Then you can examine the output carefully and make sure that it matches the data.

2.8   Summary

A data structure combines data organization with methods for accessing and manipulating the data. The "List" is a data structure that contains a number of values arranged in a linear sequence. It provides methods for inserting a value into the list, removing a value from the list, and traversing the list (i.e., processing all values in sequence, visiting each value once).

The Java library `List` interface provides the `size`, `isEmpty`, `get`, `add`, `set`, and `remove` methods, summarized in Figure 2-1. The `ArrayList` and `LinkedList` library classes implement the `List` interface. These classes assume that the values in the list have the type `Object`. If you need to put values of a primitive data type such as `int`s or `double`s into the list, you need to first convert them into objects using the appropriate wrapper class, `Integer` or `Double`.

It is assumed that the elements in the list are indexed starting from 0. "Logical" indices are used even if a list is not implemented as an array. The `size()` method returns the number of values in the list. The `get(i)` call returns the element indexed by `i`. This method and other methods that use indices generate a run-time error if an index is out of bounds.

In an `ArrayList`, the elements occupy consecutive memory locations. In a linked list, the information is stored in nodes that may be scattered in memory, but each node, in addition to the value of the element, holds a reference to (the address of) the next node. A node of a linked list can be represented by a simple class `ListNode` (Figure 2-3). If `head` is a reference to the first node in the list, the statement

```
head = new ListNode(newValue, head);
```

appends a node holding `newValue` at the beginning of the list.

A traversal of a list is an operation that visits all the elements of the list in sequence and performs some operation or displays the value of each element. The following `for` loop can be used to conveniently traverse a linked list:

```
ListNode node;
for (node = head; node != null; node = node.getNext())
{
  SomeClass value  = (SomeClass)node.getValue();
  ... // process value
}
```

The `get(i)` and `set(i)` methods work for both `ArrayList` and `LinkedList` classes. Due to the direct-access property of arrays, these methods are fast and efficient for `ArrayList`. However, they may be quite inefficient for `LinkedList` because they need to scan through the list to find the *i*-th element.

On the other hand, the specialized methods `addFirst`, `addLast`, `getFirst`, `getLast`, `removeFirst`, and `removeLast` work fast for a `LinkedList`.

Both implementations of a list, as an array or as a linked list, have their advantages and disadvantages. A programmer has to choose carefully between the two, depending on the situation.

For lists implemented as `LinkedList`, it is better to use iterators for traversing the list. `Iterator` is a library interface; a class that implements `Iterator` supplies the methods `hasNext`, `next`, and `remove`. An iterator is obtained from the list itself, by calling its `iterator` method. For example:

```
Iterator iter = list.iterator();
while (iter.hasNext())
{
  SomeClass value = (SomeClass)iter.next();
  ... // process value
}
```

A more comprehensive `ListIterator` object is returned by `List`'s `listIterator` method. A `ListIterator` can start iterations at any specified position in the list and can proceed forward or backward. For example:

```
ListIterator iter = list.listIterator(list.size());
while (iter.hasPrevious())
{
  SomeClass value = (SomeClass)iter.previous();
  ... // process value
}
```

The `ListIterator` methods are summarized in Figure 2-10.

Exercises

1. Which of the following statements compile with no errors (assuming that the necessary library names are imported)?

    (a) `List list = new List();`
    (b) `List list = new ArrayList();`
    (c) `List list = new LinkedList();`
    (d) `ArrayList list = new List();`
    (e) `ArrayList list = new ArrayList();`
    (f) `LinkedList list = new List();`
    (g) `LinkedList list = new ArrayList();`

2. Mark true or false and explain:

    (a) A list can contain multiple references to the same object. _____ ✓
    (b) The same object may belong to two different lists. _____
    (c) `java.util.List`'s `remove` method destroys the object after it has been removed from the list. _____ ✓
    (d) `java.util.List`'s `add` method makes a copy of the object and adds it to the list. _____
    (e) Two variables can refer to the same list. _____ ✓

3. Write a method

    ```
    public void removeFirstLast(List list)
    ```

    that removes the first and the last elements from the list. ✓

4. Finish the following method using indices:

    ```
    /** list contains Integer objects.  Removes the
     *  largest value from list.  (If several
     *  elements have the largest value, removes the
     *  first one of them.)
     */
    public void removeMax(List list)
    ```

5. Write a method

    ```
    public void append(List list1, List list2)
    ```

    that appends objects from `list2` to `list1` using indices. ✓

6.   What is the primary reason for using iterators rather than indices with Java library classes that implement `java.util.List`?

7.   (a)   Rewrite the method in Question 4 using an iterator.
          (b)   Rewrite the method in Question 5 using an iterator.

8.   Fill in the blanks in the initialization of `node3`, `node2`, `node1` and `head`, so that `node1`, `node2`, and `node3` form a linked list (in this order) referred to by `head`. ✓

```
ListNode node3 = new ListNode("Node 3",_____);
ListNode node2 = new ListNode("Node 2",_____);
ListNode node1 = new ListNode("Node 1",_____);
ListNode head = _____ ;
```

9.   Fill in the blanks in the following method:

```
/** Returns true if the list referred to by head
 *    has at least two nodes, false otherwise.
 */
public boolean hasTwo(ListNode head)
{
   return _____ ;
}
```

10.   Write a method

```
public ListNode removeFirst(ListNode head)
```

that unlinks the first node from the list and returns the head of the new list. Your method should throw `NoSuchElementException` when the original list is empty. ✓

11.   Write a method

```
public int size(ListNode head)
```

that returns the number of nodes in the list referred to by `head`:

(a)   using a `for` loop
(b)   using recursion.

12.   `head` is the fist node of a non-empty linked list. Write a method

```
public void add(ListNode head, Object value)
```

that appends a new node holding `value` at the end of the list. ✓

13.   Fill in the blanks in the method below that takes the list referred to by `head`, builds a new list in which nodes have the same information but are arranged in reverse order, and returns the head of the new list. The original list remains unchanged. Your solution must use a `for` loop (not recursion).

```
public ListNode reverseList(ListNode head)
{
    ListNode node, newNode, newHead = null;

    for ( _____ )
    {
        _____

        . . .
    }

    return newHead;
}
```

14.   Write a method

```
public ListNode concatenateStrings(ListNode head)
```

that takes the list referred to by `head`, builds a new list, and returns its head. The original list contains strings. The k-th node in the new list should contain the concatenation of all the strings from the original list from the first node up to and including the k-th node. For example, if the original list contains strings `"A"`, `"B"`, `"C"`, the new list should contain strings `"A"`, `"AB"`, `"ABC"`.

15.■   Write a method

```
public ListNode mix(ListNode head1, ListNode head2)
```

that takes two lists of equal length and makes a new list, alternating values from the first and the second list. For example, if `head1` refers to the list `"A"`, `"B"` and `head2` refers to the list `"1"`, `"2"`, the combined list is `"A"`, `"1"`, `"B"`, `"2"`. The method returns the head of the combined list.

16.   Write a method that is similar to the one in Question 15, but works with arguments of the type `java.util.List` and returns a `java.util.LinkedList`:

```
public LinkedList mix(List list1, List list2)
```

Use iterators on `list1` and `list2` and the `add` method for adding values to the combined list. ✓

17.▪   Write a method

```
public ListNode rotate(ListNode head)
```

that takes a linked list referred to by `head`, splits off the first node, and appends it at the end of the list. The method should accomplish this solely by rearranging links: do not allocate new nodes or move objects between nodes. The method should return the head of the rotated list.

18.▪   A list referred to by `head` contains strings arranged alphabetically in ascending order. Write a method

```
public ListNode insertInOrder(ListNode head, String s)
```

that inserts `s` into the list, preserving the order. If `s` is already in the list, it is not inserted. The method should return the head of the updated list.

19.▪   Write a method

```
public ListNode middleNode(ListNode head)
```

that returns the middle node (or one of the two middle nodes) of a linked list. Design this method using no recursion and only one loop.

20.◆   Let us say that a string matches a pattern (another string) if the pattern is at least as long as the string and for every non-wildcard character in the pattern the string has the same character in the same position. (The wildcard character is `'?'`.) For example, both `"New York"` and `"New Jersey"` match the pattern `"New ???????"`. Write a method

```
public ListNode moveToBack(ListNode head, String pattern)
```

that takes a list of strings referred to by `head` and moves all the strings that match `pattern` to the end of the list, preserving their order. Your method must work by rearranging links; do not allocate new nodes or use temporary arrays or lists.   The method should return the head of the updated list.

21.   (a)   Write a reasonably efficient method

```
public ArrayList copyToArrayList(LinkedList list)
```

that copies a given `LinkedList` into a new `ArrayList` and returns the copy. (Note that the `ArrayList` class has a constructor that lets you specify the initial capacity of the list.) ✓

(b)   The same as in Part (a) but in reverse: write a method that copies from an `ArrayList` to a `LinkedList`

```
public LinkedList copyToLinkedList(ArrayList list)
```

Use subscripts for the `ArrayList` and the efficient `addLast` method for the `LinkedList`.

22.■   A list contains $n+1$ `Double` values $a_0, ..., a_n$. Write a method

```
public double sum2(List list)
```

that calculates $a_0a_1 + a_0a_2 + ... + a_0a_n + a_1a_2 + ... + a_{n-1}a_n$ — the sum of products for all pairs of values. Do not use subscripts.

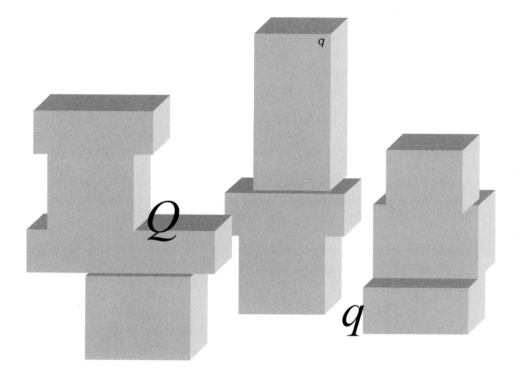

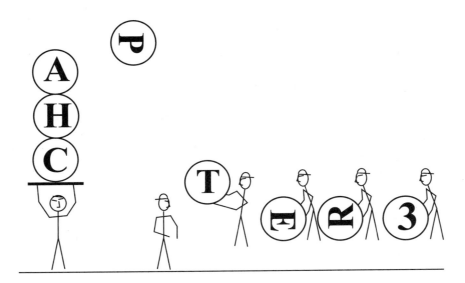

Stacks and Queues

3.1   Prologue

The *stack* is a data structure used for storing and retrieving data elements. The stack provides temporary storage in such a way that the value stored last will be retrieved first. This method is sometimes called LIFO — Last-In-First-Out.

A stack is controlled by two operations referred to as *push* and *pop*. Push adds a value to the top of the stack and pop removes the value from the top of the stack. These two operations implement the LIFO method. Values are said to be "on" the stack.

The stack mechanism is useful for temporary storage, especially for dealing with nested structures and branching processes: expressions within expressions, methods calling other methods, GUI components within GUI components, and so on. The stack mechanism helps your program untangle the nested structure and trace all its substructures in the correct order.

One example of effective stack use is in a web browser. When you click on a link, the browser saves the current URL and the place in the document so that you can retrace your steps if necessary. When you follow another link, the current location is saved again. And so on. When you press the "Back" button, the browser has to restore the location visited just before the current one. That is why a stack is appropriate for storing the sequence of visited locations.

In a *queue* data structure, data elements are retrieved in the same order as they were stored. This method is called FIFO — First-In-First-Out (as opposed to LIFO — Last-In-First-Out, the method of a stack). The queue is controlled by two operations: *enqueue* and *dequeue*. enqueue inserts a value at the rear of the queue, and dequeue removes a value from the front of the queue. These two operations implement the FIFO method.

The queue structure is usually used for processing events that have to be processed in the order of their arrival but not necessarily right away. The events are buffered in a queue while awaiting processing. One example is events handling in a Java program. Events generated by different objects (GUI components, timers, repaint requests, etc.) all go to the events queue. When the program is done with the previous event, it retrieves the next one from the queue and sends it to the appropriate "listener" for processing.

Queues are widely used at the system level for buffering commands or data between processes or devices. A personal computer has a keyboard queue implemented as a ring buffer (discussed in Section 3.5). When a key is pressed, its code does not go directly to the active program but is placed in the keyboard buffer until the program requests it. Printer output may be buffered: the characters are held in the output buffer until the printer is ready to receive them. An operating system may have a queue of print jobs waiting to be sent to a printer while other programs are running.

In this chapter we will discuss different ways for implementing the stack and queue structures in Java. The *Toy Browser* lab in Section 3.3 illustrates the use of stacks in implementing "back" and "forward" buttons in a browser. The *Teletext* lab in Section 3.6 demonstrates how messages typed in by the user are queued and later appear and scroll up on the screen.

3.2   Implementations of Stack

In Java, a stack can be implemented with the help of a list. Both the `ArrayList` and `LinkedList` classes provide methods that make programming a stack of objects very easy. One approach is to derive your stack class from one of them. However, in that case your stack will also inherit all of `List`'s methods. If you prefer to keep your stack's functionality pure, with push and pop but no `List` methods or iterators, then, instead of inheritance, embed a private field of the `ArrayList` or `LinkedList` type in your encapsulated stack class and channel the stack methods through the available `List` methods. It will look something like this:

```
import java.util.LinkedList;

public class ListStack
{
  private LinkedList list;
  ...
  public void push (Object obj) { list.addFirst(obj); }
  ...
}
```

It is also easy to program a specialized stack from scratch, using an array for holding the values. This may be useful for a stack of `ints` or `doubles`, so that you don't have to convert them into objects. This is one of the exercises at the end of this chapter. The array implementation maintains an integer index, called the stack pointer, which marks the current top of the stack. The stack usually grows toward the end of the array; the stack pointer is incremented when a new value is pushed onto the stack and decremented when a value is popped from the stack. In some implementations the stack pointer points to the top element of the stack; other programmers find it more convenient to point to the next available vacant slot on the stack. Figure 3-1 illustrates the latter implementation.

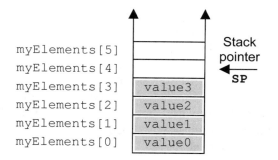

Figure 3-1. An array implementation of stack

❖   ❖   ❖

Before we start working with stacks in Java, it is appropriate to define a `Stack` interface to formalize the stack methods. We can use this interface as a basis for discussion and various implementations. The `Stack` interface in Figure 3-2 specifies the `push` and `pop` methods, the `boolean` method `isEmpty`, and an additional method `peekTop` that returns the value of the top element without removing it from the stack.[*] (The `Stack` interface in Figure 3-2 is not to be confused with the `java.util.Stack` class, which has slightly different method names.) There is no method to empty the stack — in Java you just throw it away (to the garbage collector) and create a new one.

```
public interface Stack
{
  boolean isEmpty();
  void push(Object obj);
  Object pop();
  Object peekTop();
}
```

Figure 3-2. The `Stack` interface (`Ch03\Stack.java` 💾)

---

[*] Adapted from The College Board's *AP Computer Science AB: Implementation Classes and Interfaces.*

> When you implement this `Stack` interface in a class, the `pop` and `peekTop` methods are expected to "throw" an *unchecked exception* — `IndexOutOfBoundsException` or `NoSuchElementException` — if the stack is empty.

An unchecked exception is reported as a run-time error message on the console and aborts the program. No attempt is made in the program to recover from the error. `throw` is a Java reserved word. To throw an exception, the following statement is used:

```
throw new SomeKindOfException(...);
```

For example:

```
if (isEmpty())
    throw new NoSuchElementException();
```

> If you use library classes, such as `ArrayList` or `LinkedList`, for implementing your stack class, then you don't have to worry about throwing exceptions, because library methods do it for you.

For example:

```
public Object pop()
{
  return list.removeFirst(obj);
        // throws NoSuchElementException
        //    if list is empty
}
```

Or:

```
public Object pop()
{
  return array.remove(size() - 1);
        // throws IndexOutOfBoundsException
        //    if array is empty
}
```

Figure 3-3 and Figure 3-4 show the Stack interface implemented in the ArrayStack and ListStack classes, respectively. The former relies on an embedded java.util.ArrayList field, and the latter uses an embedded java.util.LinkedList field.

```
public class ArrayStack implements Stack
{
  private java.util.ArrayList array;

  public ArrayStack()  { array = new java.util.ArrayList(); }
  public boolean isEmpty() { return array.size() == 0; }
     // Or: ... isEmpty() { return array.isEmpty(); }
  public void push(Object obj) { array.add(obj); }
  public Object pop() { return array.remove(array.size() - 1); }
  public Object peekTop() { return array.get(array.size() - 1); }
}
```

Figure 3-3. An implementation of the Stack interface based on ArrayList[*]
(Ch03\ArrayStack.java 💾)

```
public class ListStack implements Stack
{
  private java.util.LinkedList list;

  public ListStack() { list = new java.util.LinkedList(); }
  public boolean isEmpty() { return list.isEmpty(); }
  public void push(Object obj) { list.addFirst(obj); }
  public Object pop() { return list.removeFirst(); }
  public Object peekTop() { return list.getFirst(); }
}
```

Figure 3-4. An implementation of the Stack interface based on LinkedList
(Ch03\ListStack.java 💾)

---

[*] Adapted from The College Board's *AP Computer Science AB: Implementation Classes and Interfaces.*

In Java, a stack of objects holds <u>references</u> to objects. The objects potentially may change after they have been pushed on the stack (unless they are immutable). If you expect an object to change and you need to save its original state on a stack, create a copy of the object and <u>push that copy</u> onto the stack.

3.3   *Lab:* Browsing

In this lab we will implement a toy browser. Rather than browsing web pages, our browser will "browse" several lines of text in the same file. Figure 3-5 shows the classes that we have to write for this project. As usual, this is a team effort: I provide the `ToyBrowser` and `BrowserView` classes and you work on the `BrowserModel` class. We also use the `LinkedListFromFile` class from the lab in Section 2.7.

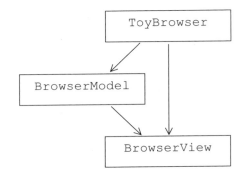

Figure 3-5. *Toy Browser* **project classes**

Our browser only understands the `<a href="#`*name*`">` and `<a name="`*name*`">` tags. To avoid complicated parsing of strings, we assume that these tags are written exactly as shown, where *name* is any non-empty alphanumeric string. If a line contains an `<a href="#...">` tag, the whole line becomes a hyperlink. As usual, when such a hyperlink is clicked, our browser finds a line with a matching `<a name="...">` tag and brings that line to the top of the screen. Our browser ignores all other tags and preserves the actual line breaks in the file rather then interpreting `<p>`, `<br>`, or other tags.

All these details are handled in my `BrowserView` class; you only need to know them if you want to create your own test data file. Or you can use the one supplied on your student disk: `ch03\Browser\lines.html` 🖫.

Our browser has "Home," "Back," and "Forward" buttons, just like a real browser. <u>An important part of your task</u> is to figure out how exactly these buttons work in a real browser (e.g., *Netscape Navigator* or *Internet Explorer*). "Home," "Back," and "Forward" in our browser should work the same way.

Now let's agree on more formal specifications.

<u>My</u> `BrowserView` <u>class</u> provides one method of interest to you:

```
public void update(List text, int n)   // 0 <= n < list.size()
```

displays several lines from `text`, as many as fit in the display, with the *n*-th line at the top of the display. Your class, `BrowserModel`, should call `update` as necessary. Note that `update` is rather general: I don't care <u>what kind</u> of list you pass to it. I use iterators to traverse the list, making it more efficient in case `text` happens to be a linked list.

<u>Your</u> `BrowserModel` <u>class</u> should provide one constructor and six methods.

`BrowserModel`'s constructor takes two arguments:

```
BrowserModel(List text, BrowserView view)
```

The first argument is a list of lines of text. (In my `ToyBrowser` class, I use `LinkedListfromFile` to load the lines from the file `lines.html` into a list.) The second argument is a `BrowserView` type of object. Your constructor should save it to be able to call `view`'s `update` method later. Don't forget to call `update` from `BrowserModel`'s constructor to initialize the view.

Four of `BrowserModel`'s methods are used for navigation:

```
void back();
void forward();
void home();
void followLink(int n);
```

I call `home`, `back`, and `forward` methods when a corresponding button is clicked. I call `followLink(n)` when a hyperlink pointing to the *n*-th line is clicked.

`BrowserModel`'s two remaining methods let me know whether the "Back" and/or "Forward" buttons should be enabled or disabled:

```
boolean hasBack();
boolean hasForward();
```

The return `true` means enable; `false`, disable.

You'll find `ToyBrowser.java` and `BrowserView.java` files on your student disk in the `Ch03\Browser` ⌹ folder. The `lines.html` ⌹ data file for testing our browser is in the same folder. We also need `LinkedListFromFile.java` — use your solution to the lab in Section 2.7 (and don't forget that it uses the `EasyReader` class). Other classes and interfaces that you might find useful are on your student disk in the `Ch03` ⌹ folder.

3.4   The Hardware Stack

What happens when a method is called? When method `caller` calls method `task`, how does `task` know where to return control after it has finished? Obviously `caller` has to pass along some return address so that `task` can send the CPU to that address when it is through. Let us consider several possible locations where that return address can be stored.

The first guess is that it could be saved in some specially reserved memory location. This could work if `task` did not call any other methods. If, however, `task` called another method, `subTask`, then its return address would go into the same memory location and overwrite the first return address. In a more elaborate scheme, the return address could go into some special memory area attached to the method code, for instance just before the beginning of the method code. This would solve the problem of methods calling other methods, because every method has its own storage for the return address. This is, in fact, how some early models of computers worked. A problem arises, however, if `task` is allowed to call itself, or when there are circular calls: `task` calls `subTask`, `subTask` calls `anotherSubTask`, `anotherSubTask` calls `task`. Then `task` will get confused about whether to return control to `anotherSubTask` or to `caller`.

The notion of a method calling itself may at first seem absurd. But, as we know, such *recursive* calls are extremely useful for dealing with nested structures or branching processes where substructures or branches are similar to the whole. Recursive methods can greatly simplify algorithms. Recursion is discussed in more detail in Chapter 4.

Practically the only solution remaining is a stack. When `caller` calls `task`, it pushes the return address on the stack. When `task` has finished, it pops the return address from the stack and passes control back to it. `task` can use the stack for its own purposes and for calling other methods: the only requirement is that it restore the stack pointer to its initial value before returning.

This way, methods can call each other without any conflict. In particular, a method can call itself or methods can call each other in a circular manner. In addition to the return address, though, we have to be careful with the parameters and local variables. If a method in the middle of its course calls itself, what becomes of its local variables? Again, the stack offers the solution. The method parameters and local variables can all reside on the stack. The stack pointer is adjusted to reserve some space for them when the method is called, and the stack pointer is restored when the method has finished its processing. That way we can use only one copy of the method code but multiple copies of the method return address, parameters, and local variables, one for every currently call in progress. The area of the stack that holds all the information for a particular method call is a **frame**. Figure 3-6 illustrates the frames created on the stack after several method calls.

In modern computers the stack method is supported in hardware. The hardware stack does not require any special memory. It is implemented simply as a stack pointer **register** that can point to a desired memory location and can be modified either directly or by the `push` and `pop` CPU instructions. The CPU instruction `call` automatically pushes the address of the next instruction onto the stack before passing control to a subroutine. The CPU instruction `ret` (return) automatically pops the return address from the stack and passes control back to that address.

When method `caller` calls method `task`, `caller` pushes the parameters that it wants to pass to `task` onto the stack, then passes control to `task`. `task` allocates some space on the stack for its own local variables. When `task` has finished its job, it wipes out its local variables from the stack. Either the caller or the called method, depending on the convention in the compiler, performs the final clean-up by removing the parameters from the stack.

The hardware stack is also used for saving the system state when it is interrupted by an external event. Pressing any key on the keyboard, for example, generates a hardware interrupt, a situation that needs the CPU's immediate attention. When this happens, the address of the current CPU instruction is pushed on stack and control is passed to the special interrupt handling routine. This routine pushes all CPU registers on stack to save the current state. Then it receives and processes the pressed key and places its code into the keyboard buffer for later use by the running application. After that the keyboard routine pops all the registers from the stack (in reverse order) and returns control to the interrupted program. The stack helps to handle nested interrupts (when one interrupt comes in the middle of processing another interrupt) properly. People often use a similar method when their tasks or conversations are interrupted.

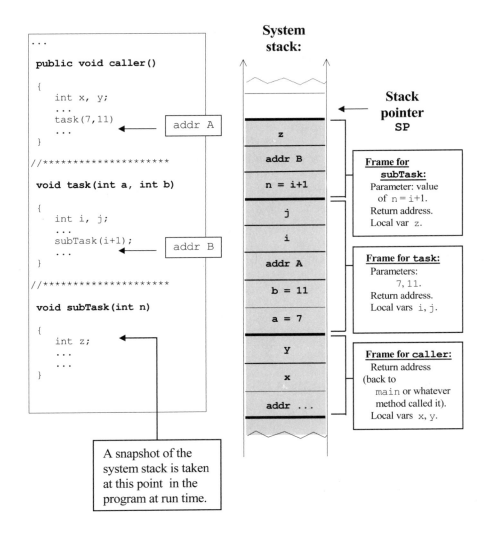

Figure 3-6. Frames on the system stack after a few method calls

3.5   Implementations of Queues

A queue can be programmed in different ways. One approach uses a linked list enhanced by an additional pointer to the tail of the list. Values are added at the tail of the list and removed at the head of the list. In Java, this implementation is based on the `java.util.LinkedList` class and its `addLast` and `removeFirst` methods.

Another implementation uses a ***ring buffer***, which is simply an array used in a circular manner. If we used an array in a regular linear manner, we would have to shift the whole array forward whenever we removed the first value. In a ring buffer we simply adjust a pointer that defines the "logical" first element. The state of the queue is maintained with the help of two indices, `front` and `rear`. `front` points to the first element in the queue, which will be returned by the next call to the `dequeue` method; `dequeue` also increments the `front` index. `rear` points to the empty slot following the last stored element. The `enqueue` method stores the next value in the slot pointed to by `rear` and increments the `rear` index. Both `front` and `rear` wrap around the end of the array to the beginning (Figure 3-7). This mechanism helps to maintain a queue without shifting the whole array.

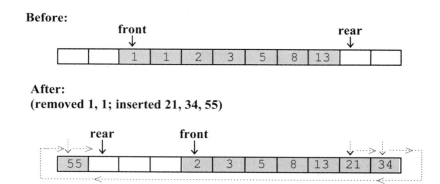

Figure 3-7.   Ring-buffer implementation of a queue

Figure 3-8 shows the `Queue` interface that serves as the basis for this discussion. If the queue is empty, the `dequeue` and `peekFront` methods "throw" an unchecked exception: `IndexOutOfBoundsException` or `NoSuchElementException`.

Either the `ArrayList` or the `LinkedList` class can be used to implement a queue, but, unless you implement a ring-buffer type of queue, an implementation based on arrays may be inefficient because it will involve shifting the values whenever an item is dequeued. On the other hand, an implementation based on a linked list with a tail is efficient and easy. Figure 3-9 shows an implementation with a `LinkedList` object embedded as a private field in the `ListQueue` class.

```
public interface Queue
{
  boolean isEmpty();
  void enqueue(Object obj);
  Object dequeue();
  Object peekFront();
}
```

Figure 3-8. The `Queue` interface [*] (Ch03\\`Queue.java` 🖫)

```
public class ListQueue implements Queue
{
  private java.util.LinkedList list;

  public ListQueue() { list = new java.util.LinkedList(); }
  public boolean isEmpty() { return list.size() == 0; }
    // Or: ... isEmpty() { return list.isEmpty(); }
  public void enqueue(Object obj) { list.addLast(obj); }
  public Object dequeue() { return list.removeFirst(); }
  public Object peekFront() { return list.getFirst(); }
}
```

Figure 3-9. An implementation of the `Queue` interface based on `LinkedList` [*]

(Ch03\\`ListQueue.java` 🖫)

Occasionally we need a class that implements both a queue and a list (for convenient traversals). In that case, we can derive our class from `LinkedList` and add the `enqueue`, `dequeue`, and `peekFront` methods as opposed to embedding a `LinkedList` field. (No need to redefine `isEmpty`, because `LinkedList` already has it.) The class then implements both the `List` and `Queue` interfaces. We will need such a class, `ListAndQueue`, for the lab in the following section.

---

[*] Adapted from The College Board's *AP Computer Science AB: Implementation Classes and Interfaces.*

3.6   *Lab:* Teletext

This application displays a list of headlines scrolling upward on the screen. The program initially loads a few headlines from a file and places them into a queue. It displays the headlines that fit in the display, starting with the first one at the top of the display. When the top line scrolls out of view, it is removed from the beginning of the queue and enqueued again at the end. Meanwhile, the user can enter new headlines. When the user presses <Enter> the new line is added to the queue. The user can also enter "delete." Then the headline currently at the top is slated for deletion: it is not enqueued again after it scrolls out of view.

We will create four classes for this project (Figure 3-10). I write `Teletext` and a sketch for `TeletextView` with missing code in two methods. You can finish `TeletextView` and write `TeletextModel` and `ListAndQueue`.

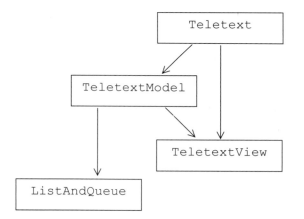

Figure 3-10.   *Teletext* project classes

<u>Your first task</u> is to write a `ListAndQueue` class that implements both the `java.util.List` interface and the `Queue` interface as described in the previous section. In addition to the no-args constructor, `ListAndQueue` should have a constructor that takes a file name as an argument and reads lines from the file into the list. A quick way to write this class is to derive it from `LinkedListFromFile`,

which you wrote in Lab 2.7. Note how we have started building a set of reusable list, queue, and stack classes (Figure 3-11).

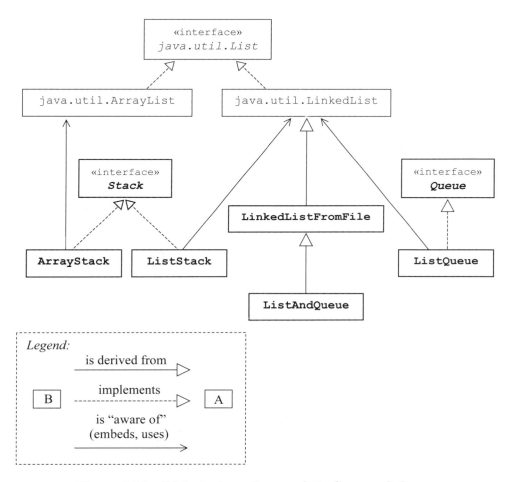

Figure 3-11. List, stack, and queue interfaces and classes

Your second task is to write the TeletextModel class with one constructor and two public methods. The constructor —

```
public TeletextModel(String fileName, TeletextView view)
```

— takes two arguments. The first argument is the name of a text file. The constructor creates a ListAndQueue type of list from that file. The constructor saves view to be able to call its update method later.

The two methods are:

```
void add(String line);
void scrollUp();
```

`add(line)` is called when the user types in a line and presses `<Enter>`. If `line` is not `"delete"`, it is added to the queue. If it is a "delete" command, then the method figures out which line is to be deleted (the first one, if most of it is still visible, or the second one) and sets a "delete counter" field accordingly, to 1 or 2.

`scrollUp()` is called to scroll the display up by one pixel. `TeletextModel` maintains the offset (in pixels) from the top of the first line to the top of the screen. The offset is zero or negative — it normally ranges from 0 to the negative height of the line. `scrollUp` decrements the offset by one pixel on each call. When the top line goes completely out of view, `scrollUp` removes that line from the queue and increments the offset by the height of one line. `scrollUp` also takes care of deleting lines. If the delete counter is 0, the line removed from the top is added back to the queue. But if the delete counter is equal to 1, `scrollUp` does not enqueue that line again. If the delete counter is positive (1 or 2), `scrollUp` decrements it. `scrollUp` updates the view on each call.

My `TeletextView` class has two methods of interest to you. `getLineHeight()` returns the height of the line (font height) in pixels. The second method, `update`, updates the view:

```
void update(List lines, int offset)
```

Its arguments are a list of lines and an offset in pixels from the top of the first line in the list to the top of the view area. The offset is the same as the one maintained by the `TeletextModel`. It is usually in the range

```
-getLineHeight() < offset <= 0
```

`update` saves parameters passed to it temporarily in the two class fields defined for that purpose, then calls `paintComponent()`.

Your third task is to supply the missing code for `TeletextView`'s `update` and `paintComponent` methods. Their code is very close to the corresponding code in `BrowserView` (in Ch03\Browser 🖫). `TeletextView.java` is available in the Ch03\Teletext 🖫 folder.

Test your program using the provided `headlines.txt` file (in Ch03\Teletext 🖫) or make you own data file.

3.7   Summary

A stack is a data structure used for storing and retrieving data elements. The values are said to be "on the stack." A stack is controlled by two operations referred to as push and pop. Push adds a value to the top of the stack, and pop removes the value from the top of the stack. These two operations implement the LIFO (Last-In-First-Out) data access method.

One possible implementation of a stack uses an array and an integer index, called the stack pointer, which marks the current top of the stack. The stack usually grows toward the end of the array; the stack pointer is incremented when a new value is pushed onto the stack and decremented when a value is popped from the stack.

In Java, it is easy to implement a stack class by utilizing one of the list classes, `ArrayList` or `LinkedList`. `ArrayList`-based implementation may be slightly more efficient, especially if the maximum needed capacity of the stack is known in advance.

The stack mechanism is useful for temporary storage, especially for dealing with nested structures or processes: it allows your program to untangle the nested structure and trace all its substructures in the correct order.

The queue data structure is used for storing and retrieving values in a First-In-First-Out (FIFO) manner. A queue can be implemented as a ring buffer, which is simply an array used in a circular way. The `front` index marks the beginning of the queue, where the next value will be removed; the `rear` index marks the end of the queue (the first available slot), where the next value will be inserted. Both pointers wrap around the end of the array. Another queue implementation may use a linked list with an additional pointer to the tail of the list where the new values will be inserted. In Java, the latter can take advantage of the `LinkedList` class.

Queues are used for processing events that have to be handled in the order of their arrival but may have to wait for available resources or an appropriate time. Queues are widely used for system tasks such as scheduling jobs, passing data between processes, and input/output buffering for peripheral devices.

Exercises

Sections 3.1-3.4

1.   Mark true or false and explain:

    (a)   A stack is especially useful as temporary storage for events that have to be handled in the order of their arrival. _____ ✓

    (b)   The Queue data structure is a special case of the Stack data structure. _____

    (c)   The `Stack` interface can be implemented in a class using either an array or a linked list. _____

2.   Which of the following is the most economical structure for the linked-list implementation of a queue: ✓

    A.   A linked list
    B.   A linked list with a reference to the tail
    C.   A circular list

3.   What is the output from the following code?

```
Stack stack = new ArrayStack();
String s;

stack.push("A");
stack.push("B");
stack.push("C");
while (!stack.isEmpty())
{
  s = (String)stack.pop();
  System.out.print(s);
}
```

4. What is the output from the following code? ✓

```
Stack stk = new ArrayStack();

stk.push("One");
stk.push("Two");
stk.push("Three");

String s;
while (!stk.isEmpty())
{
  s = (String)stk.pop();
  if (!stk.isEmpty())
  {
    s += ("-" + (String)stk.pop());
    stk.push(s);
  }
  System.out.println(s);
}
```

5. A stack `stack` contains `Integer` objects with values

```
(top) -1 3 7 -2 4 -6
```

What is its content after the following code is executed?

```
Integer obj;
Stack stackPos = new ArrayStack(),
      stackNeg = new ArrayStack();

while (!stack.isEmpty())
{
  obj = (Integer)stack.pop();
  if (obj.intValue() >= 0)
    stackPos.push(obj);
  else
    stackNeg.push(obj);
}

while (!stackPos.isEmpty())
{
  stack.push(stackPos.pop());
}

while (!stackNeg.isEmpty())
{
  stack.push(stackNeg.pop());
}
```

6. A deck of cards is represented in a program as a stack of `Card` objects. Write a method

```
public boolean moveToTop(Stack deck, int n)
```

that takes the *n*-th card (counting the top card as the first one) and moves it to the top of the deck. The method returns `true` if the deck has *n* or more cards; otherwise it leaves the deck unchanged and returns `false`. Your method may use a temporary stack, but no other arrays or lists. ✓

7. Suppose a stack is implemented as a linked list. The nodes are represented by `ListNode` objects, and the field `top` refers to the top node:

```
public class ListNodeStack implements Stack
{
  private ListNode top;
  . . .
}
```

Given the code for the push method —

```
public void push(Object value)
{
  top = new ListNode(value, top);
}
```

— supply the code for the `isEmpty`, `peekTop`, and `pop` methods. (The `peekTop` and `pop` methods should throw a `NoSuchElementException` if the stack is empty.)

8.▪ In the following code, a stack of `Integer` objects is used:

```
Point cursor;
Stack stk = new ArrayStack();
. . .
// Save cursor position:
stk.push(new Integer((int)cursor.getX()));
stk.push(new Integer((int)cursor.getY()));

show(new LoginWindow());
. . .
// Restore cursor position:
int x = ((Integer)stk.pop()).intValue();
int y = ((Integer)stk.pop()).intValue();
cursor.move(x, y);
```

(a) Find and fix a bug in the code.
(b) Suggest a way to simplify the code. ✓

9.   A stack of characters can be implemented using a `String`.

(a)   Does the following code correctly implement the `push` and `pop` methods?

```
private String stack = "";
              // Declare an empty stack of chars;
...
public void push(char ch)
{
   stack += ch;
}

public char pop()
{
   int n = stack.length() - 1;
   if (n >= 0)
   {
      char ch = stack.charAt(n);
      stack = stack.substring(0, n);
      return ch;
   }
   else
      throw new NoSuchElementException();
}
```

(b)   Discuss the merits of the above implementation of a stack. ✓

(c)   Rewrite the `push` and `pop` methods so that `pop` returns the first character in the string.

(d)■   Rewrite the above code using a `StringBuffer` object and its `append` and `deleteCharAt` methods.

10.■   Write and test a class `IntStack` that implements a stack of integers with methods similar to the ones in the `Stack` interface, but handling values of the type `int` rather than `Object`. Use an integer array of the default or specified capacity to hold the values. Use a "stack pointer" to hold the index of the first empty slot. Reallocate the array, doubling its size, if the stack runs out of space.

11.∎   The following program reads a binary number (a string of binary digits) from the console and displays the number as a decimal:

```java
public class BinToDecimal
{
  public static void main(String[] args)
  {
    Stack stack = new ArrayStack();
    EasyReader console = new EasyReader();
    String binNum = console.readWord();

    for (int i = 0; i < binNum.length(); i++)
    {
      char ch = binNum.charAt(i);
      stack.push(new Character(ch));
    }

    int dig, val = 0, power2 = 1;

    while (!stack.isEmpty())
    {
      Character obj = (Character)stack.pop();
      dig = Character.digit(obj.charValue(), 2);
      val += dig * power2;
      power2 *= 2;
    }

    System.out.println(val);
  }
}
```

Explain why the use of a stack here is overkill. Rewrite without the stack. ✓

12.✦   A book's index contains entries and sub-entries nested to several levels. Sub-entries are indicated by deeper indentation. All the sub-entries of a given entry are preceded by the same number of spaces; that number is greater than the indentation at the previous level. For example (see `Ch03\Exercises\index.dat` 🖫):

```
class
    abstract
    accessors
    constructors
      overloaded
      no-args
    modifiers
method
    private
    public
    static
stack
    for handling nested structures
    methods
      push
      pop
      peekTop
```

Write a program that reads an index file and verifies that all the entries and subentries are in alphabetical order. Skip empty lines.

13.✦   Write a program in which Cookie Monster finds the optimal path from the upper left corner (0, 0) to the lower right corner (SIZE-1, SIZE-1) in a cookie grid (a 2-D array). The elements of the grid contain cookies (a non-negative number) or barrels (-1). On each step Cookie Monster can only go down or to the right. He is not allowed to step on barrels. The optimal path contains the largest number of cookies.

The program reads the cookie grid from a file and reports the number of cookies on the optimal path. (The path itself is not reported.) A sample data file is provided in `Ch03\Exercises\cookies.dat` 🖫.

⸳ Hints: If there is only one way to proceed from the current position, then go there and update the total accumulated number of cookies. If there are two ways to proceed, save one of the possible two points (and its total) on stack and proceed to the other point. If you have reached the lower right corner, update the maximum. If there is nowhere to go, examine the stack: pop a saved point, if any, and resume from there. ⸳

Sections 3.5-3.7

14.   What is the output from the following code?

```
Queue q = new ListQueue();

for (int k = 1; k <= 3; k++)
{
  q.enqueue(new Integer(k-1));
  q.enqueue(new Integer(k+1));
}

while (!q.isEmpty())
{
  Integer obj = (Integer)q.dequeue();
  System.out.print(obj.intValue());
}
```

15.   A class `RingBuffer` implements a queue of `chars`. It has a constructor that allocates a character array of a given size and initializes it to an empty state:

```
public RingBuffer(int capacity)
{
  characters = new char[capacity + 1];
  front = 0;
  rear = 0;
  last = capacity;
}
```

(a)   Write a `void` method `flush()` that empties the queue (without deallocating `characters`). ✓

(b)   Write a `boolean` method `isEmpty()`.

(c)▪   Write a `boolean` method `enqueue(char ch)`. The method should return `true` if the operation is successful and `false` if the queue is full.

16. Suppose a class `ListNodeQueue` implements `Queue` using a linked list of `ListNode` objects with references `front` and `rear` to the first and last nodes, respectively. Given the code for the `dequeue` method —

```
public Object dequeue()
{
  if (front != null)
  {
    Object value = front.getValue();
    front = front.getNext();
    if (front == null)
      rear = null;
    return value;
  }
  else
    throw new NoSuchElementException();
}
```

— supply the code for the `isEmpty`, `peekFront`, and `enqueue` methods.

17. A Morse code message is represented in a program as a queue of strings. Each string consists of dots and dashes. The message always ends with a special terminator string

```
private final String terminator = "END";
```

Write a method

```
public void replace(Queue morseCode)
```

that replaces each question mark, represented by `"..--.."`, with a period, represented by `".-.-.-"`, leaving all other codes unchanged.

18.▪ The IBM PC BIOS uses a keyboard ring buffer of 16 bytes, starting at the address `40:1E`. The two-byte locations `40:1A` and `40:1C` represent the front and the rear of the keyboard queue, respectively. These locations hold offsets from `40:00`, stored with the least significant byte first. Each pressed keyboard key adds two bytes to the keyboard buffer: the ASCII code of the character followed by the so-called "scan code" that represents the location of the key on the keyboard. Examine the following hex memory dump and determine the current contents of the keyboard queue and the last eight characters typed. ✓

```
           0  1  2  3  4  5  6  7  8  9  A  B  C  D  E  F
0040:0010                                 28 00 28 00 30 0B
0040:0020   3A 27 31 02 61 1E 0D 1C-64 20 20 39 34 05
```

19. ▪   Complete a class `Student`:

```
public class Student
{
  private String name;
  private double GPA;
  ...
}
```

Then write a method

```
public ListQueue cutAtGPA(ListQueue students, double minGPA)
```

that removes student records one by one from the `students` queue and adds those students whose GPA is not less than `minGPA` to the new "honors" queue. The method returns the "honors" queue.

20. ▪   Write a class `ListQueueWithCopy`, which extends `ListQueue`. Add a method

```
public ListQueueWithCopy copy()
```

that builds and returns a copy of this queue (leaving the original unchanged).

21. ◆   A 6 by 6 game board contains arbitrarily arranged black and white squares. A path across this board may use only black squares and may move only down or to the right. Write and test a program that reads a board configuration from a file and finds and prints out all paths leading from the upper left corner (0,0) to the lower right corner (5,5). Use a `ListQueueWithCopy` (from Question 20) to hold partial paths and an `ArrayStack` to hold the branching points and partial paths. A sample data file is provided in `Ch03\Exercises\board.dat` 🖫.

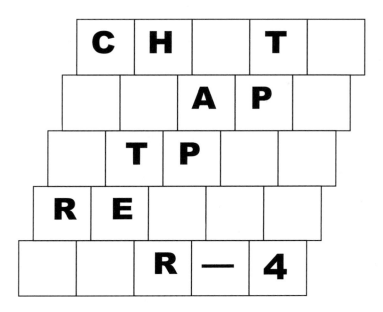

Recursion

4.1   Prologue

According to one of Euclid's axioms, "The whole is greater than the part." This may be true for the lengths of segments and the volumes of solids in geometry, but in the intangible world of computer software the whole is sometimes the same as the part, at least in terms of its structural description and use. Which is "greater," for example, a directory or a subdirectory in a tree-structured computer file system? A particular directory is "greater" than its subdirectories, because overall it contains more files (counting the files in all its subdirectories), than any subdirectory. But a directory is "the same" as its subdirectories, because any subdirectory is a directory. It holds its own files and its own subdirectories, and its structure and use are the same.

In another example, take a Java list. It can contain any type of objects as values, including other lists. In one sense, a list is "greater" than any of its elements, but in another sense, both can be lists. In an extreme case, a list even can be its own element! Java documentation says: "While it is permissible for lists to contain themselves as elements, extreme caution is advised..."

The above instances are examples of recursive structures whose substructures have the same form as the whole. Such structures are best handled by recursive procedures, which operate the same way on a substructure as on the whole structure. In computer software, recursive procedures and processes can be conveniently implemented by means of recursive functions whose code includes calls to themselves. We saw in Section 3.4 that the hardware stack mechanism implements a method call the same way, whether the method calls itself or another method. All method parameters, the return address, and the local variables are kept in a separate frame on the system stack, so several methods, including several copies of the same method, can be waiting for control to be returned to them without any conflict. Multiple copies of the same method all share the same code but operate on different data.

It is no coincidence, then, that recursive structures and processes are especially common in the computer world. It is easier to implement and use a structure or a process when its substructures and subprocesses have the same form. The same function, for example, can deal with a directory and subdirectories, a list and its elements that are also lists.

Recursion is not specific to Java: it works the same way with any language that allows functions to call themselves.

4.2   Examples of Recursive Methods

As our first example, let us consider a method that implements "deep" traversal of a linked list that may contain strings as well as similar lists as elements. In effect, it is no longer a simple list, but a whole tree. For now, let's call such a list a "branching list" (Figure 4-1).

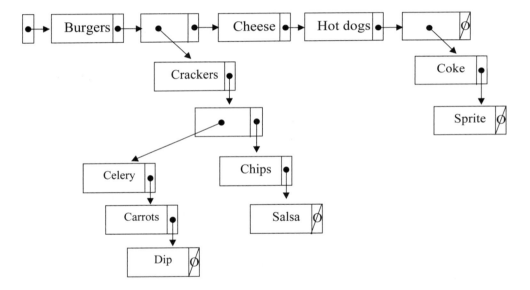

Figure 4-1.   A "Branching" list: some elements hold strings, other lists

A more formal definition of a "branching list" is recursive: a "branching list" is a list where each element is either a string or a "branching list..." Our task is to print all the strings in the list, including all the strings in all the lists that are its elements, and in all the lists that are elements of elements, and so on. Without recursion, this would be a little tricky. With recursion, it's just a few lines of code:

```
public void printAll(LinkedList list)
{
  Iterator iter = list.iterator();
  while (iter.hasNext())
  {
    Object obj = iter.next();
    String className = obj.getClass().getName();
    if ("java.lang.String".equals(className))
      System.out.println((String)obj);
    else // if ("java.util.LinkedList".equals(className))
      printAll((LinkedList)obj);
  }
}
```

In the `printAll` method, recursion helps us deal with a nested structure. For each element in a list there are two possibilities: it is either a simple string (a base case) or it is a list (a recursive case). In the base case there is no need to call the method recursively — we just print out the string. In the recursive case, `printAll` calls itself. Since structures can be nested only to some finite depth, the process eventually reaches the lowest level, the bottom, where only base case processing remains. Then recursion stops. Eventually all the recursive calls get unwound and the method finishes.

For a recursive method to terminate properly, it must explicitly or implicitly handle a base case where recursion does not happen. When a method calls itself recursively, it must be applied to a similar but "smaller" task, that eventually converges to the base case. In the above example, the "size" of the task is the total number of strings in the list and all the branches. If you make a branching list its own element or an element of one of its elements, then the method will go into infinite recursion and "blow the stack."

The above example demonstrates how compact the recursive implementation of a method can be. As usual, this method can be also implemented with a stack, but the code becomes less elegant and harder to understand:

```
public void printAll(LinkedList list)
{
  ArrayStack stack = new ArrayStack();

  Iterator iter = list.iterator();
  while (iter.hasNext() || !stack.isEmpty())
  {
    if (iter.hasNext())
    {
      Object obj = iter.next();
      String className = obj.getClass().getName();
      if ("java.lang.String".equals(className))
        System.out.println((String)obj);
      else // if ("java.util.LinkedList".equals(className))
      {
        stack.push(iter);                      // to be continued later...
        iter = ((LinkedList)obj).iterator(); // take care of this list
      }
    }
    else
    {
      iter = (Iterator)stack.pop();
    }
  }
}
```

Recursive calls actually do a similar thing, but they automate the process for you by using the system stack.

In this example we have used an `if` statement to determine the type of the node in the list. A better implementation, based on the "Composite" design pattern, discussed in Section 10.6, would avoid the explicit type checking and rely on polymorphism instead.

❖   ❖   ❖

In our second example we will generate all permutations of a string of characters. Suppose we are building a computer word game that tries to make a valid word out of a given set of letters. The program will require a method that generates all permutations of the letters and matches them against a dictionary of words. Suppose a string of *n* characters is stored in a `StringBuffer`. (We use the `StringBuffer` class rather than `String` to make rearranging characters more efficient — `Strings` are immutable objects.) Our strategy for generating all permutations is to place each character in turn in the last place in the string, then generate all permutations of the first ($n-1$) characters. In other words, `permutations` is a recursive method. The method takes two arguments: a `StringBuffer` object and the number *n* of characters in the leading fragment that have to be permutated.

In this example, the process is branching and recursive in nature although there are no nested structures. The base case is when *n* is equal to 1 — there is nothing to do except to report the permutation.

The `permutations` method below is quite short and readable; still, it is hard to grasp why it works! We will return to it in Section 4.4, which explains the best way of understanding and debugging recursive methods.

```
private void swap(StringBuffer str, int i, int j)
{
  char c1 = str.charAt(i);
  char c2 = str.charAt(j);
  str.setCharAt(i, c2);
  str.setCharAt(j, c1);
}

public void permutations(StringBuffer str, int n)
{
  if (n <= 1)
  {                                    // Base case:
                                       // The permutation is completed
    System.out.println(str);   //    -- print it out
  }
  else
  {                                    // Recursive case:
    for (int i = 0; i < n; i++)
    {
      swap(str, i, n-1);
      permutations(str, n-1);
      swap(str, n-1, i);
    }
  }
}
```

4.3   When Not to Use Recursion

Any recursive method can be also implemented through iterations, using a stack if necessary. This poses a question: When is recursion appropriate, and when is it better avoided?

There are some technical considerations that may restrict the use of recursive methods:

1. If a method allocates large local arrays, the program may run out of memory in recursive calls. A programmer has to have a feel for how deeply the recursive calls go; she may choose to implement her own stack and save only the relevant variables there, reusing the same temporary array.

2. When a method manipulates an object's fields, a recursive call may change their values in an unpredictable way unless the manipulation is done on purpose and thoroughly understood.

3. If performance is important, a method implemented without recursion may work faster.

But the most important rule is that recursion should be used only when it significantly simplifies the code without excessive performance loss. Recursion is especially useful for dealing with <u>nested</u> structures or <u>branching</u> processes. One typical example is algorithms for traversing tree structures, which are described in Chapter 5. On the other hand, when you are dealing with <u>linear</u> structures and processes, normally you can use simple iterations. The following test will help you decide when to use recursion and when iterations. If the method branches in two or more directions, calling itself recursively in each branch, it is justified to use recursion. If the method calls itself only once, you can probably do the same thing just as easily with iterations.

As an example, let us consider the `factorial(n)` method that calculates the product of all numbers from 1 to *n*. This method has a simple recursive form:

```
public long factorial(int n)
{
  if (n <= 1)      // Base case:
    return 1;
  else             // Recursive case:
    return n * factorial(n-1);
}
```

Our test shows that `factorial`'s code has only one recursive call. We are dealing with a linear process. It should be just as easy to accomplish the same thing with iterations, thus avoiding the overhead of recursive method calls:

```
public long factorial(int n)
{
  long product = n;
  while (n > 1)
  {
    n--;
    product *= n;
  }
  return product;
}
```

Both versions are acceptable, because the performance loss in the recursive version is small for small n, and the factorial of large n is far too large, anyway.

A more pernicious example is offered by the famous Fibonacci Numbers. These are defined as a sequence where the first two numbers are equal to one, with each consecutive number equal to the sum of the two preceding numbers:

1, 1, 2, 3, 5, 8, 13, ...

Mathematically this is a recursive definition:

$F_1 = 1$; $F_2 = 1$;
$F_n = F_{n-1} + F_{n-2}$ (for $n > 2$).

It can be easily converted into a recursive method:

```
public long fibonacci(int n)
{
  if (n <= 2)      // Base case:
    return 1;
  else             // Recursive case:
    return fibonacci(n-1) + fibonacci(n-2);
}
```

It may seem, at first, that this method meets our test of having more than one recursive call to `fibonacci`. But in fact, there is no branching here: `fibonacci` simply recalls two previous members in the same linear sequence. Don't be misled by the innocent look of this code. The first term, `fibonacci(n-1)`, will recursively call `fibonacci(n-2)` and `fibonacci(n-3)`. The second term, `fibonacci(n-2)`, will call (again) `fibonacci(n-3)` and `fibonacci(n-4)`. The `fibonacci` calls will start multiplying like rabbits.* To calculate the n-th Fibonacci number, F_n, `fibonacci` will actually make more than F_n recursive calls, which, as we will see in the following section, may be quite a large number.

On the other hand, the same method implemented iteratively will need only n iterations:

```
public long fibonacci(int n)
{
  long f1 = 1, f2 = 1, next;
  while (n > 2)
  {
    next = f1 + f2;
    f1 = f2;
    f2 = next;
    n--;
  }
  return f2;
}
```

For our final example of when recursion is not appropriate, let us consider the selection sort algorithm for sorting an array of n elements in ascending order. The idea is to find the largest element and swap it with the last element, then apply the same method to the array of the first $n-1$ elements. This can be done recursively:

```
public void selectionSort(int a[], int n)
{
  int i, iMax;

  if (n == 1)       // Base case: array of length 1 -- nothing to do
      return;
  else
  {
    // Find the index of the largest element:
    iMax = 0;
    for (i = 1; i < n; i++)
      if (a[iMax] < a[i]) iMax = i;

    // Swap it with the last element:
    int aTemp = a[n-1]; a[n-1] = a[iMax]; a[iMax] = aTemp;

    // Call selectionSort for the first n-1 elements:
    selectionSort(a, n-1);
  }
}
```

---

* The numbers are named after Leonardo Pisano (Fibonacci) who invented the sequence in 1202, when he considered a model for the growth of a population of rabbits.

This is a case of so-called ***tail recursion***, where the recursive call is the last statement in the method: only the return from the method is executed after that call. Therefore, by the time of the recursive call, the local variables (except the parameters passed to the recursive call) are no longer needed. A good optimizing compiler will detect this situation and, instead of calling selectionSort recursively, will update the parameter n and pass control back to the beginning of the method. Or, we can easily do it ourselves:

```
public void selectionSort(int v[], int n)
{
  int i, iMax;

  while (n > 1)
  {
    // Find the index of the largest element:
    iMax = 0;
    for (i = 1; i < n; i++)
      if (v[iMax] < v[i]) iMax = i;

    // Swap it with the last element:
    vTemp = v[n-1]; v[n-1] = v[iMax]; v[iMax] = vTemp;

    n--;
  }
}
```

To quote Niklaus Wirth, the inventor of the Pascal programming language,

> In fact, the explanation of the concept of recursive algorithm by such inappropriate examples has been a chief cause of creating widespread apprehension and antipathy toward the use of recursion in programming, and of equating recursion with inefficiency.[*]

---

[*] Niklaus Wirth, *Algorithms + Data Structures = Programs*. Prentice Hall, 1976.

4.4   Understanding and Debugging
Recursive Methods

A common way of understanding and debugging non-recursive methods is to trace, either mentally or with a debugger, the sequence of statements and method calls in the code. Programmers may also insert some debugging print statements that will report to them the method's progress and the intermediate values of variables.

These conventional methods are very hard to apply to recursive methods, because it is difficult to keep track of your current location in the hierarchy of recursive calls. Getting to the bottom of the recursive process requires a detailed examination of the system stack — a tedious and useless activity. Instead of such futile attempts, recursive methods can be more easily understood and analyzed with the help of a method known as ***mathematical induction***.

In a nutshell, mathematical induction works as follows. Suppose we have a series of statements

$P_0, P_1, P_2, \dots , P_n, \dots$

Suppose that:

1. We can show that P_0 is true (the base case);

2. We can prove that, for any $n \geq 1$, <u>if</u> P_0, ..., P_{n-1} are true (***induction hypothesis***), <u>then</u> P_n is also true.

Then, if both conditions are met, we can conclude that all statements in the series are true.

This is so because P_0 implies P_1, P_0 and P_1 imply P_2, and so on. However, we do not have to go through the entire logical sequence for every step. Instead, we can take a shortcut and just say that all the statements are true by mathematical induction.

❖   ❖   ❖

As an exercise in mathematical induction, let us estimate the running time for the recursive `fibonacci` method discussed in the previous section:

```
public long fibonacci(int n)
{
  if (n <= 2)      // Base case:
    return 1;
  else             // Recursive case:
    return fibonacci(n-1) + fibonacci(n-2);
}
```

We will prove that `fibonacci(n)` requires not less than $(3/2)^{n-2}$ calls to the method. This is true for $n = 1$ and $n = 2$ (base cases), which both require just one call:

$n=1$: $1 > (3/2)^{1-2} = (3/2)^{-1} = 2/3$;
$n=2$: $1 = (3/2)^{2-2} = (3/2)^0$

For any $n > 2$, in addition to the initial call, the method calls `fibonacci(n-1)` and `fibonacci(n-2)`. <u>From the induction hypothesis</u> the number of calls for `fibonacci(n-1)` is not less than $(3/2)^{n-3}$ and the number of calls for `fibonacci(n-2)` is not less than $(3/2)^{n-4}$. So the total number of calls for `fibonacci(n)` is not less than:

$$1 + (3/2)^{n-3} + (3/2)^{n-4} > (3/2)^{n-3} + (3/2)^{n-4} = (3/2)^{n-4}(3/2 + 1) =$$

$$(3/2)^{n-4} \cdot (5/2) > (3/2)^{n-4} \cdot (3/2)^2 = (3/2)^{n-2}, \text{ q.e.d.}$$

Assuming that a reasonably fast computer can execute a hundred million calls per second (and that we somehow manage to represent very large Fibonacci numbers in memory), `fibonacci(100)` would run for over $(3/2)^{98} / 10^8$ seconds, or more than 57 years! (The iterative implementation, by contrast, would run in less than one microsecond.)

You may notice a close conceptual link between recursion and mathematical induction. The key feature of mathematical induction is that we do not have to trace the sequence of statements to the bottom. We just have to first prove the base case and then, for an arbitrary n, show that if the induction hypothesis is true at all previous levels, then it is also true at the n-th level.

❖　❖　❖

Let us see how mathematical induction applies to the analysis of code in recursive methods. As an example, let's take the `permutations` method from Section 4.2, which generates all permutations of a string of characters:

```
public void permutations(StringBuffer str, int n)
{
  if (n <= 1)
  {                                // Base case:
                                   // The permutation is completed
    System.out.println(str);       //   -- print it out
  }
  else
  {                                // Recursive case:
    for (int i = 0; i < n; i++)
    {
      swap(str, i, n-1);
      permutations(str, n-1);
      swap(str, n-1, i);
    }
  }
}
```

We will prove two facts about this code using mathematical induction:

1. `permutations` returns the string to its original order when it is finished.

2. `permutations(str, n)` generates all permutations of the first *n* characters.

In the base case, $n = 1$, the method just reports the string and does nothing else — so both statements are true. Let us <u>assume</u> that both statements are true for any level below *n* (induction hypothesis). <u>Based on that assumption</u> let us prove that both statements are also true at the level *n*.

In the recursive case, the method swaps `str[i]` and `str[n-1]`, then calls `permutations(str, n-1)`, then swaps back `str[n-1]` and `str[i]`. <u>By the induction hypothesis</u>, `permutations(str, n-1)` preserves the order of characters in `str`. The two swaps cancel each other. So the order of characters is not changed in `permutations(str, n)`. This proves Statement 1.

In the `for` loop we place every character of the string, in turn, at the end of the string. (This is true because the index `i` runs through all values from 0 to `n-1` and, as we have just shown, the order of characters does not change after each iteration through the loop.) With each character placed at the end of the string we call `permutations(str, n-1)`, which, <u>by the induction hypothesis</u>, generates all permutations of the first *n*-1 characters. Therefore, we combine each character placed at the end of the string with all permutations of the first *n*-1 characters, which generates all permutations of *n* characters. This proves Statement 2.

The above example demonstrates how mathematical induction helps us understand and, with almost mathematical rigor, prove the correctness of recursive methods. By comparison, conventional code tracing and debugging and attempts at unfolding recursive calls to the very bottom are seldom feasible or useful.

4.5 *Lab:* The Towers of Hanoi

The "Towers of Hanoi" puzzle has three pegs, with several disks on the first peg. The disks are arranged in order of decreasing diameter from the largest disk on the bottom to the smallest on top. The rules require that the disks be moved from peg to peg, one at a time, and that a larger disk never be placed on top of a smaller one. The objective is to move the whole tower from the first peg to the second peg.

The puzzle was invented by French mathematician François Edouard Anatole Lucas[lucas] and published in 1883. The "legend" that accompanied the game stated that in Benares there was a temple with a dome that marked the center of the world. The priests in the temple moved golden disks between three diamond needlepoints. God placed 64 gold disks on one needle at the time of creation and, according to the "legend," the universe will come to an end when the priests have moved all 64 disks to another needle.

The Towers of Hanoi is probably the most famous example of recursion in computer science courses. There are hundreds of Java applets on the Internet that move disks from peg to peg, either with animation or interactively.[hanoi] In this lab, fancy display is not required.

1. Write a program that solves the puzzle and prints out the required moves for a given number of disks.

2. Examine the number of moves required for 1, 2, 3, etc. disks, find the pattern, and come up with a formula for the minimum number of moves required for *n* disks. Prove the formula using the method of mathematical induction. Estimate how long it will take your program to move a tower of 64 disks.

4.6   *Lab:* The Game of Hex

The game of "Hex" was first invented in 1942 by Piet Hein, a Danish mathematician. (The same game was apparently reinvented independently a few years later by Nobel laureate John Nash, then a graduate student of mathematics at Princeton.) Martin Gardner made the game popular when he described it in his *Scientific American* article in the late 1950s and in a later book.

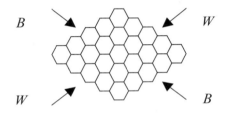

Figure 4-2.   A 5 by 5 Hex board

Hex is played on a rhombic board with hexagonal fields, like a honeycomb. A common board size is 11 by 11; Figure 4-2 shows a smaller 5 by 5 board. The game starts with an empty board. Each of the two players, *B* and *W*, is assigned a pair of opposite sides of the board. For example, *B* gets northwest and southeast, and *W* gets northeast and southwest. *B* has a pile of black stones and *W* has a pile of white stones. Players take turns placing a stone of their color on an empty field. A player who first connects his sides of the board with a contiguous chain of his stones wins.

An interesting property of Hex is that a game can never end in a tie: when the board is filled, either *B* has his sides connected or *W* has his sides connected, always one or the other, but never both. Like all finite strategy games with no repeating positions, Hex has a winning strategy for one of the players. In this case it's the first player (it never hurts to have an extra stone of your color on the board). But a winning strategy is hard to find, because the number of all possible positions is large. For a smaller board, a computer can calculate it. It is not too difficult to write such a program, relying on a recursive algorithm. However (unless you have a lot of free time) in this lab our task is more modest: only to decide whether a given Hex position is won by one of the players.

A human observer can glance at a Hex board and immediately tell whether one of the players has won. Not so in a computer program: it takes some computations to find out whether there is a chain of stones of a particular color that connects two opposite sides of the board. Our task is to develop an algorithm and to write a method that does that.

But first we have to somehow represent a Hex board position in the computer. It is not very convenient to deal with rhombuses and hexagons in a program. Fortunately, an equivalent board configuration can be achieved on a regular square board, represented by a 2-D array. Each inner field on a Hex board has six neighbors (border fields have four, and corner fields have two or three). We can emulate the same configuration on a square board using the appropriate designation of "logical" neighbors. Figure 4-3 shows which squares are supposed to be "neighbors": the rows of a 2-D array are slightly shifted so that "neighbors" share a piece of the border. Basically, a square at (*row*, *col*) has neighbors at (*row*–1, *col*–1), (*row*–1, *col*), (*row*, *col*–1), (*row*, *col*+1), (*row*+1, *col*), and (*row*+1, *col*+1), excluding those positions that fall outside the array.

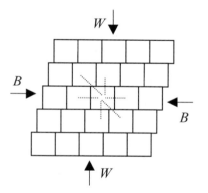

Figure 4-3. A Hex board represented as a 2-D array

Write a class `HexBoard` that represents a board position. You can represent stones of different colors using `chars`, `ints`, `Strings`, or `Colors`. If you use `chars` (e.g., `'b'` for black, `'w'` for white, and space for an empty square), then you can conveniently derive your `HexBoard` class from the `CharMatrix` class that you wrote for the *Chomp* lab in Section 1.6. To hide the implementation details, your `HexBoard` class should provide the modifiers `setBlack` and `setWhite` and the accessors `isBlack` and `isWhite`. It is also convenient to provide a private helper method isInBounds(row, col) that determines whether (*row*, *col*) refers to a legal square on the board.

It is probably easier to write a separate method that detects a win for each of the players. You need to implement only one of them. For example:

```
/**
 *   Returns true if there is a contiguous chain of black stones
 *   that starts in col 0 and ends in the last column of the board,
 *   false otherwise
 */
public boolean blackHasWon()
```

At first, the task may appear trivial: just try starting at every black stone in the first column and follow a chain of black stones to the last column. But a closer look at the problem reveals that chains can branch in tricky ways (Figure 4-4) and there is no obvious way to trace all of them. What we really need is to find a "blob" of connected black stones that touches both the left and the right sides of the board.

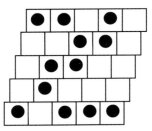

Figure 4-4. Hex: detecting a win for black stones

Finding a connected "blob" on the board falls into the category of "area fill" tasks. A very similar situation occurs when you need to flood a connected area in a picture, replacing one color with another, or to fill the area inside a given contour. It is also similar to the task of finding whether in a system of isolated networks two given points belong to the same network.

Write a public method `getBlob`. It should return a new `HexBoard` that contains only the blob that covers the black stone on a given square (r, c):

```
/**
 *   Creates and returns a HexBoard with the same dimensions as
 *   this one.  Places black stones on all squares of the new
 *   board that correspond to the black stones on this board
 *   that belong to the blob containing the black stone on (r, c).
 *   If (r, c) is not black, returns an empty HexBoard.
 *   Leaves this board unchanged.
 */
public HexBoard getBlob(int r, int c)
```

The easiest approach to extracting a blob from a Hex board is recursion. Take the given black stone, remove it from the board, and put it onto a "blob" board (or simply change its color to "gray"). Then (recursively) call "find the blob" for each of the neighboring black stones. Don't forget that in Hex, a square generally has six neighbors. Skip those that lie outside the board.

Since we want to leave the original board unchanged, we need to do some housekeeping before or after all the recursive processing. `getBlob` can perform the housekeeping tasks and use a recursive helper method to actually extract the blob. There are two approaches to separating the blob from the board while leaving the board unchanged at the end. You can use either one.

The first approach is as follows:

1. Copy the original board into `tempBoard`, leaving the original intact.

2. Create an empty board `blobBoard` that will contain the blob.

3. Call a recursive method `recursiveGetBlob`. In it:
    (a) Remove the given black stone from `tempBoard` and place it on `blobBoard`;
    (b) Call `recursiveGetBlob` for all the neighboring squares on `tempBoard` that hold black stones.

This approach calls for a private `copy` method or a copy constructor. `tempBoard` and `blobBoard` can be passed to `recursiveGetBlob` as parameters. But it is <u>not</u> a good idea to make copies of the board inside a recursive method.

> **If you allocate large local arrays in a recursive method, you may run out of memory.**

The second approach is as follows:

1. Call the recursive method `recursiveFillBlob`. In it:
   (a) Set the "color" of the given black stone to "gray" (you need to add `setGray` and `isGray` methods);
   (b) Call `recursiveFillBlob` for all the neighboring squares on the board that hold black stones.
2. When done, create an empty board `blobBoard`.
3. Restore all "gray" stones on the board back to black while simultaneously setting them to black on `blobBoard`.

The second approach may be slightly faster and more compact because you don't need to make a copy of the board, but either one does the job.

Now you need to write a `boolean blackHasWon` method that decides whether the black stones connect the left and right sides of the board. You need to determine whether at least one of the blobs touches both sides. For each black stone in the leftmost column, extract its blob, then check whether that blob has any black stones in the last column. If your `HexBoard` class is based on `CharMatrix`, `CharMatrix`'s `countInCol` method will help you do that.

Write a separate test class that has methods to read a Hex board configuration from a file and to display it. A simple console-style display will do. Test your `HexBoard`'s `getBlob` and `blackHasWon` methods.

❖   ❖   ❖

You might wonder whether there is a way to look for a win while working on a blob and quit as soon as you reach the rightmost column. This is possible, of course. However, quitting a recursive method for good is not so easy: your original call may be buried under a whole stack of recursive calls and you need to properly quit all of them. You can write a `boolean` method `foundWin` that fills the blob and returns `true` as soon as you have found what you were looking for. That would indicate that further recursion is not necessary. Something like:

```
if (foundWin(row, col-1) == true)
  return true;
if (foundWin(row, col+1) == true)
  return true;
...
```

Another variation is to define a field in your class (a local variable won't do!) and set it to `true` as soon as you find yourself in the rightmost column. Something like:

```
if (col == numCols() - 1)
   myWin = true;
if (!myWin)
   findWin(row, col-1);
if (!myWin)
   findWin(row, col+1);
...
```

Note how treacherous recursion may be: if you write what seems to be less redundant code —

```
if (col == numCols() - 1)
   myWin = true;
if (!myWin)
{
   findWin(row, col-1);
   findWin(row, col+1);
}
...
```

— you will lose the benefits of quitting early and your code will dramatically slow down!

For extra credit: make `blackHasWon` work using one of the above two variations of a more efficient method that quits as soon as it detects a win.

Test your class using a test program `Hex.java` and a sample data file `hex.dat` provided in the `Ch04\Hex` folder ⌷.

4.7   Summary

Recursion is a programming technique based on methods calling themselves.

Recursive method calls are supported by the system stack, which keeps the method arguments, return address, and local variables in a separate frame for each call. Recursion is useful for dealing with nested structures or branching processes where it helps to create short, readable, and elegant code that would otherwise be impossible.

Recursion is not essential in situations that deal with linear structures or processes, which can be as easily and more efficiently implemented with iterations.

The best way to understand and analyze recursive methods is by thinking about them along the lines of mathematical induction: attempts at unfolding and tracing recursive code "to the bottom" usually fail.

Exercises

1. What is the output from the following method when called with the argument *n* = 3? ✓

```
public void printX(int n)
{
  if (n <= 0)
    System.out.print(0);
  else
  {
    printX(n - 1);
    System.out.print(n);
    printX(n - 2);
  }
}
```

2. Consider

```
public void enigma(int n)
{
  for (int i = 0; i < n; i++)
    enigma(i);
  System.out.print(n);
}
```

Does the call `enigma(3)` terminate? If so, what is the output?

3. What is the output from the following method when called with the argument *x* = 2004? ✓

```
public void display(int x)
{
  if (x >= 10)
  {
    display(x/10);
    System.out.print(x % 10);
  }
}
```

4. Fill in the blanks in the following recursive method:

```
/**
 *   Precondition: 1 <= n <= v.length
 *   Returns the value of the largest element among the first
 *   n elements in vector v.
 */
public double max(double v[], int n)
{
  double m = v[n-1], m2;

  if ( _____ )
  {
    m2 = _____ ;

    if (m2 > m)
      m = m2;
  }
  return m;
}
```

5. A positive integer is evenly divisible by 9 if and only if the sum of all its digits is divisible by 9. Suppose you have a method `sumDigits` that returns the sum of the digits of a positive integer *n*. Fill in the blanks in the method `isDivisibleBy9(int n)` that returns `true` if n is divisible by 9 and `false` otherwise. Your method may use the assignment and relational operators and `sumDigits`, but no arithmetic operators (`*, /, %, *=, /=, %=`) are allowed. ✓

```
/**
 *   Precondition: n > 0
 *   Returns n % 9 == 0
 */
public boolean isDivisibleBy9(int n)
{
  if (_____)

    return _____ ;

  else if (_____)

    return _____ ;

  else
    return _____ ;
}
```

6.   The method below attempts to calculate x^n economically:

```
public double pow(double x, int n)
{
  double y;
  if (n == 1)
    y = x;
  else
    y = pow(x, n/2) * pow(x, n - n/2); // Line ***
  return y;
}
```

(a)   How many multiplications will be executed when pow(3.14, 5) is called? ✓

(b)   How many multiplications will be executed if we replace Line *** above with the following statements?

```
{ y = pow(x, n/2); y *= y; if (n % 2 != 0) y *= x; }
```

(c)   How many multiplications will Version (a) above take to calculate pow(3.14, 9)? Version (b)?

7.   A linked list has four nodes containing the values 10, 20, 30, and 40 (in that order) and is defined by a reference to its first node, head. The method doTheTrick below returns a reference to the head of the changed list. How many nodes will the changed list have and what values will be stored in them? ✓

```
public ListNode doTheTrick(ListNode head)
{
  if (head == null || head.getNext() == null)
    return head;

  ListNode newHead = head.getNext();
  newHead = doTheTrick(newHead);

  head.setNext(newHead.getNext());
  newHead.setNext(head);
  return newHead;
}
```

8. What happens when a method `fun1` calls `fun2` and `fun2` calls `fun1` (assuming proper method definitions)?

    A.   Compiler error
    B.   Run time "circular reference" error
    C.   The program always aborts with the "stack overflow" error
    D.   The program always goes into an infinite loop
    E.   Depends: may work fine in certain recursive programs

9. What is the return value of `mysterySum(10)`, where

```
public int mysterySum(int n)
{
  if (n == 1)
    return 1;
  else
    return mysterySum(n-1) + 2*n - 1;
}
```

Justify your answer by using mathematical induction. Explain why this is an inappropriate use of recursion. ✓

10.■ GCF(*m*, *n*), the greatest common factor of two positive integers, has the following property: if *m* is not evenly divisible by *n*, then

$$GCF(m, n) = GCF(n, m \bmod n)$$

where *m* mod *n* means modulo division (same as Java's `%` operator). Write a recursive method that calculates GCF(*m*, *n*).

11.■ Fill in the blanks in the following method:

```
/**
 *   Returns the number of all possible paths from the
 *   point(0,0) to the point(x,y), where x and y are
 *   any non-negative integers.  From any point the path
 *   may extend only down or to the right by one unit
 *   (i.e., one of the current coordinates x or y can be
 *   incremented by one).
 */
public long countPaths(int x, int y)
{
  if (x == 0 || y == 0)
    return _____;
  else
    return _____ ;
}
```

12. ▪ The notation $C(n, k)$ or $\binom{n}{k}$ (pronounced "n-choose-k") represents the number of all possible ways to choose k different items from a set of n items ($k \leq$ n). $C(n, 0)$ and $C(n, n)$ are defined as 1. These numbers are also called "binomial coefficients" because

$$(x + y)^n = C(n,0)x^n + C(n,1)x^{n-1}y + C(n,2)x^{n-2}y^2 + \ldots + C(n,n)y^n$$

Binomial coefficients have many interesting properties. Among them:

$$C(n,k) = C(n-1,k-1) + C(n-1,k), \text{ when } 0 < k < n$$

and

$$C(n,k) = \frac{n}{k}C(n-1,k-1), \text{ when } 0 < k \leq n$$

Write and test a recursive method that calculates $C(n, k)$ based on Property 1 and another version based on Property 2. Which code is more efficient? Why?

13. ▪ Rewrite the Cookie Monster program (Question 13 from Chapter 3) using recursion. For recursive handling, it often helps to restate the question in more general terms. Here we need to refer to the optimal path from (0,0) to any position (*row*, *col*). So our `optimalPath` method should now take two arguments: `row` and `col`. Note that the maximum number of cookies accumulated at a position (*row*, *col*) is related to the previous positions as follows:

```
optimalPath(row, col) = cookies[row][col] +
    the larger of the two:
    {optimalPath(row-1, col), optimalPath(row, col-1)}
```

The only problem is invalid positions: either out of bounds or "barrels." How can we define `optimalPath` for an invalid position (*row*, *col*), so that the above formula still works? Identify the base case(s) and recursive case(s).

14. On Beavis Island, the alphabet consists of three letters, A, B, and H — but no word may have two A's in a row. Fill in the blanks in the following recursive method, `allWords` that prints out all Beavis Island words of a given length:

```
/**
 *  Prints all Beavis Island words that have
 *  <code>length</code> letters.
 *  <code>word</code> contains the initial
 *  sequence of letters in a word that is being built
 *  (use an empty string buffer of capacity <code>length</code>
 *  when calling <code>allWords</code> from <code>main</code>).
 */
public void allWords(StringBuffer word, int length)
{
  if (length == word.length())  // base case
  {
    // Display the string:
    _____;
  }
  else  // recursive case
  {
    int k = word.length();
    word.append('*'); // reserve room for one char

    // Append 'A' only if last letter is not an 'A':
    if (k == 0 || word.charAt(k-1) != 'A')
    {
      word.setCharAt(k, 'A');
      _____ ;
    }
    _____; // append 'B'
    _____;

    _____; // append 'H'
    _____;

    _____;
  }
}
```

⸮ Hint: you might need `StringBuffer`'s `setLength` method that truncates the string to a specified length. ⸮

15.◆   Suppose we have a list of positive integers. We want to choose several of them so that their sum is as large as possible but does not exceed a given limit. This type of problem is called a "Knapsack Problem." For example, we may want to choose several watermelons at the market so that their total weight is as large as possible but does not exceed the airline limit for one bag.

(a)   Write a recursive method that solves a simplified Knapsack Problem: it only calculates the optimal sum but does not report the selected items:

```
/**
 *   w contains n positive integers (n <= w.length).
 *   Returns the sum of some of these integers such that
 *   it has the largest possible value
 *   without exceeding limit.
 */
public int knapsackSum(int w[], int n, int limit)
```

Use mathematical induction to prove that your code is correct.

(b)   Write a more complete version that builds a stack of the values selected for the optimal sum. Pass a Stack of Integer objects to the method as the fourth argument. The stack should be initially empty when the method is called from main (or from another method).

(c)   Can you think of an alternative algorithm that uses neither recursion nor a stack?

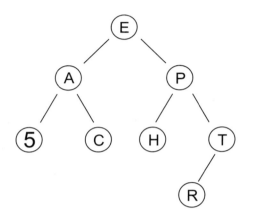

Binary Trees

5.1   Prologue

A **tree** is a branching hierarchical structure in which each element except the top one has a link to exactly one element higher in the hierarchy called its **parent** (Figure 5-1). The elements of a tree structure are referred to as **nodes**. The top node in the structure is called the **root** of the tree. Any node in the tree may be connected to one or more nodes lower in the hierarchy, called its **children**. The nodes that have no children are called **leaves**. There is exactly one path from the root to any node. The intermediate nodes in this path are referred to as the node's **ancestors** (i.e., its parent, the parent of its parent, etc.). Trees may not have circular paths.

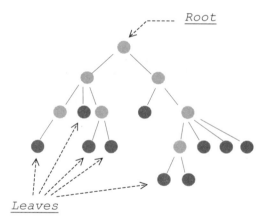

Figure 5-1. A tree structure

As you can see, computer books normally show trees "growing" down, with the root shown on top. This convention probably reflects the fact that we read from the top of the page down and also process trees starting from the root. Trees may be used for representing branching systems or processes, such as organizational charts, game strategies (Figure 5-2), decision charts, class hierarchies in Java, and other hierarchies of objects.

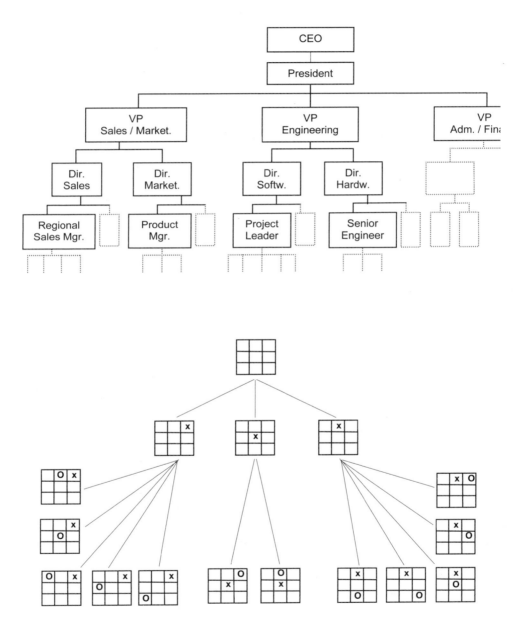

Figure 5-2. Common uses of tree structures

All the nodes in a tree can be arranged in layers with the root at level 0, its children at level 1, their children at level 2, and so on. The level of a node is equal to the length of the path from the root to that node. The total number of levels is called the **height** or the **depth** of the tree (Figure 5-3).

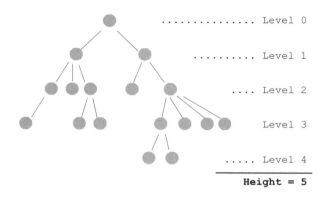

Figure 5-3. Arrangement of tree nodes in levels

One important property of trees is that we can arrange a relatively large number of elements in a relatively **shallow** (having a small number of levels) tree. For example, if each node in a tree (except the last level) has two children, a tree with h levels contains $2^h - 1$ nodes (Figure 5-4). Such a tree with 20 levels contains over one million nodes. This property may be utilized for quick searching, data retrieval, decision trees, and similar applications where, instead of going through the whole list and examining all the elements, we can go down the tree and examine just a few. (In strategy games, this property works exactly in reverse and becomes a major stumbling block: if we consider all the possible responses to a given move, then all the responses to those responses, etc., the tree of possible game paths grows so fast that it is not feasible to plan ahead beyond a few moves.)

A list can be viewed as a special case of a tree where the first node is the root, the last node is the only leaf, and all other nodes have exactly one parent and one child. A list has only one node at each level. If a tree degenerates into a near-linear shape with only a few nodes at each level, its advantages for representing a large number of elements in a shallow structure are lost.

A tree is an inherently recursive structure, because each node in a tree can itself be viewed as the root of a smaller tree (Figure 5-5). In computer applications, trees are normally represented in such a way that each node "knows" where to find all its children. In the linked representation, for example, each node, in addition to some information, holds the list of references to its children. Knowing just the root, we can find all the elements of the tree; and given any node we can find all the nodes in its subtree.

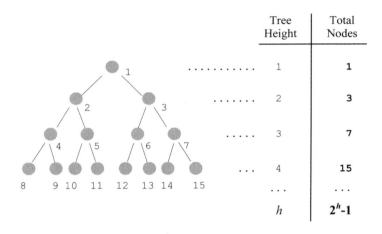

Tree Height	Total Nodes
1	1
2	3
3	7
4	15
. . .	. . .
h	2^h-1

Figure 5-4. A shallow tree can hold many nodes

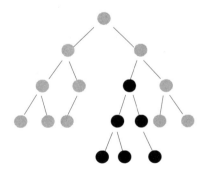

Figure 5-5. Each node in a tree is a root of its own subtree

The recursive branching structure of trees suggests the use of recursive procedures for dealing with them. The following method, for example, allows us to "visit" each node of a tree, a process known as tree *traversal*:

```
public void traverse (TreeNode root)
{
  // Base case: root == null, the tree is empty -- do nothing
  // Recursive case: tree is not empty
  if (root != null)
  {
    visit(root);
    for (... <each child of the root>)
         traverse (<that child's subtree>);
  }
}
```

This method first "visits" the root of the tree, then, for each child of the root, calls itself recursively to traverse that child's tree. The recursion stops when it reaches a leaf: all its children's trees are empty. Due to the branching nature of the process, an iterative implementation of this method would require your own stack and would be more cumbersome. In this example, therefore, the recursive implementation may actually be slightly more efficient in terms of the processing time, and it does not take too much space on the system stack because the depth of recursion is the same as the depth of the tree, which is normally a relatively small number. The major advantage of a recursive procedure is that it yields clear and concise code.

A tree in which each node has no more than two children is called a *binary tree*. The children of a node are referred to as the *left* child and the *right* child. In the following sections we will deal exclusively with binary trees. We will see how a binary tree can be used as a *binary search tree*. We will examine how a tree can be represented in Java and learn about the Java library classes, TreeSet and TreeMap, that implement binary search trees. In Chapter 7, we will look at another application of trees: priority queues and heaps.

5.2   Implementation of Binary Trees

The node of a binary tree can be represented as a class, TreeNode, which is similar to ListNode, a node in a linked list, except that instead of one reference to the next element of the list, a tree node has two references, to the left and right child of that node. In the class TreeNode in Figure 5-6, these references are called left and right and the information held in a node is represented by the object value. The class has a constructor that sets these three fields and an accessor and modifier for each of them.

```java
public class TreeNode
{
  private Object value;
  private TreeNode left;
  private TreeNode right;

  // Constructor:

  public TreeNode(Object initValue, TreeNode initLeft, TreeNode initRight)
  {
    value = initValue;
    left = initLeft;
    right = initRight;
  }

  // Methods:

  public Object getValue() { return value; }
  public TreeNode getLeft() { return left; }
  public TreeNode getRight() { return right; }
  public void setValue(Object theNewValue) { value = theNewValue; }
  public void setLeft(TreeNode theNewLeft) { left = theNewLeft; }
  public void setRight(TreeNode theNewRight) { right = theNewRight; }
}
```

Figure 5-6. TreeNode represents a node in a binary tree[*]

(Ch05\TreeNode.java 🖫)

[*] Adapted from The College Board's *AP Computer Science AB: Implementation Classes and Interfaces.*

In a linked list each node refers to the next one — a setup suitable for iterations. If, for instance, you need to count the nodes in the list, a `for` loop can do the job:

```
public int countNodes(ListNode head)
{
  int count = 0;
  for (ListNode node = head; node != null; node = node.getNext())
    count++;
  return count;
}
```

It is possible to accomplish the same task recursively, although many people may find it unnecessarily fancy:

```
public int countNodes(ListNode head)
{
  if (head == null)
    return 0;  // base case -- the list is empty
  else
    return 1 + countNodes(head.getNext());
}
```

But for binary trees, recursion is a perfect tool. For example:

```
public int countNodes(TreeNode root)
{
  if (root == null)
    return 0;  // base case -- the tree is empty
  else
    return 1 + countNodes(root.getLeft())
                      + countNodes(root.getRight());
}
```

As we will see in the following section, methods that follow a path in a tree and chose whether to go right or left in each node have simple iterative versions. But recursion is the rule. The base case in recursive methods usually handles an empty tree. Sometimes a method may treat separately another base case, when the tree has only one node, the root. Recursive calls are applied to the left and/or right subtrees.

5.3   Traversals

A method that visits all nodes of a tree and processes or displays their values is called a traversal. It is possible to traverse a tree iteratively, using a stack, but recursion makes it really easy:

```
private void traversePreorder (TreeNode root)
{
  // Base case: root == null, the tree is empty -- do nothing
  if (root != null)
  {
    process(root.getValue());
    traversePreorder(root.getLeft());
    traversePreorder(root.getRight());
  }
}
```

This is called *preorder traversal* because the root is visited <u>before</u> the left and right subtrees. In *postorder traversal* the root is visited <u>after</u> the subtrees:

```
private void traversePostorder (TreeNode root)
{
  if (root != null)
  {
    traversePostorder(root.getLeft());
    traversePostorder(root.getRight());
    process(root.getValue());
  }
}
```

Finally, in *inorder traversal*, the root is visited <u>in the middle</u>, between subtrees:

```
private void traverseInorder (TreeNode root)
{
  if (root != null)
  {
    traverseInorder(root.getLeft());
    process(root.getValue());
    traverseInorder(root.getRight());
  }
}
```

If a tree is implemented as a class with the root of the tree hidden in a private field, then the node visiting becomes restricted to some predefined method or code within the class. If you want to traverse the tree from outside the class, then, just as in the case of linked lists, you need an iterator. It is harder to program an iterator for a tree than for a list: you need to use a stack. Java library classes that implement trees provide iterators for you.

5.4   Binary Search Trees

A *binary search tree* (*BST*) is a structure for holding a set of ordered data values in such a way that it is easy to find any specified value and easy to insert and delete values. It overcomes some deficiencies of both sorted arrays and linked lists.

If we have a sorted array of elements, the "divide and conquer" Binary Search algorithm allows us to find any value in the array quickly. We take the middle element of the array, compare it with the target value, and, if they are not equal, continue searching either in the left or the right half of the array, depending on the comparison result. This process takes at most $\log_2 n$ operations for an array of n elements. Unfortunately, inserting values into the array or deleting them from the array is not easy — we may need to shift large blocks of data in memory. The linked list structure, on the other hand, allows us to insert and delete nodes easily, but there is no quick search method because there is no way of getting to the middle of the list easily.

> **Binary search trees combine the benefits of sorted arrays for quick searching and the benefits of linked lists for inserting and deleting values.**

As the name implies, a binary search tree is a kind of a binary tree: each node has no more than two children. The subtree that "grows" from the left child is called the *left subtree* and the subtree that "grows" from the right child is called the *right subtree*. The tree's nodes contain some data values for which a relation of order is defined; that is, for any two values we can say whether the first one is greater, equal, or smaller than the second. The values may be numbers, alphabetized strings, some database record index keys, and so on. Sometimes we informally say that one node is greater or smaller than another, actually meaning that that relationship applies to the data values they contain.

What makes this tree a binary search tree is the following special property: for any node, the value in the node is larger than all the values in this node's left subtree and smaller than all the values in this node's right subtree (Figure 5-7).

A binary search tree is specifically designed to support the "divide and conquer" method. Suppose we need to find a target value. First, we compare the target to the root. If they are equal, the value is found. If the target is smaller, we continue the search in the left subtree. If larger, we go to the right subtree. We will find the target value (or conclude that it is not in the tree) after a number of steps that never exceeds the number of levels in the tree. If our tree is rather "bushy," with intermediate levels filled to near capacity with nodes, the number of steps required will be close to $\log_2 n$, where n is the total number of nodes.

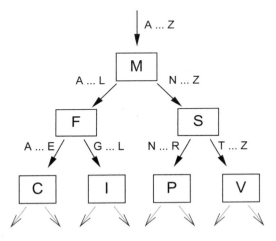

Figure 5-7. The ordering property of a binary search tree

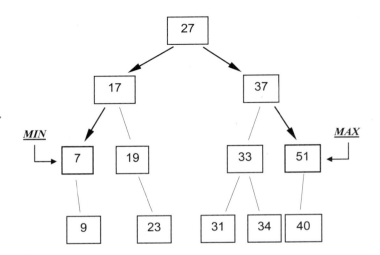

Figure 5-8. Location of the smallest and the largest values in a BST

In a binary search tree, it is also easy to find the smallest and the largest value. Starting at the root, if we always go left for as long as possible, we come to the node containing the smallest value. If we always keep to the right, we come to the node containing the largest value (Figure 5-8). The smallest node, by definition, cannot have a left child, and the largest node cannot have a right child.

The `find` method for a BST can be implemented using either iterations or recursion with equal ease. For example:

```java
// Find using iterations:
// =====================

private TreeNode find(TreeNode root, Comparable target)
{
  TreeNode node = root;
  int compareResult;

  while (node != null)
  {
    compareResult = target.compareTo(root.getValue());
    if (compareResult == 0)
      return node;
    else if (compareResult < 0)
      node = node.getLeft();
    else // if (compareResult > 0)
      node = node.getRight();
  }
  return null;
}

// Find using recursion:
// ====================

private TreeNode find(TreeNode root, Comparable target)
{
  if (root == null)           // Base case: the tree is empty
    return null;

  int compareResult = target.compareTo(root.getValue());

  if (compareResult == 0)      // Another base case: found in root
    return root;
  else if (compareResult < 0)
    return find(root.getLeft(), target);  // Search left subtree
  else // if (compareResult > 0)
    return find(root.getRight(), target); // Search right subtree
}
```

5.5   Comparable Objects and Comparators

You might have noticed in the previous section that the type of the argument `target` in the `find` method is designated as `Comparable` (pronounced com-pa′-ra-ble). This means that `target` belongs to a class that implements the library interface `Comparable`, which specifies one method, `compareTo`:

```
public int compareTo(Object other);
```

`compareTo` returns 0 if `this` is "equal to" `other`, a negative integer if `this` is "less than" `other`, and a positive integer if `this` is "greater than" `other`. To remember the order of comparison, think of `a.compareTo(b)` as "*a* – *b*."

`find`'s code calls `target.compareTo(...)` — that's why `target` has to be a `Comparable`, not just an `Object`. Many Java library methods also need to compare objects and expect or assume that they deal with comparable objects. Java library classes such as `String`, `Integer`, `Double`, and `Character`, for which "natural" order makes sense, implement `Comparable`.

You can supply a `compareTo` method for your own class, thus defining a relation of order, a way to compare your class's objects. Then state that your class `implements Comparable`. For example:

```
public class City implements Comparable
{
  ...
  public int compareTo(Object other)
  {
    return getPopulation() - ((City)other).getPopulation();
  }
  ...
}
```

Your class's objects become `Comparable` and you can store them in collections and pass them to methods that expect the `Comparable` data type, such as `find` or `Arrays.sort`.

The `compareTo` argument's type is specified as `Object`, to make the method's prototype independent of a particular class that implements it, but usually it is an object of the same class. `compareTo`'s code casts its argument back into its class's type. For example:

```
return getPopulation() - ((City)other).getPopulation();
```

> The order imposed by the `compareTo` method does not have to be totally intuitive. A programmer chooses what to call "smaller" and what "bigger." It may be easier to think of it as "earlier" and "later."

For example, if you swap the operands in the method that compares the populations of two cities —

```
public int compareTo(Object other)
{
  return ((City)other).getPopulation() - getPopulation();
}
```

— then a city with larger population becomes "smaller," that is, stands earlier in the order.

Recall that the `Object` class provides a `boolean` method `equals` that compares this object to another object for equality. Therefore, each object has the `equals` method. When you store comparable objects in a `TreeSet` or use them as keys in a `TreeMap`, it is assumed that the `compareTo` and `equals` methods for these objects agree with each other: that `this.compareTo(other)` returns `0` if and only if `this.equals(other)` returns `true`. However, `TreeSet` and `TreeMap` use only `compareTo` and will work even if `equals` and `compareTo` disagree.

> When you define a `compareTo` method for your class, it is a good idea to also define an `equals` method that agrees with `compareTo`.

For example:

```
public class MsgUser implements Comparable
{
  private String screenName;
  ...

  public int compareTo(Object other)
  {
    return screenName.compareTo(((MsgUser)other).screenName);
  }

  public boolean equals(Object other)
  {
    if (other == null)
      return false;
    return compareTo(other) == 0;
  }
}
```

❖ ❖ ❖

Defining `compareTo` gives you one way to compare the objects of your class. For instance, if you define a `compareTo` method for your class `City`, as `this.getPopulation() - other.getPopulation()`, you can sort an array of cities by population in ascending order by calling a library method `Arrays.sort`:

```
City worldCapitals[];
...
// Sort in ascending order by population:
Arrays.sort(worldCapitals);
```

But what if you sometimes need to sort them in ascending order and sometimes in descending order, or alphabetically by name? The `Comparable` abstraction becomes insufficient. Java's response to this dilemma is ***comparator*** objects.

A "comparator" is an object of a class that implements the `Comparator` interface. This interface specifies two methods: `compare` and `equals`. In most cases you don't have to define `equals`, since you can rely on the default method inherited from `Object`.

The `compare` method compares two objects passed to it:

```
public int compare(Object obj1, Object obj2)
```

The result of the comparison is an integer, sort of like `obj1 - obj2`. `obj1` and `obj2` usually belong to the same class, but that class may be different from the comparator's class. For example:

```
public class ComparatorForCityNames
        implements Comparator
{
  public int compare(Object obj1, Object obj2)
  {
    String name1 = ((City)obj1).getName();
    String name2 = ((City)obj2).getName();
    return name1.compareToIgnoreCase(name2);
  }
  ...
}
```

To use this class, create a comparator object and use it to compare cities or pass to constructors or methods that take a `Comparator` argument. For example:

```
ComparatorForCityNames alpha = new ComparatorForCityNames();
...
City worldCapitals[];
...
Arrays.sort(worldCapitals, alpha);
...
int result = alpha.compare(city1, city2);
```

> **A comparator is an object, not a class, because you may need to pass a comparator to a method and you cannot pass a class to a method.**

All comparators from the same class are the same, unless you make the `compare` method dependent on some other properties of the comparator and provide constructors and/or methods for setting these properties. For example:

```
public class ComparatorForCityPopulation
         implements Comparator
{
  private boolean ascending;

  public ComparatorForCityPopulation()
  {
    ascending = true;
  }

  public ComparatorForCityPopulation(boolean asc)
  {
    ascending = asc;
  }

  public void setPopulationOrder(boolean asc)
  {
    ascending = asc;
  }

  public int compare(Object obj1, Object obj2)
  {
    int diff = ((City)obj1).getPopulation() -
                    ((City)obj2).getPopulation();
    if (!ascending)
      diff = -diff;  // flip the result
    return diff;
  }
}
```

The second method of the `Comparator` interface, `equals`, compares comparators! In most cases it is safe to leave it out and to rely on the default `equals` method inherited from the `Object` class. Sometimes you may need to override it to improve performance.

5.6   `java.util`'s `TreeSet` and `TreeMap`

Java's `util` package provides two classes for implementing binary search trees, `TreeSet` and `TreeMap`.

> **`TreeSet` holds objects; `TreeMap` holds pairs of objects, a "key" and a "value."**

The `TreeSet` class assumes that the objects stored in the tree have some order or rank relation defined for them and arranges the objects into a BST according to that order. No two values in a BST can have the same rank.

> **A structure that holds objects, supplies "add," "remove," and "contains" methods, and does not allow duplicate values represents a "Set."**

In the `java.util` package, the set structure is formalized as the `java.util.Set` interface. Figure 5-9 summarizes a few of its commonly used methods. The `add` method inserts a given object into the set. If the set already contains an equal object, `add` ignores the duplicate value and returns `false`. The `remove` method removes a given object from the set, and the `contains` method checks whether a given object is in the set. The `iterator` method returns an iterator for the set. The order of the values generated by the iterator depends on the class that implements `Set`.

```
boolean add(Object obj);          // Adds obj to the set
                                  //    Returns true if successful,
                                  //    false if the object is already
                                  //    in the set
boolean remove(Object obj);       // Removes obj from the set
                                  //    Returns true if successful,
                                  //    false if the object is not found
boolean contains(Object obj);     // Returns true if obj is in the set,
                                  //    false otherwise
int size();                       // Returns the number of elements
                                  //    in the set
Iterator iterator();              // Returns an iterator for the set

Object[] toArray();               // Copies the objects from the set
                                  //    into an array and returns
                                  //    that array
```

Figure 5-9. Commonly used methods of `java.util.Set` (and `TreeSet`)

The `java.util.TreeSet` class implements the `Set` interface, so Figure 5-9 describes `TreeSet`'s methods as well. The `add` method inserts a given object into the tree, and the `remove` method removes a given object from the tree in such a way that the BST ordering property is preserved. For `TreeSet`, the iterator performs <u>inorder</u> traversal of the tree, delivering the values in ascending order.

> **For a BST, inorder traversal (left-root-right) visits the nodes of the tree in ascending order of values.**

(The proof of this fact is left as one of the exercises at the end of this chapter.)

The `TreeSet` class has a no-args constructor that initializes an empty tree and a constructor that takes one argument, a comparator object (see Section 5.5).

Besides BST, there are other ways to implement a set with efficient access to its elements. For example, the `java.util.HashSet` class implements the same interface `Set` but stores elements in a ***hash table***. (Hash tables and Java classes that implement them are the subject of the next chapter.)

`String`, `Character`, `Integer`, and `Double` types of objects are `Comparable`, so you can hold them in a `TreeSet`. In general, any `Comparable` objects may be placed into a `TreeSet` (or you can place any type of objects and supply a comparator). To hold values of primitive data types in a `TreeSet` you need to first convert them into objects using the corresponding wrapper class. For example:

```
TreeSet myTree = new TreeSet();
int m = ...;
...
myTree.add(new Integer(m));
...
if (myTree.contains(new Integer(2004)))
   ...
```

❖   ❖   ❖

A ***map*** establishes a correspondence between the elements of two sets of objects. The objects in one set are thought to be "keys," and the objects in the other set are thought to be "values." Each key has only one value associated with it. For example, a screen name identifies a chat room subscriber; a license plate number identifies a car in the Registry of Motor Vehicles database; a serial number identifies a computer.

"Map" is a data structure that associates keys with their values and efficiently finds a value for a given key. In Java, this functionality is formalized by the java.util.Map interface. A few of Map's commonly used methods are shown in Figure 5-10. The put method associates a key with a value in the map. If the key was previously associated with a different value, the old association is broken and put returns the value previously associated with the key. If the key had no prior association with a value, put returns null. The get method returns the value associated with a given key or null if the key is not associated with any value. The containsKey method returns true if a given key is associated with a value and false otherwise.

```
Object put(Object key, Object value);
                                 // Adds key and associated value
                                 //    to the map;
                                 //    Returns the value previously
                                 //    associated with key or null
                                 //    if no value was previously
                                 //    associated with key
Object get(Object key);          // Returns the value associated
                                 //    with key or null if no value
                                 //    is associated with key
boolean containsKey(Object key); // Returns true if key is
                                 //    associated with a value,
                                 //    false otherwise
int size();                      // Returns the number of key-value
                                 //    pairs in the map
Set keySet();                    // Returns the set of keys in
                                 //    the map
```

Figure 5-10. Commonly used methods of java.util.Map (and TreeMap)

The java.util.TreeMap class implements Map as a BST <u>ordered by keys</u>. TreeMap has a no-args constructor that initializes an empty map. Another constructor takes one argument, a comparator (see Section 5.5). If a map is constructed with the no-args constructor, then the keys must be Comparable; if a comparator is supplied to the constructor, then that comparator is used to compare two keys.

The Map interface does not specify a method for obtaining an iterator, and the TreeMap class does not have one. Instead, you can get the set of all keys by calling the keySet method, then iterate over that set. Something like this:

```
TreeMap map = new TreeMap();
SomeType key;
OtherType value;
...
Set keys = map.keySet();
Iterator iter = keys.iterator();
while (iter.hasNext())
{
  key = (SomeType)iter.next();
  value = (OtherType)map.get(key);
  ... // process value
}
```

The values will be processed in the ascending order of <u>keys</u>.

TreeMap is more general than TreeSet. Both implement BSTs, but in TreeSet the values are compared to each other, while in TreeMap, no ordering is assumed for the values and the tree is arranged according to the order of the keys. In a way, a set is a special case of a map where a value serves as its own key. In fact, the TreeSet class is based on TreeMap (or, as Java API puts it, "is backed by an instance of TreeMap," i.e., has a TreeMap field in it that does all the work). The decision of which class to use, a TreeSet or a TreeMap, is not always obvious. Sometimes it is possible to include the key in the description of a "value" object and use the TreeSet class with an appropriate comparator. But it is often easier to use a TreeMap.

5.7   *Lab:* Morse Code

Morse Hall, the Mathematics Department building at Phillips Academy in Andover, Massachusetts, is named after Samuel F. B. Morse, who graduated from the academy in 1805.

In 1838, Samuel Morse devised a signaling code for use with his electromagnetic telegraph. The code used two basic signaling elements: the "dot," a short-duration electric current, and the "dash," a longer-duration signal. The signals lowered an ink pen mounted on a special arm, which left dots and dashes on the strip of paper moving beneath. Morse's code gained wide acceptance and, in its international form, is still in use. (Samuel Morse also achieved distinction as an artist, particularly as a painter of miniatures, and between 1826 and 1845 served as the first president of the National Academy of Design.)

In 1858 Queen Victoria sent the first transatlantic telegram of ninety-eight words to congratulate President James Buchanan of the United States. The telegram started a new era of "instant" messaging — it took only sixteen and a half hours to transmit via the brand new transatlantic telegraph cable.

In this project, we will simulate a telegraph station that encodes messages from text to Morse code and decodes the Morse code back to plain text. The encoding is accomplished simply by looking up a symbol in a TreeMap that associates each symbol with its Morse code string. The decoding is implemented with the help of a binary "decoding" tree of our own design. Morse code for each letter represents a path from the root of the tree to some node: a "dot" means go left, and a "dash" means go right. The node at the end of the path contains the symbol corresponding to the code.

The "Telegraph" is implemented in two classes: Telegraph and MorseCode. In addition, MorseCode uses the TreeNode class described in Section 5.2. The Telegraph class opens two windows on the screen, "London" and "New York," and handles the text entry fields and GUI events in them. We have written this class for you. The MorseCode class implements encoding and decoding of text. <u>All the methods in this class are static</u>. The start method initializes the encoding map and the decoding tree; the private method treeInsert inserts a given symbol into the decoding tree, according to its Morse code string; the public encode and decode methods convert plain text into Morse code and back, respectively. Your task is to supply all the missing code in the MorseCode class.

The Telegraph class and the unfinished MorseCode class are in the Ch05\Morse 🖫 folder on your student disk. TreeNode.java 🖫 is provided in the Ch05 folder. Put together a project with Telegraph, MorseCode, and TreeNode and test your program.

5.8   *Case Study and Lab:* Java Messenger

In 1996, AOL introduced its subscribers to the "Buddy List," which allowed AOL members to see when their friends were online. A year later, AOL introduced the *AOL Instant Messenger (AIM)*. In this case study we implement our own instant "messaging" application, *Java Messenger*. In our application, the same user logs in several times under different screen names, and messages are sent from one window to another on the same screen. Also, in this toy version, all other logged-in users are considered "buddies" of a given user.

Our program can compensate for your friends' absence when your Internet connection is down. But even if you are online, our program has the advantage of always connecting you to a person just as smart and thoughtful as you are. (Another advantage of our program is that it illustrates the use of `java.util`'s `TreeSet` and `TreeMap` classes.)

Our *Java Messenger* application consists of four classes (Figure 5-11). The `Messenger` class initializes the program and implements GUI for logging in and adding new users. The `Server` class defines a server object that keeps track of all the registered users and all currently logged-in users. A server holds screen names and associated registered users in a `TreeMap`. The server maintains a set of all currently logged-in users in a `TreeSet`. A user is represented by an object of the `MsgUser` class. This class implements `Comparable`: its `compareTo` method compares a user to another user by comparing their screen names, case blind. When a new user logs in, the server calls its `openDialog` method, which creates a new dialog window and attaches it to that user. A dialog window is an object of the `MsgWindow` class that handles GUI for the user: a text area for typing in messages and displaying received messages and a "buddy list" for all logged-in "buddies."

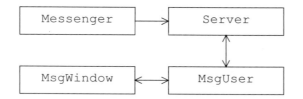

Figure 5-11. *Java Messenger* **classes**

As usual, we split the work evenly: I supply the `Messenger` and `MsgWindow` classes that deal with GUI, and you write the `Server` and `MsgUser` classes. Your `Server` class must use a `TreeMap` to associate screen names with passwords and a `TreeSet` to hold `MsgUser` objects for all currently logged-in users.

First, we have to agree on the interfaces: the constructors and public methods. The specs for your two classes are described in Table 5-1 and Table 5-2 below. Your `Server` class must supply a no-args constructor and three methods: `addUser`, `login`, and `logout`. The `addUser` and `login` methods must return correct error codes so that my `Messenger` class can display the appropriate error messages. `login` should pass a correct "buddy set" to the newly created user, which consists of all currently logged-in users excluding the new one. Your `MsgUser` class must provide a `quit` method, which I'll call when the dialog window is closed. That's pretty much all I need from your two classes.

You don't have to worry about my `Messenger` class at all, unless you are curious to see how it works. My `main` method creates a server (a `Server` object) and, to facilitate testing, registers four predefined users:

```
server.addUser("vindog1981", "no");
server.addUser("apscholar5", "no");
server.addUser("javayomama", "no");
server.addUser("lucytexan", "no");
```

You should be aware of my `MsgWindow`'s class constructor that takes two arguments, a user (who creates the dialog) and a set of that user's buddies (displayed in a combo box on the dialog window). My `MsgWindow` class also provides three methods that are useful to you: `addBuddy`, `removeBuddy`, and `showMessage`. Your `MsgUser`'s `addBuddy`, `removeBuddy` and `receiveMessage` methods simply check that your dialog window has been initialized, then pass the parameter to my corresponding method.

`Messenger.java` and `MsgWindow.java` are in the `Ch05\Messenger` 🖫 folder on your student disk.

public class Server	
Constructor:	
`public Server()`	Initializes the map of registered users and the set of logged-in users to empty.
Methods:	

`public int addUser`
`        (String name,`
`         String password)`
	Registers a new user with a given screen name and password. Returns 0 if successful or a negative integer, the error code, if failed.
	Error codes:
	−1 — invalid screen name (must be 4-10 chars)
	−2 — invalid password (must be 2-10 chars)
	−3 — the screen name is already taken

`public int login`
`        (String name,`
`         String password)`
	Logs in a new user with a given screen name and password. Returns 0 if successful and a negative integer, the error code, if failed.
	Error codes:
	−1 — user not found
	−2 — invalid password
	−3 — the user is already logged in
	This method creates a new `MsgUser` object and adds it to the "buddy lists" of all previously logged-in users (by calling their `addBuddy` method). It opens a dialog window for this user by calling its `openDialog` method and passing all previously logged-in users to it as a "buddy list." It then adds the new user to the set of logged-in users.

`public void logout` `          (MsgUser u)`	Removes a given user from the set of logged-in users and from the "buddy lists" of all other logged-in users.

Table 5-1. `Server` constructor and public methods

public class MsgUser implements Comparable	
Constructor:	

public MsgUser
   (Server server, String name,
      String password)
	Saves a reference to the server and initializes this user's and screen name and password fields.

Methods:	
public String toString()	Returns this user's screen name.
public String getPassword()	Returns this user's password.
public boolean equals (Object other)	Returns true if this user's name is equal to other's (case blind), false otherwise.
public int compareTo (Object other)	Compares this user's screen name to other's screen name, case blind.
public void openDialog (Set buddies)	Creates a dialog window passing this user and the buddies set to its constructor. Saves a reference to the new dialog window in the myWindow field.
public void addBuddy (MsgUser u)	If myWindow is initialized, adds u to this user's "buddy list" by calling myWindow.addBuddy(u).
public void removeBuddy (MsgUser u)	If myWindow is initialized, removes u from this user's "buddy list" by calling myWindow.removeBuddy(u).
public void receiveMessage (String text)	If myWindow is initialized, shows text by calling myWindow.showMessage(text).
public void quit()	Disposes of this user's dialog window. Logs out this user by calling server's logout method. (This method is called from the MsgWindow class when the "close" button is clicked on the dialog window.)

Table 5-2. MsgUser constructor and public methods

5.9   Summary

A tree is a structure of connected nodes where each node, except one special root node, is connected to one parent node and may have one or more child nodes. Each node has a unique ascending path to the root. A tree is an inherently recursive structure because each node in a tree can be considered the root of its own tree, called a subtree. A binary tree is a tree where each node has no more than two children. These are referred to as the left and right children. In the linked representation, each node of a tree contains references to its child nodes. The nodes of a tree contain some data values.

The nodes of a tree are arranged in layers: all nodes at the same level are connected to the root by a path of the same length. The number of levels in a tree is called its height or depth. One important property of trees is that they can hold a large number of values in a relatively shallow structure. A full binary tree with h levels contains 2^h-1 values.

A binary search tree is a binary tree whose data elements have some relation of order defined for them and are organized so that the data value in each node is larger than all the values in the node's left subtree and smaller than all the values in its right subtree. The binary search tree combines the benefits of a sorted array for quick binary search with the advantages of a linked list for easy value insertion and deletion.

Due to the recursive structure of trees, it is convenient to use recursive methods when working with them. The base case in such methods is when the tree is empty and, sometimes, when the tree consists only of the root. The method is usually applied recursively to the root's left and/or right subtrees.

Tree traversals can be easily implemented with recursion. Preorder traversal first visits the root of the tree, then processes its left and right subtrees; postorder traversal first processes the left and right subtrees, then visits the root; inorder traversal first processes the left subtree, then visits the root, then processes the right subtree. Inorder traversal of a BST processes its nodes in ascending order.

The `java.util` package includes two classes, `TreeSet` and `TreeMap`, that implement BSTs. The `TreeSet` class implements the `java.util.Set` interface and provides methods for adding and removing an object from the tree and for finding out whether the tree contains a given object. The `TreeMap` class implements the `java.util.Map` interface. This class is used to associate "keys" with "values" in a BST ordered by keys, and it can be used to quickly retrieve a value for a given key. A few commonly used `Set` (and `TreeSet`) and `Map` (and `TreeMap`) methods are summarized in Figure 5-9 and Figure 5-10, and in Appendix A.

Exercises

Sections 5.1-5.3

1.   Define the following tree-related terms:

> *root*
> *child*
> *leaf*
> *parent*
> *ancestor*
> *depth*

2.   What is the smallest number of levels required to store 100,000 nodes in a binary tree? ✓

3.   What is the smallest and the largest possible number of leaves
      (a)   in a binary tree with 15 nodes?
      (b)   in a binary tree containing exactly six non-leaf nodes?

4.■   Prove using mathematical induction that a binary tree of depth h cannot have more than 2^h-1 nodes. ✓

5.■   Prove using mathematical induction that in a binary tree with N nodes

$$L \leq \frac{N+1}{2}$$

where L is the number of leaves.

6.   Write a method

```
public boolean isLeaf(TreeNode node)
```

that returns `true` if node is a leaf, `false` otherwise. ✓

7.   Write a method

```
public int sumTree(TreeNode root)
```

that returns the sum of the values stored in the tree defined by `root`, assuming that the nodes hold `Integer` objects.

8.   What does the following method count? ✓

```
public int countSomething(TreeNode root)
{
  if (root == null)
    return 0;
  if (root.getLeft() == null && root.getRight() == null)
    return 1;
  else
    return countSomething(root.getLeft()) +
              countSomething(root.getRight());
}
```

9.   (a)   Write a method

```
public int depth(TreeNode root)
```

that returns the depth of the binary tree. ✓

(b)   Let us call the "bush ratio" the ratio of the number of nodes in a binary tree to the maximum possible number of nodes in a binary tree of the same depth. Using the `countNodes` method that returns the number of nodes in a tree and the `depth` method from Part (a), write a method

```
public double bushRatio(TreeNode root)
```

that calculates and returns the "bush ratio" for a given binary tree. The method should return 0 if the tree is empty.

10.   (a)   Write a method

```
public TreeNode copy(TreeNode root)
```

that creates a copy of a given binary tree and returns a reference to its root. Assume that there is enough memory to allocate all the nodes in the new tree. ✓

(b)   Write a method

```
public TreeNode mirrorImage(TreeNode root)
```

that creates a mirror image of a given binary tree and returns a reference to its root.

11.▪   Write a method

```
public int countPaths(TreeNode root)
```

that returns the total number of paths that lead from the root to any other node of the binary tree.

12.▪   (a)   Write a method

```
public boolean sameShape(TreeNode root1, TreeNode root2)
```

The method returns `true` if binary trees with the roots `root1` and `root2` have exactly the same shape and `false` otherwise.

(b)   Using `sameShape` from Part (a), write a method

```
public boolean hasSameSubtree
        (TreeNode root1, TreeNode root2)
```

`root1` and `root2` refer to the roots of two binary trees. The method returns `true` if the second tree (rooted in `root2`) is empty or has the same shape as the subtree of some node in the first tree, `false` otherwise.

13. ◆   (a)   Write a method

```
public TreeNode buildFull(int depth)
```

that builds a binary tree of the given depth with all levels completely filled with nodes. The method should set the values in all the nodes to `null` and return a reference to the root of the new tree.

(b)   Write and test a method

```
public void fillTree(TreeNode root)
```

that appends new nodes (with `null` values) to the tree until all existing levels in the tree are completely filled.

14.   An algebraic expression with parentheses and defined precedence of operators can be represented by a binary tree, called an ***expression tree***. For example:

Expression	Tree
$a + b$	<pre> + / \ a b</pre>

$(a + 1)(a - 1)$	<pre> *
	   / \
	  + -
	 /\ /\
	a 1 a 1</pre>

In an expression tree, leaves represent operands and other nodes represent operators.

(a)   Draw an expression tree for

$$\frac{2}{\dfrac{1}{x} + \dfrac{1}{y}} \quad \checkmark$$

Continued ➲

(b)   Draw an expression tree for

```
yr % 4 == 0 && (yr % 100 != 0 || yr % 400 == 0)
```

(c)   Write a class `ExpressionTree` extending `TreeNode`. Assume that
        the nodes contain `Strings`: operands are strings that represent integers
        and operators are `"+"` or `"*"`. Add a method that determines whether
        a node contains an operand or an operator and another method that
        extracts an integer value from the operand string.

(d)■   Write a recursive method

```
public static int eval(ExpressionTree root)
```

        that evaluates the expression represented by this tree.

(e)   The conventional algebraic notation is called *infix* notation. In infix
        notation, the operator is placed between the operands:

```
Infix:      x + y
```

        Write a method

```
public static String toInfixNotation(ExpressionTree root)
```

        that generates a fully parenthesized infix expression from a given
        expression tree. For example:

Continued ☞

(f)   There are two other ways to represent expressions which are useful in computer applications. They are called *prefix* and *postfix* notations. In prefix notation we place the operator before the operands; in postfix notation we place the operator after the operands:

```
Prefix:     + x y
Postfix:    x y +
```

As you can guess, prefix and postfix notations can be generated by traversing the expression tree in preorder and postorder, respectively. Prefix and postfix notations are convenient because they do not use parentheses and do not need to take into account the precedence of the operators. The order of operations can be uniquely reconstructed from the expression itself. Prefix notation is also called *Polish* notation after the Polish mathematician Łukasiewicz who invented it, and postfix notation is sometimes called *Reverse Polish Notation* (*RPN*).

Rewrite in postfix notation:

```
(x - 3) / (x*y - 2*x + 3*y)
```

(g)   Prove that the operands appear in the same order in the infix, postfix, and prefix notations — only the position of the operators is different. (This is a good test for converting one notation into another manually.) ✓

(h)   Write and test a method

```
public static int eval(String tokens[])
```

that evaluates a postfix expression. The `tokens` array contains operands — string representation of integers — and operators (e.g., "+" or "*"). ⟨ Hint: go from left to right, save "unused" operands on a stack. ⟩

(i)   Write a method

```
public static ExpressionTree toExpressionTree(String tokens[])
```

that converts a postfix expression, represented by the `tokens` array, into an expression tree and returns the root of that tree.

Sections 5.4-5.9

15. Mark true or false and explain:

    (a)   The smallest node in a binary search tree is always a leaf. _____

    (b)   If a binary search tree holds integers (with the usual order of comparison) and the root holds 0, then all the nodes of the left subtree hold negative numbers. _____ ✓

    (c)   The number of comparisons necessary to find a target node in a binary search tree never exceeds $\log_2 n + 1$, where n is the number of nodes. _____ ✓

16.   (a)   Swap two nodes in the following binary tree to obtain a binary search tree.

```
        H
       / \
      C   R
     /   / \
    A   E   S
```

    (b)   What will be the sequence of nodes when the resulting binary search tree is traversed inorder? Preorder?

17. Suppose we start with an empty binary search tree and add nodes with values

```
475, 474, 749, 623, 292, 557, 681
```

(in that order). Draw the resulting tree. How can we arrange the same numbers in a balanced binary search tree (with three levels)? ✓

18. Draw the binary search tree created by inserting the letters

```
L O G A R I T H M
```

(in that order) into an empty tree. List the nodes of this tree when it is traversed inorder, preorder, and postorder.

19. ■ Using mathematical induction, prove that inorder traversal of a BST visits the nodes in ascending order.

20.■   Write a non-recursive method

```
public TreeNode maxNode(TreeNode root)
```

that finds and returns the largest node in a BST. ✓

21.◆   Write a method

```
public TreeNode remove(TreeNode root)
```

that removes the root from a BST, repairs the tree and returns the new root.
⸗ Hint: find the smallest node xMin in the right subtree; unlink xMin from
the tree, promoting its right child into its place; place xMin into the root.
(The same works with the largest node in the left subtree.) ⸗

22.◆   (a)   Write a method

```
public TreeNode buildNCT(TreeNode root)
```

that takes a binary tree and builds a new tree. The shape of the new
tree is exactly the same as the shape of the original tree, but the values
in its nodes are different: in the new tree the value in each node is an
Integer object that represents the total number of nodes in the
subtree rooted at that node. (For example, the value at the root is equal
to the total number of nodes in the tree.) The method returns the root
of the new tree.

(b)   Suppose you have a BST and a companion "node count" tree (NCT) as
described in Part (a). Write an efficient method

```
public Object median(TreeNode bstRoot, TreeNode nctRoot)
```

that finds the median of the values stored in the BST. The median here
is the $((n + 1) / 2)$-th value in the tree, in ascending order, where n is
the total number of nodes (when the nodes are counted starting from
1). ⸗ Hints: write a more general helper function that finds the k-th
node in the tree for any given k. Use recursion or iterations building
parallel paths in the BST and the NCT from the root to the node you
are looking for. ⸗

23.   A program maintains a list of doctors on call for the current month. One doctor is on call for each day of the month. Which of the following structures is most appropriate for this task? ✓

    A.   A `TreeSet` of doctor names
    B.   A `TreeMap` keyed by doctor names
    C.   A `TreeMap` keyed by the day of the month
    D.   An `ArrayList` holding the names of doctors

24.■   (a)   Define a class `Movie` that represents a movie record from the `movies.txt` 🔲 file (in the `Ch02\movies` folder on your student disk, see Section 2.7), with fields for the release year, title, director's name, and a list (`LinkedList`) of actors. Make `Movie` objects `Comparable` by title.

    (b)   Write a program that reads the `movies.txt` file into an array of `Movie` objects and sorts them by title using the `Arrays.sort` method.

    (c)   Sort the movies array by director's last name using a `Comparator`.

    (d)   Find out the total number of different actors listed in `movies.txt` by inserting them into a `TreeSet`.

    (e)   List all the actors from `movies.txt` in alphabetical order by last name using an iterator for the `TreeSet` of actors.

25.■   A set cannot contain "equal" objects (duplicates). In the `TreeSet` implementation, which approach is used to determine whether two objects are equal?

    A.   `==` operator
    B.   `equals`
    C.   `compareTo` (or `compare` if a `TreeSet` was created with a comparator)
    D.   Both `equals` and `compareTo` (the program throws an exception if the two disagree)

Write a small program to test each hypothesis.

Chapter  6

Lookup Tables and Hashing

6.1   Prologue

In this chapter we continue our discussion of different ways to store and retrieve data in programs. But first let us briefly review what we already know about data structures.

In a list, data elements are thought of as arranged in a sequence; each element has an index assigned to it, its position in the sequence. In Java, lists are formalized by the `List` interface, which is implemented in the `ArrayList` and `LinkedList` classes. If we want to find a given value in a list, we can do a sequential search, traversing a list from the beginning until we find the value. If we represent a list as an array, it is easy to get access to an element with a given index, but inserting and removing values at the beginning or in the middle of the list takes some time. In a linked list we have to follow the links to get access to an element with a given index, but it is easy to insert and remove elements.

Stacks and queues are used for temporary storage. In these structures, access to values is defined by the order in which they were stored. A stack provides immediate access to the value stored last, while in a queue values are retrieved in the order of their arrival. Java implementation of these structures can be based on the `ArrayList` or `LinkedList` classes.

BSTs (Binary Search Trees) support quick search, similar to binary search in a sorted array, and relatively easy insertion and removal of values, as in a linked list. In Java, BSTs are thought of as a way to implement a set. A set is a collection of elements with `add`, `remove`, and `contains` methods. In Java, this concept is formalized in the `Set` interface. The `TreeSet` class implements `Set` as a BST.

Regardless of how a set is implemented, its usefulness in programs is rather limited — we can iterate over the whole set and we can tell whether a particular value is in the set, and that's about all. For example, in an instant messaging application, keeping a set of screen names can tell us whether a given name is taken, but it doesn't tell us anything else about the user who owns it. Likewise, a set of words in a dictionary can tell us whether a given string spells a valid word, but to get its meaning, pronunciation, or synonyms we need a more elaborate structure, a map.

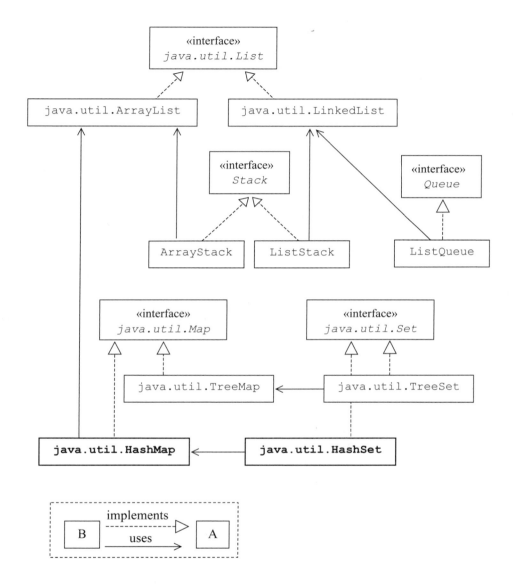

Figure 6-1. The `java.util.HashSet` and `HashMap` classes and
their relationships with other `java.util` and
our own classes and interfaces

As we have seen, a map allows us to associate keys with objects. For example, in large database systems the actual data files reside in mass storage and the search is performed not on actual records but on some index, a map that links the key with the record's location in storage. Sometimes the same file may have several indices, depending on its use. For example, the customers of a telephone company may be indexed by telephone number for billing inquiries and by name for directory assistance.

In Java, the concept of mapping is formalized in the `Map` interface. Implementations of maps parallel implementations of sets. For example, we can hold a set of values in an array; likewise, we can represent a map simply as two parallel arrays: an array of keys and an array of the respective values associated with them. If we implement a map in a BST, each node in the tree may hold a key and a reference to the value associated with that key. That's precisely what Java's `TreeMap` class does.

Is there a way to store and retrieve data faster than in a BST? The answer is yes, if we can set up a ***lookup table*** or a ***hash table***. In the remainder of this chapter we will discuss lookup tables and hashing as well as `java.util`'s `HashSet` and `HashMap` classes. Figure 6-1 shows where these two classes fit among Java implementations of other data structures that we have discussed so far. Like `TreeSet` and `TreeMap`, `HashSet` and `HashMap` implement the `Set` and `Map` interfaces respectively, but the implementations are quite different — they are based on hashing.

6.2 Lookup Tables

The idea of a lookup table is to avoid searching altogether: each key in a map itself tells us exactly where we can find it. The key is converted either directly or through some simple formula into an integer, which is used as a subscript into the lookup table array. The associated value is stored in the element of the array with that subscript. One special reserved value (e.g., `null`) may be used to indicate that a particular slot in the table is empty — the value is not in the set. The mapping from all valid keys to the computed indices must be unambiguous, so that we can go directly to the corresponding lookup table entry and store or fetch the data.

Suppose, for example, that an application such as entering shipping orders requires a database of U.S. zip codes that would quickly find the town or locality with a given code. Suppose we are dealing with 5-digit zip codes, so there are no more than 100,000 possible zip values, from 00000 to 99999. Actually, only a fraction of the 5-digit numbers represent a real zip code used by the U.S. Postal Service. But in this application it may be important to make the zip code lookup as quick as possible. This can be accomplished using a table with 100,000 entries. The 5-digit zip will be used directly as an index into the table. Those entries in the table that correspond to a valid zip code will point to the corresponding record containing the locality name; all the other entries will remain unused (Figure 6-2).

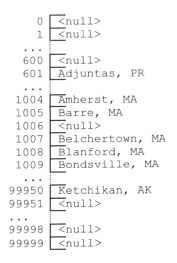

0	<null>
1	<null>
. . .	
600	<null>
601	Adjuntas, PR
. . .	
1004	Amherst, MA
1005	Barre, MA
1006	<null>
1007	Belchertown, MA
1008	Blanford, MA
1009	Bondsville, MA
. . .	
99950	Ketchikan, AK
99951	<null>
. . .	
99998	<null>
99999	<null>

Figure 6-2.   A lookup table for the United States zip codes

This type of data access is "instantaneous," but some space may be wasted if many lookup table entries are empty. At the same time, lookup tables save a little space because separate keys do not have to be stored with data values. Instead, the key is implicit in the value's location in the lookup table.

Lookup tables are useful for many other tasks, such as data compression or translating one symbolic notation into another. In graphics applications and in hardware, for example, a "logical" color code (usually some number, say, from 0 to 255) can be converted into an actual screen color by fetching its red, green, and blue components from three lookup tables.

Another common use of lookup tables is for tabulating functions when we need to speed up time-critical computations. The function argument is translated into an integer index that is used to fetch the function value from its lookup table. In some cases, when the function argument may have only a small number of integer values, the lookup table may actually take less space than the code that would be needed to implement the function! If, for example, we need to compute 3^n repeatedly for $n = 0,...,9$, the most efficient way, in terms of both time and space, is to use a lookup table of 10 values:

```
private static int n_thPowerOf3[] =
  {1, 3, 9, 27, 81, 243, 729, 2187, 6561, 19683};
...
  public int powOf3(int n)
  // precondition: 0 <= n < 10
  {
    return n_thPowerOf3[n];
  }
```

In another example, an imaging application may need to count quickly the number of "black" pixels (picture elements) in a scan line (e.g., in order to locate lines of text). In a large black and white image, pixels may be packed eight per byte to save space. The task then needs a method that finds the number of set bits in a byte. This method can easily do the job by testing individual bits:

```
// Count the number of bits in byte b that are set to 1:
int count = 0;
if ((b & 0x01) != 0) count++;  // bit 0
if ((b & 0x02) != 0) count++;  // bit 1
if ((b & 0x04) != 0) count++;  // bit 2
...
if ((b & 0x80) != 0) count++;  // bit 7
```

But, if performance is important, a lookup table with 256 elements that holds the bit counts for all possible values of a byte (0-255) may be a more efficient solution:

```
private static int bitCounts[] =
{
  0,1,1,2,1,2,2,3,1,2,2,3,2,3,3,4,    // 00000000 - 00001111
  1,2,2,3,2,3,3,4,2,3,3,4,3,4,4,5,    // 00010000 - 00011111
  ...                                   ...
  4,5,5,6,5,6,6,7,5,6,6,7,6,7,7,8     // 11110000 - 11111111
};

  ...
int i = (int)b;          // Unfortunately, in Java, byte type
if (i < 0) i += 256;     //    values are signed: -128 <= b <= 127
int count = bitCounts[i];
```

6.3   *Lab:* Cryptogram Solver

Almost everyone is sooner or later tempted to either send a message in code or to decode an encrypted message. In a simple cryptogram puzzle, a small fragment of text is encrypted with a substitution cipher in which each letter is substituted with another letter. Something like: "Puffm, Cmafx!" To solve a cryptogram we usually look for familiar patterns of letters, especially in short words. We also evaluate frequencies of letters, guessing that in English the most frequent letters stand for 'e' or 't', while the least frequent letters stand for 'j' or 'q'. The purpose of this lab is to solve a cryptogram and to master the use of lookup tables and distributions in the process.

Our *Cryptogram Solver* program is interactive. After opening an encrypted text file the user sees the encrypted text on the left side of the screen and the decoded text on the right. Initially, nothing is decoded — the decoded text has only dashes for all the letters. The user then enters substitutions for one or several letters, clicks the "Refresh" button, and immediately sees an updated version of the decoded text. In addition, the program offers decoding hints based on the frequencies of letters in the encrypted text.

Cryptogram Solver can also create cryptograms. If you enter random substitutions for all letters (or click the "Encode" menu item) and then type in your text fragment on the left side (or load it from a text file), then the text shown on the right side will be an encrypted version of your text.

Your task is to write a class `Enigma`, named after the famous German encryption machine.[enigma] Enigma was invented in 1918 and was first used in the banking business, but it very quickly found its way into the military. Enigma's codes were considered "unbreakable," but they were eventually broken, first by Polish codebreakers in 1932 and later, during WWII, by the codebreakers of the Bletchley Park project in Great Britain, led by Alan Turing,[turing] one of the founders of modern computer science. The battle between Enigma codemakers and codebreakers lasted through WWII, and the dramatic successes of Allied cryptanalysts provided invaluable intelligence information.

Your `Enigma` class must maintain a lookup table for substitutions of the letters 'A' through 'Z'. The easiest way to store the table is simply in a string of text. Initially the lookup table contains only dashes. For example:

```
private String lookupTable = "--------------------------";
```

The lookup table is based on the fact that the letters 'A' through 'Z' have consecutive Unicode codes. `Character.getNumericValue(ch)` returns a positive integer that corresponds to ch's Unicode code. If ch is an upper-case letter, then

```
int i = getNumericValue(ch) - getNumericValue('A');
```

sets i to an integer in the range from 0 to 25, which can be used as a subscript into our lookup table (array or string) of 26 letters.

My GUI class `Cryptogram` needs four methods from your `Enigma` class:

```
void setSubstitutions(String subs);
String decode(String text);
void countLetters(String text);
int getFrequencyPos(int k);
```

The first two methods support decoding (or encoding) of text; the last two support computer-generated hints based on letter counts.

The `setSubstitutions(String subs)` method assumes that subs contains 26 letters and saves it as the lookup table.

The `decode(String text)` method takes a string of characters and decodes all the letters in it according to the current lookup table. decode leaves all characters that are not letters unchanged and preserves the upper or lower case of letters. It returns the decoded string, which has the same length as text.

The `countLetters(String text)` method counts the number of occurrences for each of the letters 'a' through 'z' in text (case blind) and saves these 26 counts in an array for future use. You must count all letters in one sweep over text. First zero out all the counters, then increment the appropriate counter for each letter.

Finally, the `getFrequencyPos(int k)` method helps generate decryption hints. My `Cryptogram` code defines a string of 26 letters of the alphabet, arranged in the order of their frequency in average English text. I simply took a small plain text file, sample.txt, counted occurrences for the 26 letters, then arranged the letters in increasing order of frequency:

```
private static final String frequentLetters =
                "JQXZKBVWFUYMPGCLSDHROANITE";
```

If we arrange the letters in the encrypted text in the same manner, according to frequency count, then we can match them against `frequentLetters` and use a character from `frequentLetters` as a possible guess for the corresponding letter of the encrypted text. Your `getFrequencyPos(int k)` method returns the rank of the *k*-th letter of the alphabet by frequency: i.e., its position in the string of all 26 letters arranged in increasing order of their frequency in the encrypted text. The method's code is very short once you figure out the algorithm. Try to figure it out yourself or read the (encrypted) hint below.

Kzddnkg anzo vmukk kusgk tfg vnzqtk wno mgttgok pq tfg uooua vnzqtgok pq anzo vmukk. Pt uddguok ut wpokt tfut anz qggh tn knot `vnzqtgok` tn wplzog nzt cfgog `vnzqtgok[b]` ktuqhk pq tfg knotgh uooua. Uvtzumma, knotpql vuq ig usnphgh fgog. Pqktguh, xzkt wplzog nzt fnc yuqa sumzgk pq tfg `vnzqtgok` uooua uog igmnc `vnzqtgok[b]`. Nw tfnkg sumzgk tfut uog gezum tn `vnzqtgok[b]`, vnzqt nqma tfnkg tfut uog tn tfg mgwt nw `vnzqtgok[b]` (p.g., cfnkg pqhgj pk mgkk tfuq b).

(The above paragraph is also available in `Ch06\Cryptogram\hint.txt` 🖫 on the student disk — you can use *Cryptogram Solver* on it even before you get the hints part working correctly. Just use a ***stub*** method for `getFrequencyPos` that always returns 0.)

Note that if you load `sample.txt` (a plain text file) into the program, the hint displayed for each letter should be that same letter, because I used `sample.txt` to arrange the letters in `frequentLetters`. This is an easy way to test your `countLetters` and `getFrequencyPos` methods.

Combine your `Enigma` class with my `Cryptogram` class, located on the student disk in the `Ch06\Cryptogram` folder 🖫. The project also needs the `EasyReader` and `EasyWriter` classes. Test your program with `sample.txt`, then try to decode `secret.txt`. Both these files are in the `Ch06\Cryptogram` folder 🖫, too.

Unfortunately, as you can see, our computer-generated hints have turned out to be entirely unhelpful, except for the most frequent letter 'e'. Apparently we need a more sophisticated tool for solving cryptograms automatically — perhaps counting 2-D distributions for all pairs of adjacent letters, or even 3-D distributions for all triplets of letters, or look for other patterns in the text.

6.4   Hash Tables

The *hashing* technique builds on the lookup table concept. In a lookup table, a key is either used directly or converted through a very simple formula into an integer index. Different keys translate into different indices in the lookup table. This method is not practical, however, when the range of possible key values is large. It is also wasteful when the mapping from keys to integer indices is very sparse — many lookup table entries remain unused.

We can avoid these problems by using a better system of mapping from keys to integer indices in the table. The purpose of the mapping is to map all possible key values into a narrower range of indices and to cover that range more uniformly. Such a transformation is called a *hash function*; a table used with it is a *hash table*.

The price of hashing is that we lose the one-to-one correspondence between the keys and the table entries: two different keys may be mapped into the same location in the hash table. Thus when we try inserting a new value into the table, its slot may already be occupied. These situations are called *collisions*. We have to devise some method of dealing with them. When we retrieve a value, we have to verify that its key indeed matches the target; therefore, the key must be explicitly stored in the table with the rest of the record.

The design of a hash table thus hinges upon successful handling of two problems: how to choose a good hash function and how to handle collisions. There is room for ingenious solutions for both.

A good hash function must have the following properties:

1. It must be easy to calculate.

2. It must map all possible values of keys onto a range that is not too large.

3. It must cover that range uniformly and minimize collisions.

To devise such a function, we can try some "random" things akin to the transformations used for generating random numbers in a specified range. If the key is a string of characters, we can use some numeric codes (e.g., Unicode) for them. We then chop the key into pieces and combine these together using bitwise or arithmetic operations — hence the term "hashing." The result must be an integer in the range from 0 to `tableSize-1`.

Overly simplistic hash functions, such as simply truncating the key or converting it modulo the table size —

```
public int hashCode(long key) { return (int)(key % tableSize); }
```

— may create unexpected clusters of collisions resulting from some peculiar clustering in the data. Fortunately, we can evaluate our hash function on some simulated and real data before using it in an application.

❖   ❖   ❖

There are two principal approaches to resolving collisions. In the first approach, each entry in the hash table is itself implemented as a structure that can hold more than one value. This approach is called *chaining* and the table entry is referred to as a *bucket*. A bucket may be implemented as a linked list, a sorted array, or even a binary search tree (Figure 6-3). This approach works well for densely populated hash tables.

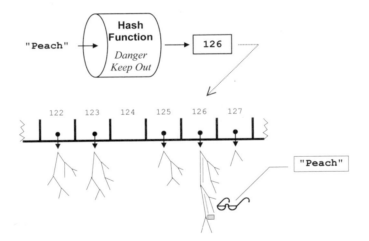

Figure 6-3.   Resolving collisions in a hash table by chaining

The second approach to resolving collisions is by storing the colliding value in a different slot of the same hash table. This approach is known as *probing*. We calculate the index into the table using the hash function as usual. If the slot is already occupied, we use some *probing function* to convert that index into a new index; we repeat this step until we find a vacant slot:

```
. . .
int index = hashCode(target.getKey());
while (hashTable[index] != null)
   index = probe(index);
hashTable[index].setValue(target.getValue());
. . .
```

The same probing function, of course, must be used for finding a value:

```
. . .
int index = hashCode(key);
while (hashTable[index] != null &&
       !key.equals(hashTable[index].getKey())
   index = probe(index);
target = hashTable[index];
. . .
```

The simplest form of the probing function is to increment the index by one or by some fixed number:

```
int probe(index) { return (index + INCR) % tableSize; }
```

This is called *linear probing* (Figure 6-4).

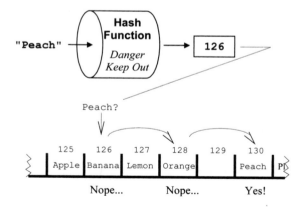

Figure 6-4. Resolving collisions in a hash table by linear probing

After the table has been in use for a while, linear probing may degrade the uniform distribution of the hash table population — a condition called ***clustering***. In so-called ***quadratic probing***, the sequence of examined slots is

```
index, index+1, index+4, index+9, ...
```

In more elaborate probing schemes, the next location may depend not only on the consecutive number of the attempt, but also on the value of the key. In addition, some rehashing function may be used instead of `% tableSize`:

```
...
int index = hashCode(target.getKey());
int attempt = 1;
while (hashTable[index] != null)
  index = rehash(index, hashTable[index].getKey(), attempt++);
...
```

Probing should be used only with relatively sparsely populated hash tables so that probing sequences are kept short. The sequence of probing attempts required to insert a value is repeated each time we search for that value.

As we can see, the performance of a search in a hash table varies with the details of implementation. In the best case, the data access is instantaneous. But with many collisions, the performance may deteriorate. If a hash table resolves collisions by chaining, the ratio of the entries stored in a hash table to the total number of buckets is called the hash table's ***load factor***. If a load factor is too small, a lot of space is wasted. When the load factor becomes very high, all the advantages of hashing are lost. Then it may be time to rehash all the entries into a new table with a larger number of buckets. A reasonable load factor may range from 0.5 to 2.0. `java.util`'s `hashSet` and `hashMap` classes have constructors that take the maximum allowed load factor as a parameter. Their no-args constructors set the load factor limit to 0.75.

6.5   `java.util`'s `HashSet` and `HashMap`

The `HashSet` class has the same methods as the `Set` interface and the `TreeSet` class. Likewise, the `HashMap` class has the same methods as the `Map` interface and the `TreeMap` class. We list the more commonly used ones here again for convenience (Figure 6-5 and Figure 6-6) — they are the same as in Figure 5-9 and Figure 5-10 in Section 5.6.

```
boolean add(Object obj);      // Adds obj to the set
                              //   Returns true if successful,
                              //   false if the object is already
                              //   in the set
boolean remove(Object obj);   // Removes obj from the set
                              //   Returns true if successful,
                              //   false if the object is not found
boolean contains(Object obj); // Returns true if obj is in the set,
                              //   false otherwise
int size();                   // Returns the number of values
                              //   in the set
Iterator iterator();          // Returns an iterator for the set

Object[] toArray();           // Copies the objects from the set
                              //   into an array and returns
                              //   that array
```

Figure 6-5. Commonly used methods of `java.util.Set` (and the `TreeSet` and `HashSet` classes)

```
Object put(Object key, Object value);
                              // Adds value and associated key
                              //   to the map;
                              //   Returns the value previously
                              //   associated with key or null
                              //   if no value was previously
                              //   associated with key
Object get(Object key);       // Returns the value associated
                              //   with key or null if no value
                              //   is associated with key
boolean containsKey(Object key); // Returns true if key is
                              //   associated with a value,
                              //   false otherwise
int size();                   // Returns the number of key-value
                              //   pairs in the map
Set keySet();                 // Returns the set of keys in
                              //   the map
```

Figure 6-6. Commonly used methods of `java.util.Map` (and the `TreeMap` and `HashMap` classes)

The HashSet class has a no-args constructor that creates an empty hash table with a default initial capacity (the number of buckets) and a load factor limit. If you know in advance the maximum number of entries to be stored in the table, it is better to use another constructor —

```
HashSet(int initialCapacity)
```

— to avoid unnecessary reallocation and rehashing of the table when it runs out of space. initialCapacity is the number of buckets to be used in the table; it should be roughly twice the number of entries expected to be stored. The third constructor takes two arguments, the initial capacity and the load factor limit.

The HashMap class provides similar constructors.

❖   ❖   ❖

The main difference between Java's BST classes and hashing classes is that objects stored in a HashSet and keys mapped in a HashMap do not have to be Comparable and do not use comparators. An iterator for a hash set produces the set's values in no particular order. Instead of ordering, you have to worry about a reasonable hashing function. When you call the HashSet's add(obj) or contains(obj) method, the obj's hashCode method is called. Likewise, key.hashCode() is called when you call a HashMap's put(key, value) or containsKey(key) method.

The Object class has a hashCode method defined, and, therefore, each object has a hashCode method. Unfortunately, this method is hardly usable because it is based on the object's current address in memory and does not reflect the object's properties.

> **It is important to override Object's built-in hashCode method with a hashCode method appropriate for your class if you plan to store the objects of your class in a HashSet or use them as keys mapped in a HashMap.**

Java library classes such as String, Double, and Integer have suitable hashCode methods defined for their objects. For example, String's hashCode method computes the hash code as

$$s_0 \cdot 31^{n-1} + s_1 \cdot 31^{n-2} + \ldots + s_{n-1}$$

where s_i is Unicode for the i-th character in the string. (It uses integer arithmetic, ignoring overflows.)

> **Normally, you do not have to invent your own hash code formula for your class but can rely on the library `hashCode` methods for one or several fields of your class.**

For example:

```
public class MsgUser
{
  ...
  private String screenName;
  ...
  public int hashCode()
  {
    return screenName.hashCode();
  }
}
```

But, no matter how simple it is, it is important not to forget to supply a `hashCode` if you plan to use your objects in a `HashSet` or a `HashMap`. In fact, it is a good idea to always supply a reasonable `hashCode` method for your class if there is a chance that you or someone else will reuse this class in a future project and place its objects (or objects of a derived class) into a hash table.

You don't have to worry about the range of values returned by a `hashCode` method.

> **Java library `hashCode` methods return an integer from the whole integer range. `HashSet` and `HashMap` methods further map the hash code onto the range of valid table indices for a particular table (e.g., by taking it modulo table size).**

6.6   *Lab:* Search Engine

We have already built a couple of games, a movie actor database, a browser, and a messaging program, but one can hardly imagine life without a search engine. In this lab we design and program our own search engine, which we call "Giggle." Rather than searching the Internet for keywords or phrases, *Giggle* searches a single file for all lines of text that contain a given word. *Giggle*'s code uses lists, BSTs, and hash tables. More precisely, it takes advantage of `java.util`'s `List`, `Set`, and `Map` interfaces and `LinkedList`, `TreeSet`, and `HashMap` classes.

Before you start searching, you need to create an index for the file you are going to search. This is analogous to the indexing process in which real search engines constantly update their indices and "crawl" the web looking for new web pages. In

Giggle, the index is a map that associates each word in a text file with a list of all lines in the file that contain that word. With a little more work, we can upgrade *Giggle* to build an index for multiple files.

As usual, I'll supply a GUI class, `Giggle`, that loads files, accepts user input, and displays the search results. You write the `SearchEngine` class that builds the index for a file and generates the search results. Your class <u>must</u> use a `Map` object to hold the word index. In this map, a key is a word (in lowercase letters) and the associated value is a `List` of `Strings`. The list holds all the lines from the file that contain the corresponding keyword.

Here are the specs for your class:

<u>Fields:</u>

```
private String myURL;   // holds the name for the "url" (file name)
private Map myIndex;    // holds the word index
```

<u>Constructor:</u>

```
public SearchEngine(String url)
```

Saves `url` in `myUrl`; initializes `myIndex` to an empty <u>HashMap</u> with an initial capacity of 20,000. Note: this constructor does not load the file; the `Giggle` class reads the file and passes one line at a time to `SearchEngine`.

<u>Public methods:</u>

```
public String getURL()
```

Returns `myUrl`. I call this method from `Giggle` to display the name of the file in which hits were found. In the present version I already know the file name, but eventually an expanded version of `Giggle` may need to index several files.

```
public void add(String line)
```

Extracts all words from `line`, and, for each word, adds `line` to its list of lines in `myIndex`. This method obtains a set of all words in `line` by calling a private method `parseWords(line)` (see below). <u>Use an iterator</u> to extract each word from that set. Use a `LinkedList` object to represent a list of lines associated with a word.

```
public List getHits(String word)
```

Returns the list associated with `word` in `myIndex`.

Private methods:

```
private Set parseWords(String line)
```

Returns a set of all words in `line`. For our purposes here, a "word" is defined as any string of alphanumeric characters. In `line`, "words" are delimited by non-alphanumeric characters or border the beginning or the end of `line`. Scan `line` once, extracting all the words and adding them to the set. Convert each word to lower case before adding it to the set. `parseWords` must represent the set of words as a <u>TreeSet</u> object. We use a set, as opposed to a list, because we don't want to index the same line multiple times when the same word occurs several times in it. A set does not allow duplicate values, so when we add words to the set, duplicates are automatically eliminated.

Combine your class with the `Giggle` class, located on the student disk in the `Ch06\Giggle` folder 🖫, and with `EasyReader`. Test `Giggle` thoroughly on a small text file. Be sure to try searching for words that are not in the file as well as those that appear in several lines and multiple times in the same line.

6.7   Summary

In a lookup table, each key is converted through some simple formula into a non-negative integer, which is used as an index into the lookup table array. The associated value is stored in the element of the array with that index. Lookup tables can be used when the keys can be easily mapped onto integers in a relatively narrow range. All allowed keys correspond to valid indices in the table, and different keys correspond to different indices. Lookup tables provide "instantaneous" access to data, but a sparsely populated lookup table may waste a lot of space.

In the hashing approach, the key is converted by some hashing function into an integer which is used as an index into a hash table. Different keys may be hashed into the same index, causing collisions. The chaining technique resolves collisions by turning each slot in the hash table into a "bucket" that can hold several values. The probing technique stores the colliding objects in free slots chosen according to a predefined probing function. The performance and space requirements for hash tables may vary widely depending on implementation. In the best scenario a hash table provides "instantaneous" access to data, but the performance may deteriorate with a lot of collisions. One disadvantage of hash tables over a binary search tree or a sorted list is the difficulty of quickly traversing the table in ascending order of keys. This may be a serious consideration in some applications.

`java.util`'s `HashSet` and `HashMap` classes implement the `Set` and `Map`, interfaces, respectively, using hash tables. The objects kept in `HashSet` and keys mapped in a `HashMap` do not have to be `Comparable` and do not use comparators. Instead, you have to make sure that these objects have a reasonable `hashCode` method defined for them. Java library classes, such as `String`, `Double`, and `Integer`, have suitable `hashCode` methods defined. You can often write a reasonable `hashCode` method for your own class by calling library `hashCode` methods for one or several fields of your class.

A `hashCode` method may return an integer from the whole integer range. `HashSet` and `HashMap` methods further map the hash code onto the range of valid table indices for a particular table.

Exercises

1.   Define:

hashing
hash function
collisions
chaining
bucket
probing

2.   Mark true or false and explain:

(a)   Access time in a lookup table of size n is proportional to n _____   ✓
(b)   Probing is feasible only when the population of a hash table is relatively sparse. _____
(c)   Access time in a hash table is never greater than $T \cdot n$, where n is the size of the table and T is some constant that depends on the time necessary to compute the hashing function. _____
(d)   It is easy to traverse a hash table in ascending order of keys. _____
(e)   One of the advantages of hash tables over binary search trees is the faster access time for adding and removing data values. _____   ✓

3.   A class `LookupState` implements a lookup table that helps to find full names of states from their two-letter postal abbreviations (both letters uppercase). The lookup table is implemented as an array of 676 entries (676 is 26 times 26) of which only 50 are used.

```
public class LookupState
{
  private static String stateNames[] = new String[676];

  public static void add(String abbr, String name)
  {
    . . .
  }

  public static String find(String abbr)
  {
    . . .
  }

  private static int lookupIndex(String abbr)
  {
    . . .
  }
}
```

Devise a method for mapping a two-letter state abbreviation into an integer index from 0 to 675 returned by the `lookupIndex` method, write the `add` and `find` methods, and test your class.

⟨ Hint: `Character.getNumericValue(ch)` returns the Unicode code for `ch` as an integer. ⟩

4.   The class `PhoneCall` represents a record of a telephone call:

```
public class PhoneCall
{
    ...
    public int getStartHour() { ... }  // Military time: 0 -- 23
    public int getStartMin() { ... }
    public int getDuration() { ... }   // in seconds
    ...
}
```

Write a method

```
public int busiestHour(List dayCalls)
```

that returns the hour (a value from 0 to 23) in which the largest number of calls originated. Count only those calls that lasted at least 30 seconds. Your method must scan the list only once, using an iterator. ✓

5.   A class `RecordsHashTable` implements a set of `Record` objects as a hash table —

```
private ListNode hashTable[] = new ListNode[1000];
```

It resolves collisions by chaining, with buckets implemented as linked lists (references to `ListNode` bucket).

(a)   Assuming that a class `Record` has a method `hashCode` that returns an integer from 0 to 999 and a method `equals(Object other)`, write a `RecordsHashTable`'s method

```
public boolean contains(Record record)
```

that returns `true` if `record` is found in the set, `false` otherwise.

(b)■   Suppose a reference takes 4 bytes and `Record` information takes 20 bytes. The average number of collisions is 5. Suppose we can convert our hash table into a lookup table by using 12 times more slots and a different `hashCode` method. Will we use more or less space? By approximately what percentage? How many times faster, on average, will the retrieval operation run, assuming that computing the old and the new `hashCode` method and comparing two records takes the same time? ✓

6.■   A hash table has sixty entries. Devise and test a hash function for English words such that all the different words from this paragraph are hashed into the table with no more than four collisions. Do not call any `hashCode` methods.

Compare performance of your method with the more standard `Math.abs(word.hashCode()) % 60`.

7.■   In the `HashSet` implementation of a set, which approach is used to determine whether two objects are equal?

A.   `==` operator
B.   `equals`
C.   `compareTo`
D.   Both `equals` and `hashCode` (a `HashSet` works properly only when the two agree)
E.   Both `compareTo` and `hashCode`

Write a small program to test each hypothesis.

8.♦   ***Radix Sort*** is a sorting method that is not based on comparing keys but rather on applying the lookup or hashing idea to them. Suppose we have a large list of data records but all their keys are integers from 0 to 9. We can create 10 buckets, corresponding to the 10 possible keys. In one pass through the list we add each value to the appropriate bucket. Then we scan through the ten buckets in ascending order and collect all the values together. The result will be the list sorted in ascending order.

Now suppose the keys are integers in the range from 0 to 99999. Suppose memory limitations do not allow us to have 100000 buckets. The Radix Sort technique lets us sort the keys one digit at a time: we can complete the task with only 10 buckets, but we will need five passes through the list. We have to make sure that the buckets preserve the order of inserted values; for instance, each bucket can be a list with the values inserted at the end (or a queue). We start with the least significant digit in the key and distribute the data values into buckets based on that digit. When we are done, we scan all the buckets in ascending order and collect the data back into one list. We then take the second digit (the tens digit) and repeat the process. We have to make as many passes through the data as there are digits in the key. After the last pass, the list is sorted.

Continued ⇨

The Radix Sort method works for data with any keys that permit positional representation. For integers, using hexadecimal digits or whole bytes is actually more appropriate than decimal digits. A program that sorts words in lexicographic order can perform a radix sort with a bucket for each letter or symbol. In the latter case, we have to pad all the words with blanks to the maximum length and start sorting from the last character position.

(a)   Implement Radix Sort for a list of words (`String` objects):

```
public LinkedList sort(LinkedList words)
```

The method takes a list of words and returns a linked list of these words sorted alphabetically in ascending order. Assume that all the words are made up of uppercase letters 'A' through 'Z'. Recall that `Character.getNumericValue(ch)` returns the Unicode code for `ch` as an integer. Use an `ArrayList` to hold the temporary buckets; each bucket is a `LinkedList` of words. Don't forget to "pad" (logically) shorter words with "spaces": the first bucket should be reserved for words that are shorter than the letter position at the current pass, so you need to use 27 buckets. Use the `LinkedList`'s `addAll` method to collect the buckets into a new list. `addAll` concatenates another list to this list. (You can also use an iterator for each bucket to append the words from the bucket to the new list.) Don't forget to start with empty buckets on each pass.

(b)   Rewrite the method from Part (a) using `ListQueue` objects (`Ch03/ListQueue.java` 🖫) for buckets.

chapter7 =
remainingChapters.removeMin();

Priority Queues

7.1   Prologue

When you are swamped with requests and can't keep up with them, perhaps you need to respond to the most pressing ones first. Some computer applications, too, need to maintain a list of items that are ranked in some way in order of priority and be able to access the top-priority item quickly. A structure that supports this functionality is called a ***priority queue***.

Consider, for example, a credit card authorization processing system in which pending transactions are phoned in from merchants to the bank's central office for authorization. In addition to checking available credit limits, the system may run all its transactions through a special fraud detection module that ranks them according to the likelihood of fraud. All the transactions that receive a significant fraud score may be inserted into a priority queue, ranked by their score, for review by specially trained operators.

In everyday life we talk about "top priority" or "highest priority," but in computer science people usually say that they remove the <u>smallest</u> value from a priority queue. In this convention the <u>smallest</u> value has the highest priority! This is not very important, of course — what is smaller and what is bigger depends on how you rank or compare items. In the credit card fraud example above, for instance, the fraud score might be a negative number, so a higher absolute value would indicate a higher fraud risk.

> **In this book we will follow the same convention: the <u>smallest</u> value has the "highest priority."**

One obvious way of implementing a priority queue is to keep all the items in an ordered list. In an array list we would put the smallest item last; in a linked list, first. This would make it very easy to access and remove that item, but to insert a new item in order, we would need to scan through the list until we found the spot corresponding to its rank. If the list were long, this could take considerable time. In an application where values are frequently inserted and removed, the insert operation would create a bottleneck that would offset the advantage of instantaneous removal.

A binary search tree can store items according to their rank, and it takes relatively little time to insert a new node and to remove the smallest node (just follow the left-child link as far as you can go — see Figure 5-8 on page 125). However, if we use a BST as a priority queue, with lots of removals and insertions of values, our BST may quickly deteriorate into a nearly linear structure. We will need to spend time re-balancing our tree back into shape.

It turns out that binary trees of another type, called ***heaps***, help us implement the priority queue in such a way that both insertion and removal of items is quick and the tree always keeps its shape. In a heap, the smallest node is in its root, and each node holds the smallest value of the subtree rooted in it. In other words, in a heap each subtree is also a heap. Inserting or removing a value takes a number of steps that is less than or equal to the height of the tree, which is only $\log_2 n$ for a tree with n nodes. For a tree with a million nodes, we would have to run through at most 20 steps, as opposed to the average of half a million steps in a sequential list implementation.

The algorithm for quick insertion of nodes into a heap requires going from a node to its parent. In the linked representation of a tree, we could add to the node structure a reference to the node's parent. A more efficient way of implementing heaps, however, is based on non-linked representation of binary trees. In this approach, all nodes are stored in an array in a certain order so that it is easy to find the children and the parent of any given node.

In the following sections we will discuss a more formal representation of priority queues as a Java interface. We will then learn about heaps and implement an efficient priority queue class based on a heap. In Chapter 9, we will utilize priority queues in a mock-up of a stock trading application.

7.2   The `PriorityQueue` Interface

A priority queue contains items ranked according to some relation of order and provides methods to add an item and to remove and return the smallest item. The items in a priority queue do not have to all be different; if several items have the smallest rank, the removal method can remove and return any one of them. In Java implementation, we assume that the items are `Comparable` objects or that a comparator is supplied for them.

The Java library packages do not supply an interface specifically for priority queues. The `PriorityQueue` interface shown in Figure 7-1 defines four methods: `isEmpty`, `add`, `removeMin`, and `peekMin`. The latter returns the smallest value without removing it from the priority queue. The methods in this interface are analogous to the ones in the `Stack` interface (Figure 3-2 on page 64) and the `Queue` interface (Figure 3-8 on page 73).

The Java library does not supply a class that implements a priority queue. A naïve class that implements a priority queue can be put together very quickly based on `java.util`'s `ArrayList` or `LinkedList`. However, as the term suggests, for priority queues efficiency is a priority. A more satisfactory and efficient implementation can be based on **heaps**, which are the subject of Sections 7.3 and 7.4.

```
public interface PriorityQueue
{
  boolean isEmpty();
  void add(Object obj);
  Object removeMin();
  Object peekMin();
}
```

Figure 7-1. The `PriorityQueue` interface[*] (`Ch07\PriorityQueue.java` 💾)

7.3   Binary Trees: Non-Linked Representation

A binary tree is called *full* if all its levels are filled with nodes. A full tree with h levels has 2^h-1 nodes. Each level contains twice as many nodes as the preceding level; the number of nodes in the last level is 2^{h-1}.

A binary tree is called **complete** if it has no gaps on any level. The last level may have some leaves missing on the right. Figure 7-2 shows the shapes of a full tree and a complete tree.

---

[*] Adapted from The College Board's *AP Computer Science AB: Implementation Classes and Interfaces.*

If we have a complete tree, we can number all its nodes starting from 1 at the root, then proceeding from left to right at each consecutive level (Figure 7-3). Since the tree is complete, there are no gaps between its nodes, so a node's number tells us exactly where in the tree we can find it. The left and right children of the i-th node, if they are present, have the numbers $2i$ and $2i+1$, and its parent has the number $i/2$ (truncated to an integer).

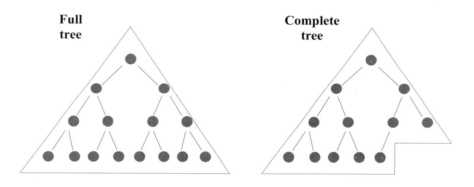

Figure 7-2.   The shapes of *full* and *complete* trees

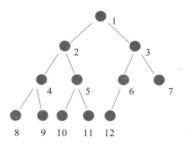

Figure 7-3.   Numbering of the nodes in a complete tree

We have numbered all the nodes of a complete tree from 1 to n in such a way that knowing the number of a node lets us easily find the numbers of its left and right child and its parent. This property allows us to store a complete tree in an array where the element `items[i]` corresponds to node number i (Figure 7-4). This is one of a few cases where it is convenient to count the elements starting from 1, as opposed to the Java convention of indexing the elements of an array starting from 0. In the Java implementation, it is convenient to leave `items[0]` unused.

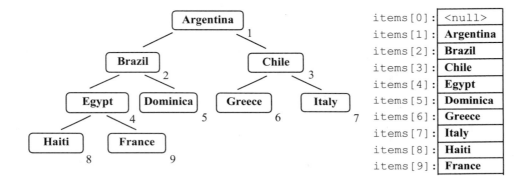

Figure 7-4. Representation of a complete binary tree in an array

7.4   Heaps and Priority Queues

A *heap* is a binary tree that satisfies two conditions:

1.   It is a complete tree;

2.   The value in each node does not exceed any of the values in that node's subtree.*

Unlike binary search trees, heaps are allowed to have more than one data item with the same value, and values in the left subtree do not have to be ranked lower than values in the right subtree.

> **The root of a heap holds its smallest value. This fact, together with efficient algorithms for adding and removing nodes, makes heap a perfect tool for implementing a priority queue.**

The best way to program a heap is by using the array representation of a complete binary tree, discussed in the previous section. We will use an array of `Objects` called `items` to hold the items. The element `items[1]` of the array corresponds to the root node. The element `items[0]` remains unused, as shown in Figure 7-4 above. Figure 7-5 shows the beginning of our `HeapPriorityQueue` class, its fields, four constructors, and the `isEmpty` and `peekMin` methods.

---

* As with priority queues, the terminology for heaps depends on convention. Many people distinguish a "min heap" with the smallest value at the root from a "max heap" with the largest value at the root. Here we call a "min heap" simply a "heap" for consistency with `removeMin` in `PriorityQueue`.

```java
import java.util.*;

public class HeapPriorityQueue
     implements PriorityQueue
{
  private static final int DFLT_CAPACITY = 1024;
  private Object items[];
  private int numItems;
  private Comparator comparator;

  public HeapPriorityQueue()
  {
    this(DFLT_CAPACITY, null);
  }

  public HeapPriorityQueue(Comparator c)
  {
    this(DFLT_CAPACITY, c);
  }

  public HeapPriorityQueue(int initialCapacity)
  {
    this(initialCapacity, null);
  }

  public HeapPriorityQueue(int initialCapacity, Comparator c)
  {
    items = new Object[initialCapacity + 1];
    comparator = c;
  }

  public boolean isEmpty()
  {
    return numItems == 0;
  }

  public Object peekMin()
  {
    if (numItems == 0)
    {
      throw new NoSuchElementException();
    }

    return items[1];
  }
  ...
}
```

Figure 7-5. Fields, constructors, and `isEmpty` and `peekMin` methods in `HeapPriorityQueue` (Ch07\HeapPriorityQueue.java 💾)

The no-args constructor allocates an array, setting its size to some default capacity. Another constructor allocates an array of a given size. A separate field `numItems` holds the number of items currently stored in the array. We assume the items are `Comparable` objects or that a comparator is supplied for them. Two other constructors, which take a comparator object as an argument, are provided.

Since the smallest value in a heap is in its root, it is not too difficult to find it — the `peekMin` method is really simple. However, if we remove the root, we need to repair the heap, restoring both its shape as a complete tree and its node ordering property. The shape is restored by cutting off the last leaf and placing it into the root. To repair the order we apply the "reheap down" procedure, in which the value from the root moves down the heap until it falls into place. At each step down that value is swapped with its smaller child. In the actual code, the swapping is logical: the root is saved and an "empty node" moves down the tree until it falls into place, then the saved root value is stored in that node. Figure 7-6 illustrates the procedure and Figure 7-7 shows the code for the `removeMin` and `reheapDown` methods.

The `add` method works in a similar way but in the reverse direction: first we add the new node as the last leaf, then apply the "reheap up" procedure to restore the ordering property of a heap. "Reheap up" moves the new node up the tree, swapping places with its parent until the order is restored (Figure 7-8).

Note that if the `items` array runs out of space, we have to allocate a new, larger array and copy all the items into it. In this case we'll do what Java's `ArrayList` and other library classes do: double the size of the array. If the approximate maximum heap size is known in advance, it is better to construct a heap of sufficient capacity at the outset (using one of the constructors that takes the initial capacity as a parameter).

The complete code for the `PriorityQueue` interface and the `HeapPriorityQueue` class is in the `Ch07` folder ⊟ on the student disk.

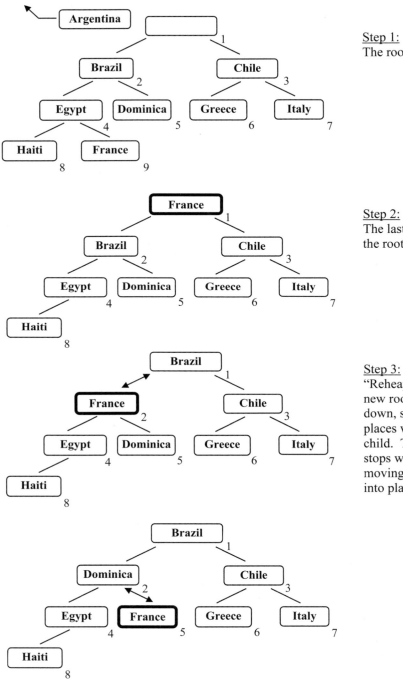

Step 1:
The root is removed

Step 2:
The last leaf replaces
the root

Step 3:
"Reheap down": the
new root value moves
down, swapping
places with its smaller
child. The process
stops when the
moving value falls
into place.

Figure 7-6. Removing the root node from a heap

```
...

public Object removeMin()
{
  if (numItems == 0)
  {
    throw new NoSuchElementException();
  }

  Object min = items[1];
  items[1] = items[numItems];
  numItems--;
  reheapDown();
  return min;
}

private void reheapDown()
{
  Object root = items[1];  // save root
  int iParent = 1, iChild = 2;

  while (iChild <= numItems)
  {
    if (iChild < numItems && lessThan(items[iChild+1], items[iChild]))
      iChild++;  // set iChild to the smaller right child
    if (!lessThan(items[iChild], root))
      break;
    items[iParent] = items[iChild];
    iParent = iChild;
    iChild = 2 * iParent; // left child
  }
  items[iParent] = root;
}

private boolean lessThan(Object obj1, Object obj2)
{
  if (comparator != null)
    return comparator.compare(obj1, obj2) < 0;
  else
    return ((Comparable)obj1).compareTo(obj2) < 0;
}

...
```

Figure 7-7. `removeMin` and `reheapDown` methods in `HeapPriorityQueue`

```
...

public void add(Object obj)
{
  numItems++;
  if (numItems >= items.length)
    doubleCapacity();
  items[numItems] = obj;
  reheapUp();
}

private void reheapUp()
{
  Object temp = items[numItems];  // save last leaf
  int iChild = numItems, iParent = iChild / 2;

  while (iParent >= 1 && lessThan(temp, items[iParent]))
  {
    items[iChild] = items[iParent];
    iChild = iParent;
    iParent = iChild / 2;
  }
  items[iChild] = temp;
}

private void doubleCapacity()
{
  Object tempItems[] = new Object[2 * items.length - 1];
  for (int i = 0; i <= numItems; i++)
    tempItems[i] = items[i];
  items = tempItems;
}

...
```

Figure 7-8. add and reheapUp methods in HeapPriorityQueue

7.5   *Lab:* Heapsort

A priority queue, implemented as a heap, can be used for sorting. All you have to do is add all the items to a priority queue in any order, then remove them one by one. The items will be returned in ascending order. This efficient algorithm is called **Heapsort**.

Write an application that sorts a file alphabetically using Heapsort. The program reads lines form the input file and writes lines into an output file sorted in alphabetical order. Use one priority queue but <u>no other temporary arrays or lists</u>.

As an extension to the project, sort the lines alphabetically by substrings that start in a specified column n. The file may contain transactions or other data formatted in such a way that each field starts in a fixed position. For example:

```
03-01-05  253        41.50 7996 17018103250 SEA WORLD OF CALIFO   SAN DIEGO   CA
02-12-27  253       199.50 5311 16018104277 WALMART #9201        ˙SAN DIEGO   CA
03-01-08  252      1134.67 9999 00099999970 PAYMENT THANK YOU
03-01-02  254       200.00 6012 10991111120 SEARS DCSI C/A        RIVERWOODS IL
03-01-02  253        43.61 5311 16450026740 MERVIN'S 267          EL TORO     CA
```

Sorting this file by the substring starting at column 0 will sort it by date, while sorting starting at column 13 will sort transactions by amount. Make sure that your program can handle lines that are shorter than n characters; put all such lines at the beginning of the sorted file.

Hint: you need a comparator — see Section 5.5.

7.6   **Summary**

A binary tree is called complete if all its levels are completely filled with nodes without gaps up to the last level, which may have nodes missing on the right. A heap is a complete binary tree that holds some ranked data items in such a way that the root holds the smallest item and each node holds an item ranked not higher than all the items in its subtree. A heap is allowed to have several items of the same rank. The heap structure is an efficient way of implementing a priority queue in which we can insert items in any order and remove the smallest item (the item of the highest priority). The heap allows us to insert or remove an item in $\log_2 n$ steps, where n is the total number of items in the heap.

A good way of implementing a heap is through the non-linked representation of a complete binary tree. In this implementation the tree nodes are represented by the elements of an array. If `items` is the array, the root corresponds to `items[1]`; subsequent slots in the array store the nodes in each consecutive level from left to right. In a Java implementation, it is convenient to leave `items[0]` unused. With this numbering of nodes, the children of the node `items[i]` can be found in `items[2*i]` and `items[2*i+1]`, and the parent of `items[i]` is in `items[i/2]`.

In Java, the "Priority Queue" data structure can be formalized as an interface `PriorityQueue` with `isEmpty`, `add`, `removeMin`, and `peekMin` methods. We have implemented this interface in the `HeapPriorityQueue` class. The `add` and `removeMin` methods add and remove an object, respectively. These methods rearrange a number of nodes in the heap to preserve the heap structure, keeping it a complete tree with the heap ordering property. `add` uses the "reheap up" procedure and `removeMin` uses the "reheap down" procedure. These elegant algorithms involve no more than one node at each level and therefore require a number of steps no greater than the depth of the tree. They can be implemented in concise iterative code.

The efficient Heapsort algorithm sorts a collection of items by inserting them into a priority queue in any order, then removing them one by one in ascending order.

Exercises

1.   Mark true or false and explain:

    (a)   A heap is a kind of binary search tree. _____ ✓
    (b)   All nodes in a heap must contain different values. _____
    (c)   The largest value in a heap, if unique, is always a leaf. _____ ✓
    (d)   At most one node in a heap may have one child. _____
    (e)   If a heap has n nodes, a new node can be inserted using at most $\log_2 n + 1$ comparisons. _____ ✓
    (f)   The most economical implementation of a heap is a linked binary tree with pointers from each node to its parent. _____

2.   The nodes of a complete binary tree are represented by the following array (starting with the first element):

```
12 17 4 65 50 17 2 76 72 74 73 18 57
```

(a)   Draw the tree.
(b)   Swap the root with one of the leaves to obtain a heap.

3.   In an array representation of a complete binary tree, `x[0]` is unused, `x[1]` represents the root, and so on. The heap contains *n* nodes.

(a)   Write the indices of the parent, left child, and right child of the node `x[i]` in terms of `i`. ✓
(b)   Write a condition for `i` that determines whether `x[i]` is a leaf. ✓
(c)▪   Write an expression for the depth of the tree.

4.▪   Write and test a method

```
public void traverseInOrder(int x[], int n)
```

that would traverse inorder a heap of integers with *n* nodes and with the root in `x[1]`. Hint: use a recursive helper method with a third argument.

5.▪   Consider a heap

```
         5
       /   \
      8     34
     / \
    21  55
```

Nodes are inserted by appending them at the bottom level and then using the "Reheap Up" procedure. Nodes are removed by removing the root, putting the last leaf at the top, and then using the "Reheap Down" procedure.

(a)   Draw the resulting heap after inserting `13`, then `3`. ✓
(b)   Draw the heap after removing the smallest value three times from the result of (a).

6.▪   Implement `PriorityQueue` as an `ArrayList` sorted in descending order. Use binary search to find the place where a new value is to be inserted. Is this implementation more or less efficient than a heap? Explain.

7.■   (a)   The class `Message` has a method `int getPriority()` that returns an integer from 0 to 4 (0 being the highest priority). Write and test a class `MessagePriorityQueue` that implements the `PriorityQueue` interface. The class implements a priority queue for `Message` objects based on the value returned by the `getPriority` method. Use an array of five queues (`ListQueue` objects, see `Ch03\ListQueue.java` ▣), one queue for each priority value.

(b)   How does the time efficiency of this implementation with a separate queue for each priority compare to a heap?

(c)◆   Using `MessagePriorityQueue`, write a simulation in which a `Message` event with a random priority from 0 to 4 occurs with the probability 0.2 each "minute" (iteration). Pretend that processing of a message takes four "minutes." Determine the average waiting time for messages of different priorities. ⸮ Hint: add the "time of arrival" field and a `getArrivalTime` method to `Message`. ⸮

8.◆   Modify *Giggle* in Section 6.6 so that it displays the lines that contain a search word in descending order by the number of hits in each line. Modify the `getHits` method in the `SearchEngine` class: rather than returning a list of lines that contain a given word, make `getHits` scan the list and build and return a `PriorityQueue`. Use a `HeapPriorityQueue` constructed with a comparator. Provide a comparator class that compares two strings based on how many times a search word occurs in each of them; provide a comparator's constructor that takes a search word as an argument. The updated `Giggle` class is provided for you in `Ch07\Exercises\Giggle.java` ▣.

Chapter 8

Analysis of Algorithms

8.1   Prologue

By now, no doubt, you know how to describe algorithms using flowcharts or pseudocode, have learned many standard algorithms, and have designed a few of your own. Still, a formal definition of an algorithm remains elusive.

> **Informally, an** *algorithm* **is a more or less abstract, formal, and general step-by-step recipe that tells how to perform a certain task or solve a certain problem on a computer.**

When discussing algorithms, we have to keep in mind the following three important properties. First, the description of an algorithm is usually relatively short: a meaningful algorithm uses iterations or recursion to fold a long computation into one or several fragments repeated multiple times. This property makes an algorithm different from a straightforward cookbook recipe, which typically has the same number of instructions as there are steps followed by the cook. (That would not be very useful for computers that can execute millions of instructions per second.) Like a recipe, an algorithm describes all the necessary intermediate steps for getting from the initial state to the final state; however, it usually includes instructions to repeat certain sequences of steps a number of times.

Second, an algorithm must be rather general. The same algorithm applies to a whole set of initial states and produces corresponding final states for each of them. For example, a sorting algorithm must be applicable to any list regardless of the values of its elements. Moreover, an algorithm must also be independent of the *size* of the task. The concept of the size of a task is hard to formalize, too. It applies when the domain of all the initial states can be parameterized by a positive integer which is in some way related to the total number of steps necessary to do the task. The size can be the length of a list, the dimensions of a 2-D array, and so on. For example, the number of elements in the list determines the size of a list-sorting task. In an iterative or recursive procedure for finding n-factorial or the n-th Fibonacci number, n is the size. The generality of an algorithm ensures that the same algorithm applies to different sizes of the same task.

Third, algorithms are described and discussed at a certain level of abstraction that ignores specific details. For example, the same sorting algorithm applies to any type of values for which there is a relation of order. It does not matter whether the values are integers, floating-point numbers, or some records that have to be sorted by some key. What is important for sorting is that for any two values we can say whether the first is less than, equal to, or greater than the second, and that the values in the list can swap places. The abstract formulation of algorithms allows us to talk about algorithms for searching, sorting, and so on, without referring to specific data types and other details (and certainly ignoring the specifics of a programming language or a hardware platform).

These properties let us study algorithms in an abstract, theoretical way. Algorithms are often analyzed in terms of their time efficiency and space requirements. These are the concerns of a branch of computer science called ***computational complexity*** or ***operations research***. In this book we concentrate on time efficiency. One obvious way to measure the time efficiency of an algorithm is to implement it in a computer program, run that program on various sets of input data, and measure the running time. Computer practitioners call this type of measurement a ***benchmark***.

It may seem that benchmarks leave little room for theory, but that first impression is incorrect. While benchmarks depend on the details of implementation, such as the actual code, the programming language and optimizing capabilities of the compiler and so on, as well as on the CPU speed and other hardware characteristics, it turns out it is possible to study the efficiency of algorithms excluding all these practical matters. The ***big-O*** concept serves this purpose. You probably already know something about the way "big-O" notation is used to describe the efficiency of algorithms. In this chapter we will discuss it in a more mathematically rigorous way.

The theoretical study of algorithms relies on an abstract model of a computer as a device with some defined capabilities, such as the capability to perform arithmetic operations and to store and retrieve data values in memory. The abstract model disregards specific features of a particular computer system, such as the CPU speed or RAM size. The theoretical approach requires two simplifications. First, we have to stop measuring performance in real time (which depends on CPU speed, etc.). Nor do we measure it in terms of the number of required program instructions or statements (which depends on the language, compiler, implementation, etc.). Instead, we discuss performance in terms of some abstract "steps" that are necessary to complete the task. What constitutes a "step" depends on the nature of the task. In a searching task, for example, we may define one step as one comparison between the target value and a data value in the list. In calculating a Fibonacci number iteratively, one step may be defined as one addition. The total number of required steps may depend on the size of the task, but it is assumed that each step takes the same amount of time. With this approach we cannot say how long a particular implementation of an algorithm might run on a particular computer system, but we can compare different algorithms that accomplish the same task.

The second simplification is that our theoretical analysis applies only when the task size is a large number. Let us denote the total number of steps that an algorithm requires to complete the task as $T(n)$. $T(n)$ is some function of the task size n. The theoretical approach focuses on the behavior of $T(n)$ for large n, which is called *asymptotic behavior*. In the following section we will see why knowing the asymptotic behavior of an algorithm is important and how it can be expressed in formal mathematical terms.

In the remainder of this chapter we will discuss a more formal definition of "big-O," consider some examples, and review sorting algorithms and their big-O performance.

8.2   Big-O Notation

As a starting point for our discussion, let us compare two searching algorithms in an array, Sequential Search and Binary Search. We will assume that the elements in the array are arranged in ascending order.

In the Sequential Search algorithm we simply try to match the target value against each array value in turn until we find a match or finish scanning the whole array. If the array contains n elements, the maximum possible number of "steps" (comparisons with the target) will be

$$T(n) = n$$

This is "the worst case." If we assume that the target is randomly chosen from the values in the array, on average we will need to examine only half of the elements, so

$$T_{avg}(n) = n / 2$$

Suppose this algorithm is implemented as follows:

```
int i;
for (i = 0; i < n; i++)
  if (a[i] == target)
    break;
```

The total running time includes the initialization and several iterations through the loop. In this example, the initialization is simply setting i equal to 0. Assuming that the average number of iterations is $n/2$, the average time may be expressed as:

$$t(n) = t_{init} + t_{iter} \cdot n / 2$$

where t_{init} is initialization time and t_{iter} is the time required for each iteration. In other words, the average time is a linear function of n:

$$t(n) = An + B$$

As n increases, An also increases, and the relative contribution of the constant term B eventually becomes negligible as compared to the linear term An, even if A is small and B is large. Mathematically, this means that the ratio

$$\frac{t(n)}{An} = \frac{An + B}{An} = 1 + \frac{B}{An}$$

becomes very close to 1 as n increases without bound.

Therefore, <u>for a large n</u> we can drop the constant term and say that the average time is approximately An. That means that the average time for the Sequential Search algorithm **grows linearly** with n (Figure 8-1 (a)).

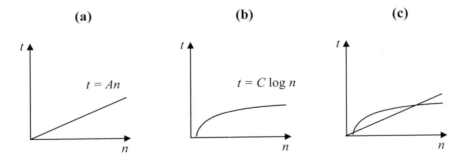

**Figure 8-1. (a) Linear growth   (b) Logarithmic growth
(c) log growth is slower**

Now let us consider the Binary Search algorithm applied to the same task. For this algorithm it is important that the values be arranged in ascending order. We compare the target with the middle element in the array. If the target is smaller, we continue searching in the left half, and if it is larger, in the right half.

For $n=3$, if we are lucky, we find the element on the first try; in the worst case we need 2 comparisons. For $n=7$, we first try a[3] and then, if it does not match the target, continue with a[0]...a[2] or a[4]...a[6]. In the worst case we need 3 comparisons. In general, if n is between 2^{h-1} and 2^h-1, the worst case will require h comparisons. Thus, the number of comparisons in the worst case is

$$T(n) = \log_2 n + 1 \text{ (truncated to an integer)}$$

For a value randomly chosen from the values in the array, the average number of steps in a binary search is (approximately, for large n) only one less than the worst case.

Let us assume that the algorithm is implemented as follows:

```
static public int binarySearch(int a[], int target)
{
  int left = 0, right = a.length - 1, middle;
  int i = -1;

  while (left <= right)
  {
    middle = (left + right) / 2;

    if (target > a[middle])
      left = middle + 1;
    else if (target < a[middle])
      right = middle - 1;
    else  // if (target == a[middle])
    {
      i = middle;
      break;
    }
  }
  return i;
}
```

Again, the total average time consists of the initialization time and the average number of iterations through the loop:

$$t(n) = t_{init} + t_{iter} \cdot \log_2 n$$

Following the same reasoning as for the sequential search, we conclude that the execution time of the binary search is, for large n, approximately proportional to the logarithm of n:

$$t(n) = C \log_2 n$$

The coefficient C is determined by the time spent in one iteration through the loop. Figure 8-1 (b) shows the general shape of this curve. $\log_2 n$ approaches infinity as n increases, but it does so more <u>slowly</u> than the linear growth of a straight line.

Note that "one step" in the sequential search is not exactly the same as "one step" in the binary search, because besides comparing the values, we also need to modify some variables and control the iterations. Thus, the coefficients A and C may be different; for example, C may be larger than A. For some small n, a sequential search may potentially run faster than a binary search. But, no matter what the ratio of A to C, the linear curve eventually overtakes the logarithmic curve for large enough n (Figure 8-1 (c)).

In other words, <u>asymptotically</u>, binary search is faster than sequential search. Moreover, it is not just 5 times faster or 100 times faster. It is faster <u>in principle</u>: you can run sequential search on the fastest computer and binary search for the same task on the slowest computer, and still, <u>if n is large enough</u>, binary search will finish first.

This is an important theoretical result of our comparison of the two searching algorithms. The difference in their asymptotic behavior provides an important new way of looking at their performance. Binary search time grows logarithmically and sequential search time linearly, so no matter what specific coefficients of the growth functions we use, linear time eventually surpasses logarithmic time.

In this context it makes sense to talk about the <u>order of growth</u> that characterizes the asymptotic behavior of a function, ignoring the particular constant coefficients. For example, $f(n) = n$ has a higher order of growth than $g(n) = \log_2 n$, which means that for any positive constant C

$$n > C \log_2 n$$

when n is large enough. Two functions that differ only by a constant factor have the same order of growth.

The following definition of **big-O** (order of growth) notation helps us formalize this terminology and refine our ideas about the order of growth. "Big-O" is defined as follows:

> **Given two functions $t(n)$ and $g(n)$, we say that**
> $$t(n) = O(g(n))$$
> **if there exist a positive constant A and some number N such that**
> $$t(n) \leq A\, g(n)$$
> **for all $n > N$.**

The big-O definition basically means that $t(n)$ asymptotically (for large enough n) grows <u>not faster than</u> $g(n)$ (give or take a constant factor). In other words, the order of growth of $t(n)$ is not larger than $g(n)$.

So, in terms of order of growth, $f = O(g)$ is like "$f \leq g$." In practice, when the performance of algorithms is stated in terms of big-O, it usually refers to the "tightest" possible upper bound. In this book, we have chosen to follow the widely accepted practice of using big-O in the sense of "growth of $f = g$." For example, in our analysis of the two searching algorithms we say that both the worst and average time is $O(n)$ for the sequential search and $O(\log_2 n)$ for the binary search.

❖ ❖ ❖

One set of functions that are often used for describing the order of growth are, naturally, powers of n:

$$1,\ n,\ n^2,\ n^3,\ \dots$$

The order of growth for n^k is higher than n^{k-1}.

If a function is a sum of several terms, its order of growth is determined by the fastest growing term. In particular, if we have a polynomial

$$p(n) = a_k n^k + a_{k-1} n^{k-1} + \dots + a_1 n + a_0$$

its growth is of the order n^k:

$$p(n) = O(n^k)$$

Thus, any second-degree polynomial is $O(n^2)$. This is called **quadratic** growth.

> Note that no one uses such things as $O(3n)$ or $O(n^2 / 2)$ because they are the same as $O(n)$ or $O(n^2)$, respectively.

❖ ❖ ❖

Let us consider a common example of code that requires $O(n^2)$ operations. Suppose we have two nested loops:

```
... // set up the outer loop
for (i = 1;   i < n;   i++)
{
   ... // set up the inner loop
   for (j = 0;   j < i;   j++)
   {
      ... // do something
   }
}
```

This kind of code may be used for finding duplicates in an array or in a simple sorting method (e.g., Selection Sort), or in some operations on matrices (e.g., transposing a matrix by flipping an *n* by *n* 2-D array symmetrically over its diagonal).

The outer loop runs for *i* from 1 to *n*–1, a total of *n*–1 times, and the inner loop runs for *j* from 0 to *i*–1, a total of *i* times. The code inside the inner loop will, therefore, execute a total of

$$1 + 2 + ... + (n{-}1)$$

times. Since this is an arithmetic sequence, its sum can be found by taking the total number of terms and multiplying it by the average of the first and the last term:

$$1 + 2 + ... + (n-1) = (n-1)\,\frac{1 + (n-1)}{2} = \frac{(n-1)n}{2}$$

If the setup time for the outer loop is t_{setup1}, the setup time for the inner loop is t_{setup2}, and the time inside the inner loop is t_{iter}, the total time for this code can be expressed as

$$t(n) = t_{setup1} + t_{setup2} \cdot (n-1) + t_{iter} \cdot \frac{(n-1)n}{2}$$

This is a second-degree polynomial of n:

$$t(n) = \frac{t_{iter}}{2}n^2 + (t_{setup2} - \frac{t_{iter}}{2})n + (t_{setup1} - t_{setup2})$$

Therefore,

$$t(n) = O(n^2)$$

❖   ❖   ❖

As we know from the Change of Base Theorem, for any $a, b > 0$, and $a, b \neq 1$

$$\log_b n = \frac{\log_a n}{\log_a b}$$

Therefore,

$$\log_a n = C \log_b n$$

where C is a constant equal to $\log_a b$.

Since functions that differ only by a positive constant factor have the same order of growth, $O(\log_2 n)$ is the same as $O(\log n)$. Therefore, when we talk about logarithmic growth, the base of the logarithm is not important, and we can say simply $O(\log n)$.

❖   ❖   ❖

The time efficiency of almost all of the algorithms discussed in this book can be characterized by one of very few growth rate functions:

I. $O(1)$ — *constant time*. This means that the algorithm requires the same fixed number of steps regardless of the size of the task.

Examples:

    A.   Finding a median value in a sorted array
    B.   Calculating $1 + 2 + ... + n$ using the formula for the sum of an arithmetic sequence
    C.   Push and pop operations in an efficiently implemented stack; enqueue and dequeue operations in a queue
    D.   Finding a key in a lookup table or a sparsely populated hash table

II. $O(n)$ — *linear time*. This means that the algorithm requires a number of steps proportional to the size of the task.

Examples:

    A.   Traversing a list with n elements, (e.g., finding max or min)
    B.   Calculating iteratively n-factorial; finding iteratively the n-th Fibonacci number
    C.   Traversing a tree with n nodes

III. $O(n^2)$ — *quadratic time*. The number of operations is proportional to the size of the task squared.

Examples:

    A.   More simplistic sorting algorithms, such as a Selection Sort of n elements
    B.   Comparing two two-dimensional arrays of size n by n
    C.   Finding duplicates in an unsorted list of n elements (implemented with two nested loops)

IV. $O(\log n)$ — *logarithmic time*.

Examples:

    A.   Binary search in a sorted list of n elements
    B.   Finding a target value in a binary search tree with n nodes
    C.   "Add" and "removeMin" operations in a priority queue, implemented as a heap, with n nodes

V. $O(n \log n)$ — *"n log n" time*.

Examples:

    A.   More advanced sorting algorithms, such as Mergesort and Quicksort

VI. $O(a^n)$ $(a > 1)$ — *exponential time*.

Examples:

    A.   Recursive Fibonacci implementation ($a \geq 3/2$; see Section 4.3)
    B.   The Towers of Hanoi ($a = 2$; see Lab 4.5)
    C.   Generating all permutations of n symbols

The best time in the above list is obviously constant time, and the worst is exponential time, which overwhelms even the fastest computers even for relatively small *n*. **Polynomial** growth (linear, quadratic, cubic, etc.) is considered manageable as compared to exponential growth.

Figure 8-2 shows the asymptotic behavior of the functions from the above list. Using the "<" sign informally, we can say that

$$O(1) \ < \ O(\log n) \ < \ O(n) \ < \ O(n \log n) \ < \ O(n^2) \ < \ O(n^3) \ < \ O(a^n)$$

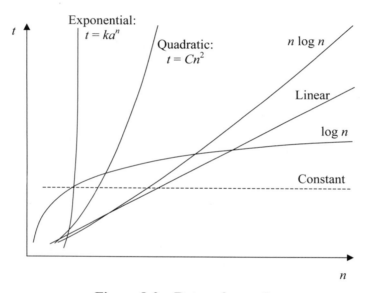

Figure 8-2. Rates of growth

The slow asymptotic growth of $\log_2 n$ (in comparison to linear growth) is especially dramatic. The thousand-fold increase in the size of a task results in only a fixed, fairly small increment in the required number of operations. Consider the following:

$$\log_2 1000 \approx 10; \quad \log_2 10^6 \approx 20; \quad \log_2 10^9 \approx 30; \quad ... \text{ etc.}$$

This property is used in many efficient "divide and conquer" algorithms such as Binary Search and is the basis for using binary search trees and heaps.

8.3   Sorting: a "Big-O" Review

We assume that you are already familiar with several sorting algorithms. **Selection Sort**, **Insertion Sort**, and **Mergesort** are described in Chapter 12 of *Java Methods*[*], and **Quicksort** is the subject of Exercise 17 in that chapter. **Heapsort** is described in Lab 7.5 of this book. In this section we quickly review the sorting algorithms and discuss their big-O properties more formally.

In general, the task of sorting is understood as rearranging the values of a list in ascending (or descending) order. The usual abstract formulation of this task assumes that we need to compare two values from the list to decide which one is smaller. What matters is the result of each comparison, not the values themselves. As we have seen in Exercise 8 for Chapter 6, such methods as Radix Sort allow us to sort values using some kind of lookup tables without any comparisons at all. These methods rely on information about the range and "composition" of values in the list. For example, if we know that the values in the list are in the range from 0 to 9, we can simply count the number of occurrences for each value and then recreate the list in order. The performance of such algorithms is $O(n)$. But here we deal with the algorithms that require actual comparisons.

Mathematically speaking, we assume that we have a list of objects, $X = \{x_0, ..., x_{n-1}\}$, and that an ordering relation $<$ is defined on X. This relation is called **total ordering** if for any two values a and b in X, exactly one of three possibilities is true: either $a < b$, or $b < a$, or $a = b$. An ordering relation must be **transitive**: if $a < b$ and $b < c$, then $a < c$. A sorting algorithm is a strategy for finding a permutation of the indices $p(0), p(1), ..., p(n-1)$ such that

$$x_{p(0)} \leq x_{p(1)} \leq ... \leq x_{p(n-1)}$$

(A permutation is a one-to-one mapping from the set of integers $\{0, 1, 2, ... n-1\}$ onto itself.) The sorting strategy is based on pairwise comparisons of values; the next pair of values to be compared may be based on the results of all the previous comparisons.

In these terms, how fast can we sort? Clearly if we compare each value with each other value, it will take n^2 comparisons. As we know, Mergesort, Quicksort, and Heapsort can do the job in only $O(n \cdot \log n)$ comparisons. Can we do any better? The answer is no.

---

[*] *Java Methods: an Introduction to Object-Oriented Programming.* Skylight Publishing, 2001.

If you are limited to "honest" comparison sorting, any sorting algorithm in its worst case scenario takes *O*(*n*·log *n*) steps.

To prove this, envision your sorting strategy as a binary decision tree: in each node we compare two values, then go left or right depending on the result (Figure 8-3). Each leaf, at the end of each path from the root, holds a different permutation of values. The number of comparisons in the worst case is the length of the longest path. If the length of the longest path in the tree is *h* then the number of leaves does not exceed 2^h. The number of all possible permutations of *n* values is *n*!. So we must have

$$2^h \geq n!$$

and, therefore

$$h \geq \log_2 (n!)$$

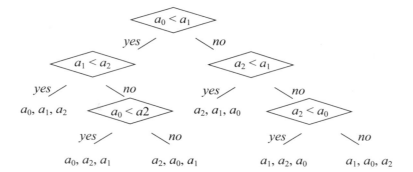

Figure 8-3. A sorting algorithm as a decision tree (for three values)

For example, for *n* = 4, *n*! = 24, so the best algorithm needs 5 comparisons; for *n* = 5 it needs 7 comparisons. An algorithm with 7 comparisons for 5 values indeed does exist, but it is not at all obvious.

Stirling's approximation (from calculus) tells us that for large *n*

$$n! \approx \sqrt{2\pi n} \left(\frac{n}{e}\right)^n$$

Asymptotically, $\log_2 (n!) = n \cdot \log n$, so faster sorting is not possible.

This is as far as we want to go with theory. Now let us review a few slower $O(n^2)$ algorithms and then a few more advanced, $O(n \cdot \log n)$ algorithms.

8.3.1 $O(n^2)$ Sorts

Sorting by Counting

In the most simplistic approach, we can compare each value in X to each other value. This means $n \cdot (n-1)$ or $O(n^2)$ comparisons. Indeed, for each x_i from X a computer program can simply count how many other values x_j do not exceed x_i. (If $x_j = x_i$ we only count it when $j < i$.) Then the position of x_i in the sorted list, $p(i)$, is set to the resulting count. This is called sorting by counting:

```
for (i = 0; i < n; i++)
{
  count = 0;
  for (j = 0; j < n; j++)
    if (a[j] < a[i] || (a[j] == a[i]  && j < i))
      count++;
  b[count] = a[i];
}
```

The algorithm is inefficient because it makes a lot of redundant comparisons. If we have already compared x_i to x_j, there is no need to compare x_j to x_i.

Selection Sort

A slight improvement is achieved in Selection Sort. In this method we find the largest value in the list and put it out of the way by swapping it with the last element in the list. We then reduce by one the length of the fragment of the list that remains to be sorted and repeat the procedure until only one element is left.

```
while (n > 1)
{
  iMax = 0;
  for (i = 1; i < n; i++)
    if (a[i] > a[iMax]) iMax = i;

  swap(a, iMax, n-1);
  n--;
}
```

This cuts the number of comparisons by half, but the big-O for the Selection Sort algorithm is still $O(n^2)$.

The number of comparisons in the counting algorithm and in Selection Sort does not depend on the initial arrangement of the values in the list. For example, if the list is already sorted, these algorithms still go through all the prescribed steps. There is no "best case" and no "worst case" scenario: the number of executed steps is always the same.

Insertion Sort

Slightly more sophisticated sorting algorithms may take advantage of a particular initial arrangement of values in the list to reduce the number of comparisons. For example, Insertion Sort keeps the beginning fragment of the list sorted and inserts each next element into it in order. At first, the beginning fragment is just one element; then it grows as we go along:

```
for (i = 1; i < n; i++)
{
  temp = a[i];
  for (j = i; j > 0 && a[j-1] > temp; j--)
    a[j] = a[j-1];
  a[j] = temp;
}
```

On average, Insertion Sort takes half the number of comparisons of Selection Sort, but it is still an $O(n^2)$ algorithm. In the worst case, when the array is sorted in reverse order, the number of comparisons is the same as in Selection Sort, $n \cdot (n-1) / 2$. But if the array is already sorted, the inner `for` loop performs only one comparison. If the array is nearly sorted, with only a couple of elements out of place, then Insertion Sort takes only $O(n)$ comparisons.

Bubble Sort

Another variation on the $O(n^2)$ sorting theme is Bubble Sort. In this algorithm we scan the list repeatedly from the beginning, swapping pairs of neighboring elements that are out of order. Each scan "bubbles up" the largest value to the end of the list, so the number of scanned elements can be reduced after each scan, and $n-1$ scans always sort the array. However, you can quit early after a "clean" scan that finds all values in order and no swapping necessary:

```
disorder = true;
while (n > 1 && disorder)
{
  disorder = false;
  for (i = 1; i < n; i++)
  {
    if (a[i] > a[i-1])
    {
      swap(a, i, i-1);
      disorder = true;
    }
  }
  n--;
}
```

Bubble Sort works best when only a few values in the list are out of order and not too far from where they belong. In the best case, when the array is already sorted, it takes only one scan through the list, $O(n)$ comparisons.

8.3.2 $O(n \cdot \log n)$ Sorts

Mergesort

In Mergesort, we split the array into two equal (or almost equal) halves. We sort each half recursively, then merge the sorted halves into one sorted array. All the comparisons are actually performed at the merging stage — the sorting stage merely calls the method recursively for each half of the array:

```
private void sort (double a[], int from, int to)
{
  if (to == from)
    return;

  int middle = (from + to) / 2;
  sort(a, from, middle);
  sort(a, middle + 1, to);

  // Merge two sorted halves into temp:

  int i = from, j = middle + 1, k = from;

  while (i <= middle && j <= to)
  {
    if (a[i] < a[j])
      temp[k++] = a[i++];   // temp is declared and initialized
    else                    //   outside of this recursive method
      temp[k++] = a[j++];
  }
  while (i <= middle)
    temp[k++] = a[i++];
  while (j <= to)
    temp[k++] = a[j++];

  // Copy back from temp to a:

  for (k = from; k <= to; k++)
    a[k] = temp[k];
}
```

This version of Mergesort predictably takes $O(n \cdot \log n)$ comparisons regardless of the initial configuration of the array. With a shortcut, discussed in Question 15 in the exercises, it only takes n comparisons when the array is already sorted.

Quicksort

The idea of Quicksort is to choose one element, called the pivot, then partition the array in such a way that all the elements to the left of the pivot are smaller than or equal to it, and all the elements to the right of the pivot are greater than or equal to it.

After partitioning, Quicksort is applied (recursively) to the left-of-pivot part and to the right-of-pivot part.

Partitioning is accomplished by going from both ends of the array towards the meeting point as far as possible, comparing the elements with the pivot. When the elements are out of order on both sides, then you swap them:

```
private int sort(double a[], int from, int to)
{
  if (from >= to)
    return;

  // Choose pivot:
  int p = (from + to ) / 2;
    // The choice of the pivot element may vary:
    //   you can also use p = from or p = to or use
    //   a fancier method, say, the median of the above three.

  // Partition:

  int i = from;
  int j = to;
  while (from <= to)
  {
    if (a[i] <= a[p])
      i++;
    else if (a[j] >= a[p])
      j--;
    else
    {
      swap (a, i, j);
      i++;
      j--;
    }
  }

  // Place pivot in its correct position:

  if (p < j)
  {
    swap (a, j, p);
    p = j;
  }
  else if (p > i)
  {
    swap (a, i, p);
    p = i;
  }

  // Sort recursively:
  sort(a, from, p-1);
  sort(a, p+1, to);
}
```

The Quicksort algorithm was invented by C.A.R. Hoare.[*] Although its performance is less predictable than Mergesort's, it averages a faster time for random arrays.

In general, you have to be careful with this type of recursion: you have to think not only about performance, but also about the required stack space. If everything goes smoothly, Quicksort partitions the array most of the time into approximately equal halves. Then the array length is divided roughly by two for each recursive call, recursion quickly converges to the base case, and the required stack space is only $O(\log n)$. But what happens if we always choose the first element of the array as the pivot and the array happens to be sorted? Then partitioning does not really work: one half is empty, while the other has all the elements except the pivot. In this case, the algorithm degenerates into a slow version of the Selection Sort and takes $O(n^2)$ time. What's worse, the depth of recursion becomes $O(n)$, and, for a large array, it may overflow the stack. (There is a version of Quicksort that overcomes the possible stack overflow problem by handling the shorter half of the array recursively and the longer half iteratively.)

<u>Heapsort</u>

In Lab 7.5 you sorted a file using Heapsort. The idea of the algorithm is simple: add all the values to a heap, then remove them one by one.

The Heapsort algorithm can also be used for sorting an array. You don't really have to create a temporary heap — use the same array to hold the heap. Gradually build a maximum heap, with the largest value in the root, by repeatedly applying the "reheap down" procedure to each node, starting from a[n/2] and going backwards to a[1]. (a[n/2] is the last node with children, assuming that a[0] is not used, the list starts at a[1], and the heap's root is in a[1]). After you are done, your array becomes a real inverted heap (with the largest value in the root). Now repeatedly swap the root element with the last element, fix the heap by applying the reheap down procedure to the root, and decrement the logical size of the heap. You will end up with the array sorted in ascending order.

Heapsort was proposed by J. Williams.[*] This is a magical algorithm: if you look at the code without a model of a heap in mind, you will never figure out what's going on or how it works. But if you know the code is actually based on a heap, then it becomes clear. Heapsort is predictable and it does not use any temporary space. Its shortcoming is that it does not take advantage of the situation when the array is already sorted.

---

[*] C.A.R. Hoare. Quicksort. *Comp. J.*, Vol. 5, No. 1 (1962), pp. 10-15.
[*] J.W.J. Williams. Heapsort (Algorithm 232). Comm. ACM, Vol. 7, No. 6 (1964), pp.347-48.

8.4   Summary

The efficiency of algorithms is usually expressed in terms of asymptotic growth as the size of the task increases toward infinity. The size of a task is basically an intuitive notion: it reflects the number of elements involved or other similar parameters. The asymptotic growth may be expressed using "big-O" notation, which gives an upper bound for the order of growth. In practice, the big-O estimate is usually expressed in terms of the "tightest" possible upper bound.

The most common orders of growth (in increasing order) are

$O(1)$ — constant;
$O(\log n)$ — logarithmic;
$O(n)$ — linear;
$O(n \log n)$ — "n log n";
$O(n^2)$ — quadratic;
$O(a^n)$ — exponential.

Logarithmic growth is dramatically slower than linear growth. This explains the efficiency of "divide and conquer" algorithms, such as Binary Search, and of binary search trees and heaps. Discovering an $O(\log n)$ algorithm instead of an $O(n)$ algorithm or an $O(n \cdot \log n)$ instead of $O(n^2)$ algorithm for some task is justifiably viewed as a breakthrough in time efficiency. Exponential growth is unmanageable: it quickly puts the task out of reach of existing computers, even for tasks of rather small size.

Sorting algorithms provide a fertile field for formulating and studying general properties of algorithms and for comparing their efficiency. Simplistic sorting algorithms, such as Sorting by Counting, Selection Sort, Insertion Sort, and Bubble Sort, accomplish the task in $O(n^2)$ comparisons, although Insertion Sort and Bubble Sort may work much faster when applied to an array that is already sorted or almost sorted. More advanced algorithms, such as Mergesort, Quicksort, and Heapsort, accomplish the task in $O(n \cdot \log n)$ comparisons.

Sorting is a very well studied subject. There are hundreds of other algorithms and variations. There is no one "best" sorting algorithm. In the real world, the choice depends on specific properties of data and additional constraints and requirements.

Exercises

Sections 8.1-8.2

1.   Mark true or false and explain:

    (a)   In comparing the order of growth, $f = O(g)$ is like "$f \leq g$." _____ ✓
    (b)   We often informally say $f = O(g)$ when we actually mean that the order of growth of f and g is the same. _____
    (c) $\log_2 n = O(\log_{10} n)$. _____ ✓
    (d)   If $f(n) = 1 + 2 + \ldots + n$, then $f(n) = O(n^2)$. _____
    (e)■ $(\log_2 n)^2 = O(n)$. _____ ✓

2.   What is the big-O of the number of operations required to perform the following tasks, assuming reasonably optimized implementation?

    (a)   Transposing a square matrix of size n ✓
    (b)   Reversing an array of n elements
    (c)   Finding the number of pairs of consecutive double letters in a character string of length n ✓
    (d)   Selection sort of an array with n elements.
    (e)◆   Generating all the Beavis Island words of length n (see Question 14 for Chapter 4).

3.   What is the big-O of the number of operations in the following methods, assuming reasonable implementations?

    (a)   `addFirst` in a `LinkedList` with n nodes ✓
    (b)   `dequeue` in a `ListQueue` with n nodes
    (c)   `traverseInOrder` in a BST with n nodes ✓
    (d)   `contains` in a `TreeSet` with n nodes
    (e)■   `removeMin` in a `HeapPriorityQueue` with n nodes

4. What is the big-O of the number of operations, in terms of n, in the following method: ✓

```
/**
 * Converts n into an array of binary digits
 */
public char[] longToBin(long n)
{
  char binDigits[] = new char[100];
  int i = 99;
  while (i >= 0 && n > 0)
  {
    if (n % 2) binDigits[i] = '1';
    else binDigits[i] = '0';
    i--;
    n /= 2;
  }
  while (i >= 0)
  {
    binDigits[i] = '0';
    i--;
  }
  return binDigits;
}
```

5. What is the worst-case running time (big-O, in terms of n) of the following methods?

(a)

```
public int maxCluster(double v[], double d)
{
  int n = v.length, i, j;
  int count, maxCount = 0;
  for (i = 0; i < n; i++)
  {
    count = 0;
    for (j = 0; j < n; j++)
      if (Math.abs(v[i] - v[j]) < d)
        count++;
    if (count > maxCount)
      maxCount = count;
  }
  return maxCount;
}
```

Continued ☞

(b)

```java
public boolean isPalindrome(String w)
{
  int n = w.length(), i = 0, j = n-1;
  while (i < j && w[i] == w[j])
  {
    i++;
    j--;
  }
  return i >= j;
}
```

(c)

```java
/**
 *   root refers to the root of a non-empty BST
 *   with n nodes.
 */
public TreeNode minNode(TreeNode root)
{
  TreeNode node = root;
  while (node.getLeft() != null)
    node = node.getLeft();
  return node;
}
```

(d) ✓

```java
/**
 *   Assumes n >= 0.   Returns x^n.
 */
public double pow(double x, int n)
{
  double y = 1;
  if (n > 0)
  {
    y = pow(x, n/2);
    y *= y;
    if (n % 2 != 0)
      y *= x;
  }
  return y;
}
```

6.   Indicate whether the specified task requires logarithmic (L), polynomial (P) or exponential (E) time (assuming an optimal implementation):

(a)   Counting how many numbers in a set of n values are equal to the average of two or more values in the same set

(b)   Concatenating all strings of length 5 stored in a matrix

```
private String words[][] = new String[n][n];  ✓
```

(c)   Finding the highest power of 2 that evenly divides a given positive integer n

(d)■   Generating all possible shapes of binary trees with n nodes ✓

7.■   The code below calculates the sum of the elements in a 2-D array m that belong to a "cross" formed by an intersection of a given row and column:

```
int sum = 0;

for (r = 0; r < nRows; r++)
{
  for (c = 0; c < nCols; c++)
  {
    if (r == row || c == col)
      sum += matrix[r][c];
  }
}
```

Find the big-O for this code and rewrite the code to improve it.

8.◆   Suppose the array s contains a digitized seismogram recorded for 5 seconds
during a remote earthquake. We want to find the moment of the arrival of
the seismic wave. Suppose the seismogram is digitized at n samples per
second and the array contains $5n$ amplitudes of the signal. The code below
averages the signal over one-second intervals and chooses the largest average
to detect the arrival of the first wave:

```
double sum, max;
int i, k, kMax;

// Find the sum starting at i = 0:
sum = 0.0;
for (i = 0; i < n; i++)
  sum += s[i];
max = sum;
kMax = 0;

for (k = 1; k < 4*n; k++)
{
  // Find the sum starting at i = k:
  sum = 0.0;
  for (i = k; i < k + n; k++)
    sum += s[i];

  // Update max:
  if (sum > max)
  {
    max = sum;
    kMax = k;
  }
}
return kMax;
```

What is the big-O for this code in terms of n? Is there a way to improve it?

9.◆   Suppose we have an integer function $f(k)$ with an integer argument and define a sequence g_k as follows:

$$g_0 = 1; \ g_i = f(g_{k-1}) \ \text{for } k > 0.$$

We want to know whether the values $g_0, g_1, \ldots$ start repeating before too long. In other words, for a given n we want to know whether there exist k and m, $0 \le k < m \le n$, such that $g_k = g_m$ and find the smallest such k.

Consider the following code written for this task:

```
private int g(int k)
{
   if (k == 0) return 1;
   else return f(g(k-1));
}

public int hasRepeats(int n)
{
   for (int k = 0; k < n; k++)
     for (int m = k+1; m <= n; m++)
        if (g(k) == g(m))
           return k;
   return -1;
}
```

What is the big-O for the time and space requirements for this code in terms of n? Can they be improved? Can this task be done in $O(n)$ time?

Sections 8.3-8.4

10.   What is the total number of swaps performed in sorting the array 5, 3, 2, 4, 9, 0 in ascending order using Bubble Sort ? ✓

11.   Mark true or false and explain:

(a)   The Mergesort procedure is more suitable for use with linked lists than with arrays. _____ ✓

(b)   Quicksort is sensitive to data; the performance is $O(n \log n)$ only if most splits divide the array into two halves that are approximately equal in size. _____

(c)   Quicksort requires an auxiliary array that is as large as the original array. _____ ✓

(d)■   Heapsort takes $O(n)$ time if the array is already sorted.

12. Complete each sentence with the word *always*, *sometimes*, or *never*:

    (a) Selection Sort in an array of *n* elements _____ works in $O(n^2)$ time. ✓

    (b) Bubble Sort in an array of *n* elements _____ works in $O(n)$ time.

    (c) Insertion Sort _____ works faster than Quicksort. ✓

    (d) Quicksort is _____ slower than Mergesort.

13. What is the state of the array after the "split" phase of the Quicksort algorithm is applied, at the top level of recursion, if its initial values are

```
int a[9] = {6, 9, 74, 10, 22, 81, 2, 11, 54};
```

and the middle element is chosen as a pivot? ✓

14. Suppose the Insertion Sort algorithm for sorting an array has been modified: instead of sequential search, binary search is used to find the position for inserting the next element into the already sorted initial segment of the list. What is the big-O for the average number of <u>comparisons</u> (in terms of the length of the array *n*)? What is the big-O for the best and for the worst cases?

15. The Mergesort algorithm, as presented on page 208, always takes $O(n{\cdot}\log n)$ comparisons. Add a shortcut —

```
if (...)
    return;
```

— so that the algorithm works in $O(n)$ time when the array is already sorted.

16. ▪ A queue q holds Comparable objects. Write two versions of a recursive method

```
public Queue sorted(Queue q, int n)
```

The method builds and returns a new queue (a ListQueue) that contains the first n objects from q, sorted in ascending order.

    (a) Use the Mergesort algorithm. ✓

    (b) Use the Quicksort algorithm with the first element as the pivot.

CHPT 9.00 (+1.00)

Data Structures in Action:
A Case Study

9.1   Prologue

In this chapter we consider a larger, more realistic case study. Our project is to implement a miniature stock exchange. A stock exchange is an organization for trading shares in publicly owned companies. In the OTC ("Over the Counter") system, stocks are traded electronically through a vast network of securities dealers connected to a computer network. There is no physical "stock exchange" location. In the past few years, thousands of investors have started trading stocks directly from their home computers through Internet-based online brokerage firms.

In this project we will program our own stock exchange and electronic brokerage, which we call *SafeTrade*. Not too long ago, some unscrupulous online brokerage firms started encouraging "day trading," in which traders hold a stock for a few hours or even minutes rather than months or years. As a result, quite a few people lost all their savings and got into debt. Actually, this case study would be more appropriately placed in Chapter 11: in the U.S. code of bankruptcy laws,[uscode] "Chapter 11" deals with reorganization due to bankruptcy. But we only have ten chapters in this book. With our *SafeTrade*, you stay safely offline and out of trouble and don't pay commissions to a broker.

> **We have picked this project because it illustrates appropriate uses of many of the data structures that we have studied. It also gives us an opportunity to discuss object-oriented design in a more realistic setting. This project is large enough to warrant a meaningful team development effort.**

In the following sections we describe the general project specifications, the data structures used, object-oriented design, and detailed design. Many programmers might be tempted to skip this discussion and rush off to write code. But if you do that, you will waste a lot of time and won't learn much either. Read the discussion sections first.

9.2   *SafeTrade* Specifications

The stock exchange system keeps track of buy and sell orders placed by traders and automatically executes orders when the highest "bid" price (order to buy stock at a certain price) meets the lowest "ask" price (offer to sell stock for a certain minimum price). There are also "market" orders to buy or sell stock at the current "ask" or "bid" price. The stocks are identified by their trading symbols. For example, Sun Microsystems is "SUNW" and Microsoft is "MSFT."

"Shares" (of a particular stock) are usually sold in multiples of 100. Not very long ago, NASDAQ (National Association of Securities Dealers Automated Quotation System) switched from its traditional binary fractions notation for prices (like 7 and 1/2 or 12 and 3/8) to the decimal notation (like 7.50 or 12.38). In the real world, very small stock prices may include fractions of cents, but in *SafeTrade* we only go to whole cents.

SafeTrade maintains a list of registered users and allows them to log in and trade stocks. The program keeps track of all active buy and sell orders for each stock. A trader can request a quote for a stock which includes the last sale price, the price and the number of shares offered in the current highest bid and lowest ask, the day's high and low price for the stock, and volume — the total number of shares traded during the day. In our model, a "day" is one run of the program. A stock is identified by its trading symbol, a string of one to five letters.

A trader can place buy and sell orders, specifying the price for a "limit" order or choosing a "market" order. Each order deals with only one stock. The order for a given stock holds a reference to the trader who placed it, the buy or sell indicator, the number of shares to be traded, the market or limit indicator, and the price for a limit order. *SafeTrade* acknowledges a placed order by sending a message back to the trader.

When a new order comes in, *SafeTrade* checks if it can be executed and, if so, executes the trade and reports it to both parties by sending messages to both traders. In *SafeTrade*, all orders are "partial" orders. This means that if an order cannot be executed for the total number of shares requested in it, the maximum possible number of shares changes hands and an order for the remaining shares remains active.

SafeTrade executes a market buy order at the price of the lowest ask, and a market sell order at the price of the highest bid. Normally, market orders can be executed immediately when they arrive. If both buy and sell orders are limit orders and the bid happens to be higher than the ask, the trade is executed at the ask price. In the unlikely event that there is only a market sell and a market buy, *SafeTrade* executes them at the last sale price. At the beginning of the day, the last sale price is carried over from the "previous day." *SafeTrade* sets the "last sale" price when a stock entry is created.

SafeTrade <u>does not</u> keep track of the availability of money or shares on the trader's account. If you want, you can add this functionality. For example, you can keep all transactions for a given trader in a list and have a separate field to hold available "cash."

At a first glance, this appears to be a pretty large project. However, it turns out that with careful planning and an understanding of the requirements, the amount of code to be written is actually <u>very</u> small. The code is simple and splits into a number of small pieces, which can be easily handled either by one programmer or by a team of several programmers. I'll contribute one GUI class, `TraderWindow`.

One of the challenges of a project like this is thorough testing. Actually, one of the members of the team should specialize in QA (Quality Assurance). While other team members work on the design and coding, this team member develops a comprehensive test plan, tests the finished pieces as they become available, and works with programmers on fixing bugs and improving the "look and feel."

9.3   *SafeTrade*: Structural Design

Our design process for *SafeTrade* consists of three parts. The first part is structural design, which determines the data structures that will be used in the program. The second part is object-oriented design, which determines the types of objects to be defined and the classes and interfaces to be written. The third part is detailed design, which determines the fields, constructors, and methods in all the classes. In this section we discuss the structural design. In the following sections we will discuss the OOD and the detailed design.

SafeTrade has to keep track of all registered traders and all currently logged-in traders. This is very similar to the *Java Messenger* project from Chapter 5. As in *Messenger* it is reasonable to hold all registered traders in a map, keyed by the trader's screen name. Again we can hold all logged-in traders in a set. But what kind of map and set? Now we can choose between a BST and a hash table — both are in our toolbox. A hash table may potentially work faster but may waste space. We hope that thousands of traders will register, so we can't afford to waste any space in our database. Besides, the response time for a new registration is not very important, as long as it takes seconds, not hours. So our choice is a BST. As in *Messenger*, we will use a `TreeMap` from `java.util` to hold all registered traders.

Similar considerations apply to the set of logged-in traders. There may be many of them, and a BST will work fast enough to let us know who is logged in and who isn't. The time is not as critical here. So we opt to use a `TreeSet` to hold all logged-in traders.

A trader may log in, place a few orders, and log out. Meanwhile, *SafeTrade* may execute some of the trader's orders and send messages to the trader. But the trader may already not be there to read them. So the messages must be stored in the trader's "mailbox" until the trader logs in again and reads them. We are lucky: this is a perfect example of a queue. *SafeTrade* implements a mailbox for each trader as a `Queue`, more specifically as a `ListQueue`, since we already have that class (see Chapter 3).

SafeTrade also needs to maintain data for all traded stocks. A stock is identified by its trading symbol, and it is convenient to use a map where the stock symbol serves as the key for a stock. The number of all listed stocks is limited, perhaps two or three thousand, and the list does not change very often. *SafeTrade* must be able to find a stock immediately for real-time quotes and especially to execute orders. Traders will get upset if they lose money because their order was delayed. Therefore, a good choice for maintaining listed stocks is a hash table, a `HashMap`.

Finally, *SafeTrade* must store all placed buy and sell orders for each stock in such a way that it has quick access to the highest bid and the lowest ask. Both adding and executing orders must be fast. This is a clear case for using priority queues. We need two of them for each stock: one for sell orders and one for buy orders. Naturally, we will use the `HeapPriorityQueue` class (see Chapter 7) for both priority queues. For <u>sell</u> orders the order with the <u>lowest</u> ask price is on the top of the heap, while for <u>buy</u> orders the order with the <u>highest</u> bid price is on top. Therefore, we need to provide a comparator class and two differently configured comparator objects — one for the buy priority queue and one for the sell priority queue.

Our structural design decisions are summarized in Table 9-1. We are lucky we have a chance to use some of the data structures discussed earlier in this book.

Data	Structure => *interface* => class
Registered traders	BST => *Map* => TreeMap
Logged-in traders	BST => *Set* => TreeSet
Mailbox for each trader	Queue => *Queue* => ListQueue
Listed stocks	Hash table => *Map* => HashMap
Sell orders for each stock	Priority queue => *PriorityQueue* => HeapPriorityQueue (with ascending price comparator)
Buy orders for each stock	Priority queue => *PriorityQueue* => HeapPriorityQueue (with descending price comparator)

Table 9-1. Structural design decisions for *SafeTrade*

9.4   *SafeTrade*: Classes and Objects

We begin by listing a few types of objects that we have mentioned in our informal discussion of this project: a stock exchange, a brokerage, a trader, a stock, a trade order, a quote, a message, a comparator. Do we need to write a class for each of them? Do we need other types of objects? These decisions depend on how we plan to use objects of a particular type and, in part, on our plans to extend the project and reuse the classes involved.

In the real world, traders connect to brokerage firms that pass orders on to the stock exchange. In *SafeTrade* we decided to eliminate brokerage firms and let traders go directly to the exchange. This makes our life easier.

9.4.1   SafeTrade, GUILogin, Exchange, and Trader

Our `Exchange` class is analogous to the `Server` class in the *Messenger* project in Section 5.8: it keeps track of all the registered and logged-in traders. In addition, `Exchange` keeps all listed stocks in a hash table and provides methods for receiving orders and executing orders from traders.

As in *Messenger*, `Exchange` needs a GUI login class that displays a login window and accepts logins and new registrations. Normally, we would be able to reuse *Messenger*'s class as is, without any changes. Unfortunately, when we wrote the *Messenger* project we cut corners and made the GUI login class, `Messenger`, somewhat specific to the *Messenger* application. Not only did we name the class inappropriately, we also put `main` into it and allowed it to interact with a particular type of server, calling `Server`'s `addUser` and `login` methods. Of course, we could fix `Messenger` a little: rename it from `Messenger` to, say, `SafeTrade` and, instead of creating a `Server` object and calling its methods, create an `Exchange` object and call its methods. But then we would end up with two copies of essentially the same code floating around and it would be hard to maintain both of them. And in our next project we would have to fix this class again.

Perhaps now is the time to do it right and to make our GUI login class reusable and independent of other classes. We need to <u>isolate</u> that class from any particular type of server to which the user logs in. To do this, let's define an interface with two methods:

```
public interface Login
{
  int addUser(String name, String password);
  int login(String name, String password);
}
```

Now, instead of dealing with a specific type of server, our GUI login class can deal with <u>any</u> `Login` server. We can pass the server object to `GUILogin`'s constructor as an argument. Polymorphism will take care of the rest. All we have to do is declare that `Server` (in *Messenger*) and `Exchange` (in *SafeTrade*) implement `Login`. Let us rename our class `GUILogin` and take `main` out of it, into a separate small application-specific class, say, `SafeTrade` (Figure 9-1).

Figure 9-2 shows the relationships between the `SafeTrade`, `GUILogin`, and `Exchange` classes. You can also see why the `Login` interface is called an "interface" — the `GUILogin` class doesn't know that the `Exchange` class exists.

```
import java.awt.event.*;

public class SafeTrade
{
  public static void main(String[] args)
  {
    Exchange server = new Exchange();

    //*** Temporary -- for testing:

    server.addUser("stockman", "fido");
    server.login("stockman", "fido");

    server.addUser("mstrade", "rex");
    server.login("mstrade", "rex");

    //***************************

    GUILogin window = new GUILogin("Safe Trade", server);
    window.addWindowListener(new WindowAdapter()
      { public void windowClosing(WindowEvent e) { System.exit(0); }});
    window.setBounds(0, 0, 360, 140);
    window.show();
  }
}
```

Figure 9-1. The `SafeTrade` class

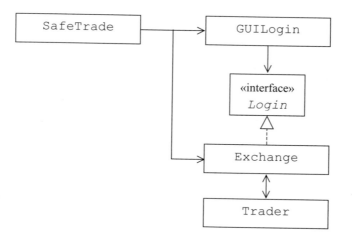

Figure 9-2. High-level classes and the `Login` interface in _SafeTrade_

This may be a good place to begin putting the *SafeTrade* project together. Our first step is to make *Messenger* work under a different name with a project-independent `GUILogin` class. Follow these steps:

1. Copy all four *Messenger* classes, `Messenger.java`, `Server.java`, `MsgUser.java`, and `MsgWindow.java` from the `Ch05\Messenger` folder 💾 and your solution to that lab into a new folder, `SafeTrade`. Rename `Messenger` to `GUILogin`, `Server` to `Exchange`, `MsgUser` to `Trader`, `MsgWindow` to `TraderWindow`. Make global changes in the code to reflect these name changes.

2. Define the `Login` interface, as described above, and add the declaration `implements Login` to `Exchange`.

3. Take `main` out of `GUILogin` and place it in a separate class `SafeTrade`, as shown above. Fix `GUILogin` a little to make it work with any `Login` type object, passed to its constructor, rather than with the specific `Server` type object. Pass an application title to `GUILogin`'s constructor, too.

4. Compile and test the project — the former *Messenger*, now *SafeTrade*, should work exactly as before.

All this work for nothing? Actually this is a good start: we've finished half of our project even before writing any code!

9.4.2   Stock, TradeOrder, and PriceComparator

Stock

In addition to the classes shown in Figure 9-2, we need a class `Stock` that represents one stock: stock symbol and company name, last sale price, total volume traded, day's high and low prices, and the priority queues for pending buy and sell orders. This class provides methods for getting a stock quote and executing an order.

TradeOrder

We need a way to represent information about a trade order: who placed it, buy or sell, price or market, number of shares. This information is passed up from a `TraderWindow` object to a `Trader`, then to the `Exchange`, then to a `Stock`.

Potentially we could simply pass this information in separate variables or encode it in a string, but this would be old-fashioned and inconvenient.

A better way, and more in OOP style, is to define a class, TradeOrder, which will allow us to consolidate all the data items in one object. Besides, we need to place orders into priority queues, and it is more efficient to store TradeOrder objects, for which all the data items are readily available, than strings, which would need to be parsed repeatedly.

TradeOrder is a "passive" class: it has one constructor that sets all the fields and an accessor method for each field. The primary purpose of such a class is to hold a few data items together. It does need one modifier method, which subtracts a number of shares from the order when a particular trade is executed.

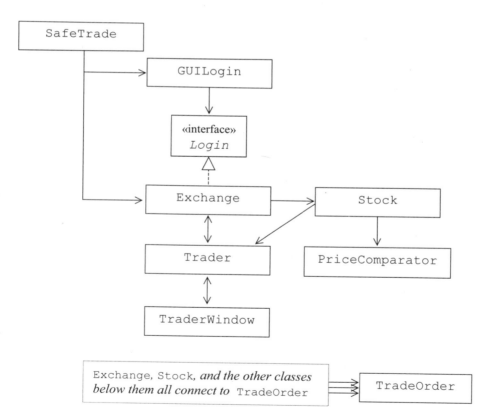

Figure 9-3. All the classes in the *SafeTrade* project

PriceComparator

We also need a class `PriceComparator` that implements a `Comparator` for orders based on their prices. We can use two objects of the same class to compare prices in ascending and descending order by defining a field that specifies the order of comparison. We will discuss this in more detail later, when we deal with the detailed design.

Our final layout for all the *SafeTrade* classes is shown in Figure 9-3.

9.5   *SafeTrade*: Detailed Design

Perhaps a good starting point for detailed design is the trader's screen. The one we have designed (Figure 9-4) is implemented in the `TraderWindow` class supplied on your student disk in the `Ch09\SafeTrade` 🖫 folder. The view in Figure 9-4 will help us design fields, constructors, and methods for our classes, going from the bottom up. If you have time, program your own `TraderWindow` class as an exercise.

Figure 9-4.   A trader's window in *SafeTrade*

public class TradeOrder	
Constructor:	
```public TradeOrder(Trader trader, boolean buyOrder, boolean marketOrder, int numShares, double price)```	Constructs an order for a given trader, with a given buy indicator, market indicator, number of shares, and price.
Methods:	
`public Trader getTrader()`	Returns a reference to the trader who placed this order.
`public boolean isBuy()`	Returns `true` if this is a buy order, `false` otherwise.
`public boolean isSell()`	Returns `true` if this is a sell order (i.e., not a buy order), `false` otherwise.
`public boolean isMarket()`	Returns `true` if this is a market order, `false` otherwise.
`public boolean isLimit()`	Returns `true` if this is a limit order (i.e., not a market order), `false` otherwise.
`public int getShares()`	Returns the number of shares to be traded.
`public double getPrice()`	Returns the price of the shares to be traded.
```public void subtractShares (int shares)```	Subtracts a given number of shares from the shares to be traded.

Table 9-2. `TradeOrder` constructor and public methods

9.5.1   Detailed Design: `TradeOrder` and `Trader`

<u>TradeOrder</u>

The trader's screen shows us what goes into the `TradeOrder` class. Besides a field for a trader who places the order, it needs a `boolean` field that defines whether this is a sell (or a buy) order and another `boolean` field that defines whether this is a market (or a limit) order. An integer field holds the number of shares to be traded, and a `double` field holds the limit price. The class has a constructor that sets all the fields and accessors for all the fields. We also need a modifier method that subtracts a given number of shares from the order — this is for situations where only a part of the order is executed. The public interface for the `TradeOrder` class is formalized in Table 9-2.

<u>Trader</u>

The trader's screen in Figure 9-4 shows two buttons: "Get quote" and "Place order." Each of these buttons generates a call to the corresponding method of the `Trader` class. A trader object requests a quote or places an order with the `Exchange`, receives a quote or an acknowledgement message back from the `Exchange`, and shows it in the window's message area on the right by calling its window's `showMessage` method.

So it turns out that our `Trader` class is fairly simple. Its public constructors and methods are listed in Table 9-3.

`public class Trader` `   implements Comparable`	
Constructor:	

`public Trader (Exchange server,`
`                String name,`
`                String password)`
	Initializes a reference to the server and the trader's screen name and password fields.

Methods:	
`public String toString()`	Returns this trader's screen name.
`public String getPassword()`	Returns this trader's password.
`public boolean equals` `             (Object other)`	Returns `true` if this trader's name is equal to `other`'s, case blind, `false` otherwise.
`public int compareTo` `             (Object other)`	Compares this trader's screen name to `other`'s screen name, case blind.
`public void openDialog()`	Creates a `TraderWindow` window and saves a reference to it in the `myWindow` field. Removes and shows all the messages from the mailbox queue by calling `myWindow.showMessage` as necessary.
`public void receiveMessage` `             (String text)`	Adds `text` to this trader's mailbox. If `myWindow` is initialized, removes and shows all the messages from the mailbox queue.
`public void getQuote` `             (String symbol)`	Requests a quote for `symbol` from `Exchange`.

`public void placeOrder`
`      (String symbol,`
`       TradeOrder order)`
	Places `order` for `symbol` with `Exchange`.

`public void quit()`	Disposes of this user's dialog window. Logs out this user by calling `Exchange`'s `logout` method.

Table 9-3. `Trader` constructor and public methods

Compare Table 9-3 to the specs for the `MsgUser` class (Table 5-2 on page 138). They are very similar. It should not take long to update the `Trader` class that we copied earlier from `MsgUser`. Globally replace `MsgWindow` with `TraderWindow`. Remove all references to a "buddy list" (other traders are not your buddies!). Add and initialize a `mailbox` field to hold a queue of messages. In `receiveMessage`, rather than sending a message directly to `myWindow`, add it to `mailbox`, then, if `myWindow` is open (trader is logged in), show all the messages from `mailbox`. Also show all the messages from `mailbox`, if any, in the `openDialog` method. Finally, add the `getQuote` and `placeOrder` methods. These methods simply pass the request on to `Exchange`.

For extra credit: when the trader logs in, make the `Exchange` send a "Welcome to SafeTrade" message, but only if the trader's mailbox is empty.

You might want to test your `Trader` class separately, before `Exchange` is ready. To do that, temporarily "short-circuit" the `getQuote` and `placeOrder` methods, providing "stubs" that don't go to the `Exchange` and just fake a message received from `Exchange` (call `receiveMessage`).

Now one or two members of the development team are ready to go to work. One person codes the simple `TradeOrder` class. Another person (or the same person) modifies the `Trader` class. When they are done, the "project leader" collects all the classes that are ready — `SafeTrade`, `GUILogin`, `Login`, `Exchange` (still the old version, the one we made by renaming `Server` from the *Messenger* project), `TradeOrder`, and also `Queue` and `ListQueue` (from Ch03 ⊟) — and builds an application. Then the QA person can test the first prototype of *SafeTrade*.

9.5.2   Detailed Design: `Exchange`

While a few members of the team are working on the `Trader` and `TradeOrder` classes, the Chief Software Architect can decide how the actual trades are executed. This brings us to the design of the `Stock` and `Exchange` classes. These two classes work together to provide quotes and execute orders.

The `Exchange` server holds a hash table of stocks, keyed by their trading symbols. In this project we do not want to bother listing or unlisting stocks interactively — instead we let `main` list a half-dozen stocks for us. For example:

```
server.listStock("RAMD", "Ramblecs Design Associates", 12.33);
server.listStock("NSTL", "Nasty Loops Inc.", 0.25);
server.listStock("GGGL", "Giggle.com", 28.00);
server.listStock("MATI", "M and A Travel Inc.", 28.20);
server.listStock("DDLC", "Dulce De Leche Corp.", 57.50);
server.listStock("SAFT", "SafeTrade.com Inc.", 322.45);
```

The `Exchange` class provides a `listStock` method that constructs a new stock with the given symbol, name, and initial price and adds it to the map of listed stocks.

Each `Stock` object holds all the information about the stock including priority queues of sell and buy orders for that stock. The `Exchange` server channels the quote requests and the trading orders to particular stocks. For a quote request, the stock returns a string that contains the quote; the server passes the quote string to the requesting trader by calling the trader's `receiveMessage` method. For a trading order, the stock "executes" the order and sends messages directly to all the traders involved.

This is the way we've designed it. There is an alternative design in which a trader requests a reference to a particular stock from the `Exchange` server, then deals with that stock directly. This design would reduce the messages passed back and forth between a trader, the server, and a stock, and would allow us to eliminate a couple of one-line methods. However, we have rejected this alternative because it contradicts the spirit of our model. Even though our model runs on a single computer, we should pretend that many traders are trading concurrently. We cannot allow a trader to modify a stock object directly because presumably another trader may be working with it at the same time. So all orders and requests must go in an orderly way through the central exchange.

It appears that we need to add two methods besides `listStock` to the `Exchange` class: `getQuote` and `placeOrder` — the same names as in the `Trader` class. `Exchange`'s `getQuote` method takes two arguments, the stock symbol and the requesting trader. It finds the stock, passes the quote request to that stock, then sends the returned quote back to the trader. Something like this:

```
public class Exchange implements Login
{
  ...
  public void getQuote(String symbol, Trader trader)
  {
    Stock stock = ... // get stock for symbol
    String msg;

    if (stock != null)
      msg = stock.getQoute();
    else
      msg = symbol + " not found";

    trader.receiveMessage(msg);
  }
  ...
}
```

Exchange's placeOrder method is equally short:

```
public void placeOrder(String symbol, TradeOrder order)
{
  Stock stock = ...  // get stock for symbol
  if (stock != null)
    stock.placeOrder(order);
  else
    ...
}
```

The public interface for the Exchange class is formalized in Table 9-4.

9.5.3   Detailed Design: Stock

Note that our development effort so far has consisted of rehashing some old code, making minor changes and straightforward additions to several classes, and writing one simple class, TradeOrder. This is how it is supposed to be in OOP. But eventually you get to code a class that does actual work and involves some logic. Now that we are ready to program the Stock class, where trading orders actually get executed, this moment has come.

The public interface for the Stock class is described in Table 9-5. The Stock class has the following fields:

```
private String companySymbol;
private String companyName;
private double loPrice, hiPrice, lastPrice;
private int volume;
private PriorityQueue buyOrders, sellOrders;
```

public class Exchange	
Constructor:	
`public Exchange()`	Initializes the map of registered users, the set of logged-in users, and a map of listed stocks (a `HashMap`) to empty.
Methods:	

`public void listStock`
`        (String symbol,`
`         String companyName,`
`         double price);`
	Adds a new stock with given parameters to the map of all stocks, with `symbol` as the key.

`public int addUser`
`        (String name,`
`         String password)`
	See Table 5-1 on Page 138.

`public int login`
`        (String name,`
`         String password)`
	See Table 5-1 on Page 138. Also (optional) sends a welcome message to the logged-in trader if the trader's mailbox is empty.

`public void logout(Trader u)`	See Table 5-1 on Page 138.

`public void getQuote`
`        (String symbol,`
`         Trader trader)`
	Requests a quote from the `Stock` object associated with `symbol` and sends the quote message to `trader`. Notifies `trader` if `symbol` is not found.

`public void placeOrder`
`        (String symbol,`
`         TraderOrder order)`
	Places `order` for the stock specified by `symbol`. Notifies the trader who placed the order if `symbol` is not found.

Table 9-4. Exchange constructor and public methods

public class Stock	
Constructor:	

public Stock(String symbol,
            String name,
            double price)
	Initializes the stock's symbol and company name. Sets low, high and last sale prices to price. Sets volume to 0. Creates empty priority queues for buy and sell orders (see also PriceComparator).

Methods:	
public String getQuote()	Returns a quote for this stock, including the company name, symbol, last sale price, day's low, high, and volume, and, if available, highest bid and lowest ask price and size.
public void placeOrder (TraderOrder order)	Sends an acknowledgement to the originating trader listing the details of the order. Adds order to the appropriate queue. Executes as many orders as possible.

Table 9-5. Stock constructor and public methods

The constructor initializes the stock symbol and name and sets the low, high, and last prices to a specified price. It also creates empty priority queues for buy and sell orders, each configured with an appropriate price comparator (discussed below).

The getQuote method summarizes all the stock information: company name, stock symbol, last sale price, day's low and high prices and volume, and the price and size for the top ask and bid orders, if available. It returns all the information in one string. It is better to format the quote string into several lines (by embedding "\n") to make the quote look better on the trader's screen. For example:

```
Giggle.com (GGGL)
Price: 10.00  hi: 10.00  lo: 10.00  vol: 0
Ask: 12.75 size: 300  Bid: 12.00 size: 500
```

The placeOrder method first sends an acknowledgement message to the trader who placed the order: this includes the company name and stock symbol, the number of shares ordered to buy or sell, and the market or limit price. After that, placeOrder actually has to figure out what to do with the order. If you try to treat all the different possibilities for a buy or sell order and the top bid and ask, you will very quickly get confused. The way we (programmers) solve such problems is by adding the order to the appropriate priority queue first and asking questions later. More precisely, first add the order to the appropriate queue, then call a private method that moves the queues along, executing as many full or partial orders as possible.

9.5.4   Detailed Design: `PriceComparator`

While somebody is working on the `Stock` class, another team member can take care of the last remaining detail, a `PriceComparator` for `TradeOrder` objects. This class is needed for configuring the priority queues of trading orders. If you need to review comparators, see Section 5.5. The `PriceComparator` class implements `java.util.Comparator` and provides one method:

```
public int compare(Object obj1, Object obj2)
```

The parameters actually passed to `compare` will be `TradeOrder` objects, so `compare` casts `obj1` and `obj2` into that type. Note that `compare` returns an `int`.

If both orders are market orders, they are deemed to be "equal," and `compare` returns 0. If one order is a market order and the other is a limit order, the market order is deemed "smaller" (i.e., has higher priority), regardless of the configuration of the comparator.

If both orders are limit orders, then we need to look at the prices they specify. `compare` converts each price into an integer — the number of cents, rounded to the nearest cent. It then returns the difference of these numbers.

But which operand should we subtract from which? This should be configurable for a particular comparator object. `PriceComparator` has a `boolean` field `ascending` that defines the sign of the comparison result. Supply a no-args constructor that sets `ascending` to `true` and another constructor with one `boolean` argument that sets `ascending` to a given value. If `ascending` is `true`, then `compare` returns `cents1 - cents2`. If `ascending` is `false`, the order is reversed. Thus you can configure a `PriceComparator` object for either a min or a max priority queue. The `Stock` object that creates the queues is then able to create an appropriate `PriceComparator` object for each queue.

9.6   Testing

While the programmers were busy writing code, the QA person has developed a comprehensive testing plan. Proper testing for an application of this size is in many ways more challenging than writing the code. Entering and executing a couple of orders won't do. The tester has to make a list of all possible scenarios and to develop a strategy for testing them methodically. In addition, the tester must make a list of features to be tested. The most obvious are, for example: Do the "login" and "add user" screens work? Does the "Get quote" button work? When a trader logs out and then logs in again, are the messages preserved? And so on.

When the project leader finally puts the project together, the tester is ready to go to work. By now the project involves no less than 13 source files:

```
SafeTrade.java              TraderWindow.java
GUILogin.java               Ch03\Queue.java
Login.java                  Ch03\ListQueue.java
Exchange.java               Ch07\PriorityQueue.java
Stock.java                  Ch07\HeapPriorityQueue.java
PriceComparator.java
Trader.java
TradeOrder.java
```

The tester puts the testing plan into action and gives bug reports to the project leader. The project leader works with the individual programmers to fix the found bugs.

The tester can also evaluate the user interface (unless you want to invite a special "human factors" consultant for that). The user interface specialist evaluates screen layouts, formatting, and message readability and may come up with some recommendations for improvement.

9.7   Summary

While it is not possible to describe a large real-world project in one chapter, our *SafeTrade* case study gives you a flavor of what it might be like.

Careful structural design helps a software architect to choose the data structures appropriate for a software system. Java's powerful libraries supply the necessary tools for implementing a variety of data structures easily.

The object-oriented approach helps us split a fairly large project into smaller manageable pieces that we can code and even test independently. It also helps us reuse classes from previous projects. And, with little additional effort, we can structure at least one of our classes (GUILogin) to be reusable in future projects.

An object-oriented designer tries to reduce the coupling (i.e., interdependencies between different classes) in the project. The detailed design defines the public interface — constructors and public methods — for each class. Individual programmers work out the implementation details for their classes.

Although it is possible to test individual software components in a project to some extent, a comprehensive test plan is needed for testing a software application as a whole. Developing and implementing such a test plan may actually be more challenging than writing the code.

Exercises

1. *SafeTrade* does not use much inheritance or polymorphism in user-defined classes.

    (a) Give one example where it does. ✓
    (b) Explain why buy and sell orders are not implemented as subclasses of TradeOrder.

2. Derive a class Guest from Trader. A guest is allowed to get quotes but is not allowed to trade stocks — a "Login required" message should be displayed when a guest attempts to place a trade order. Make Exchange create and log in a Guest object, rather than a Trader object, when the supplied login name is "guest". Add a guest to loggedUsers under a unique user name (e.g., "guest"+uniqueNum). Don't allow new users to register with "guest" as their login name.

3.   Add a time stamp to a `TradeOrder` object. To keep things simple, make it a `long time` field in the `TradeOrder` class and set it to `System.currentTimeMillis()` when the order is placed (unless you want to learn about the rather convoluted `java.util.Calendar` class and handle the date and time properly). Modify the `PriceComparator` class so that if two orders have the same price or both are market orders, the one placed earlier is executed first.

4.■   In this project we make it possible for a trader to list all his or her active orders.

(a)   Add two private fields to `TradeOrder` to hold the stock symbol and company name and provide accessors and modifiers for these fields. Initialize these fields to empty strings and make `Stock`'s `PlaceOrder` method set them appropriately when the order is placed. Also add a `toString` method to `TradeOrder`, moving into it the code from `Stock`'s `placeOrder` method.

(b)   Modify the `Trader` class, adding a list of active orders for each trader. Provide `addOrder` and `removeOrder` methods to add an order to the list and remove an order from the list, respectively. Also add a private method `listOrders`. When a trader types ">list" in the "Stock symbol" field and clicks on the "Get quote" button, the program should display the list of all the active orders (or a "No active orders" message).

(c)   Modify the `Stock` class, adding appropriate calls to `Trader`'s `addOrder` and `removeOrder` methods. When an order is executed completely, it must be removed from the trader's list.

5.■   In this project we make it possible for the Exchange to make old orders expire. We assume that an order has a time stamp (see Question 3) and carries its stock symbol (see Question 4).

(a)   Create a priority queue class with a `remove` method. One approach is to replace the `HeapPriorityQueue` class in the project with a simpler implementation based on `ArrayList`. (You can use, for example, `BinarySearchPriorityQueue` from Question 6 in Chapter 7.) Make the `ArrayList` field in this class `protected`, so that derived classes have access to it. Extend this class into `PriorityQWithRemove`, adding a method

```
public boolean remove(Object obj)
```

Another approach is to add a `remove` method to `HeapPriorityQueue`. You will need to figure out an algorithm for removing an arbitrary node from a heap.

If you'd like, learn about the decorator design pattern (see Section 10.5) and make `PriorityQWithRemove` a decorator for your priority queue class.

(b)   Make the `Stock` class use `PriorityQWithRemove` rather than `PriorityQueue`. Add a method that removes an order from the appropriate queue and notifies the trader that his or her order has expired.

(c)   Add a list (e.g., an `ArrayList`) of all outstanding trade orders to the `Exchange` class and add each new order to that list. Create a timer that fires periodically (e.g., every second) and, when it fires, check the list for expired orders. Scan the list using an iterator and cancel all orders that are too old (e.g., more than 2 minutes old). Remove expired orders from the list by calling the iterator's `remove` method. Also remove an expired order from the appropriate `Stock`'s priority queue.

6.♦♦   The following suggested projects require structural and detailed design, implementation, and testing. They also involve some adaptations of the `TradeWindow` GUI class. These projects work best as team projects.

(a)   Convert *SafeTrade* into an online store inventory system. Adapt the `Stock` class into the `StockItem` class with fields for the inventory code, full name, unit price, and quantity in stock. Adapt the `TradeOrder` class into a `PurchaseOrder` class. Let a buyer (a trader) request a quote (price, quantity in stock) and place purchase orders. Orders are executed right away if the item is in stock in sufficient quantity; otherwise the buyer receives an "Out of stock" message.

Add the capability to queue orders when the item is out of stock. Also add the capability to re-supply an item. To achieve this, derive a class `StoreManager` from `Trader` and make the manager's orders re-supply the item by <u>adding</u> a specified quantity and changing the price to the manager's specified price (as opposed to purchasing an item the way customers' orders do). A re-supply order should move the queue of pending orders along as far as possible.

(b)   Convert *SafeTrade* into a system for swapping baseball cards. Instead of stocks, the system maintains a database of card swap offers. A card is described by the player's name. A swap offer holds the name of a card on hand, the name of a desired card, and a reference to the user who requested the swap. When the user enters a new swap offer, the system examines all the current offers and tries to arrange a swap between two or three users. If possible, it executes the swap and notifies all the participants of that swap. If a swap is not immediately possible, the offer is added to the database of swap offers.

The `Exchange` class keeps all the active swap offers in a `HashMap`, keyed by the card name. Associated with each key is a list of all the offers to swap that card. Eliminate the `Stock` class and adapt the `TradeOrder` class for this application.

Continued ☞

(c)   Convert *SafeTrade* (or the baseball card trading system from Part (b)
into the *SafeAirways* flight reservation system. Instead of stocks, the
system maintains a database of Safe Airways's direct flights. Each
flight is described by its origin's airport code, destination's airport
code, departure time, flight duration, and fare. The airport codes are
three-letter strings; for example, Boston Logan airport is BOS, San
Juan is SJU, and Greenville, South Carolina is GSP. (A complete list
is available on many travel sites on the Internet.)

When the user enters the origin and destination codes, the system
should list all the possible itineraries that have at most two plane
changes with no more than a 180-minute wait between the flights. The
system calculates the total fare by adding up the fares for all the legs of
the itinerary. The user can request that itineraries be displayed in
ascending order by price or by total travel time.

The Exchange class (or whatever you want to call it now) keeps all
the direct flights in a HashMap, keyed by the origin's airport code.
Associated with each key is a list of all the flights from that origin.
Add a method to load all flights into this hash table from a file. The
file describes each flight on a separate line; the flights are listed in the
file in no particular order.

Eliminate the Stock and TradeOrder classes and add the Flight
and Itinerary classes. Add the price and travel-time comparators
for the itineraries. To produce the requested display, add all found
itineraries to a priority queue, then remove them one by one and show
to the user.

chapter

peach   *crate*   *heart*
teach   *caret*   *earth*
reach   *carpet*
preach   *chart*

10

Design Patterns

10.1 Prologue

Object-oriented design is not easy — it often takes more time than coding, and design errors may be more costly than errors in the code. **Design patterns** represent an attempt by experienced designers to formalize their experience and share it with novices. Design patterns help solve common problems and avoid common mistakes.

The idea of design patterns came to OOP from an influential writer on architecture, Christopher Alexander.[alexander] In his books, *The Timeless Way of Building*[*] and *A Pattern Language*,[**] Alexander introduced design patterns as a way to bring some order into the chaotic universe of arbitrary architectural design decisions. In *A Pattern Language*, Alexander and his co-authors catalogued 253 patterns that helped solve specific architectural problems and offered standard ideas for better designs.

No one has a good formal definition of a "pattern" — somehow we recognize a pattern when we see one. In fact we humans, and especially programmers, are very good at pattern recognition. We recognize a pattern as some recurring idea manifested in diverse situations. We talk about organizational patterns and patterns of behavior, grammatical patterns, musical patterns, speech patterns, and ornament patterns. Recognizing patterns helps us structure our thoughts about a situation and draw on past experiences of similar situations.

Experts, researchers, and volunteers have published some OO software design patterns in books, magazine articles, and on the Internet. The first and most famous book on the subject, *Design Patterns*, was published in 1995.[***] Since then, hundreds of patterns have been published, some rather general, others specialized for particular types of applications. Apparently many people enjoy discovering and publishing new design patterns. Great interest in design patterns is evident from the numerous conferences, workshops, discussion groups, and web sites dedicated to collecting and cataloguing patterns.[patterns]

A more or less standard format for describing patterns has emerged. A typical description includes the pattern name, a brief statement of its intent or the problem it

---

[*] C. Alexander, *The Timeless Way of Building*. Oxford University Press, 1979.
[**] C. Alexander, S. Ishikawa, & M. Silverstein, *A Pattern Language*. Oxford University Press, 1977.
[***] The famous "Gang of Four" book. *Design Patterns: Elements of Reusable Object-Oriented Software*, by Erich Gamma, Richard Helm, Ralph Johnson, and John Vlissides. Addison-Wesley, 1995.

solves, a description of the pattern, the types of classes and objects involved, perhaps a structural diagram, and an example, sometimes with sample code.

With too many patterns around, there is a danger that a novice may get lost. It may be a good idea to start with only a handful of the most commonly used ones and to understand exactly when and how they are used. One shouldn't feel inadequate if his initial design doesn't follow an "officially" named pattern. But if the design manifests a problem, the designer may try to find a pattern that deals with that kind of problem, fix the design, and follow the pattern in the future. Fortunately, unlike buildings, programs are not set in concrete — it is often possible to change the design through minor restructuring of classes while keeping most of the code intact. We have seen an example of this in the case study in the previous chapter. Once you find a standard pattern that fits your situation really well, it may bring you great satisfaction.

> **Being aware that OO design patterns exist helps you pay more attention to the design stage of your project before rushing to write code.**

In the following sections we briefly review and illustrate six common design patterns, "Façade," "Strategy," "Singleton," "Decorator," "Composite," and "MVC" (Model-View-Controller).

10.2 Façade

When you design a complex software system, it is often split into subsystems, each implemented in several classes. The Façade design pattern solves the problem of a complicated interface to a subsystem, replacing complex interfaces to several classes with one simpler interface to the whole subsystem. This is achieved by hiding the functionality of the subsystem's classes and their interactions in one "black-box" class.

One example is our `EasyReader` class, which provides a façade for the rather complicated system of Java input stream library classes. If you look at `EasyReader`'s code, you will see that this class hardly does any work — it simply delegates its responsibilities to the library classes. For example:

```
public EasyReader(String fileName)
{
  ///
  try
  {
    myInFile = new BufferedReader(new FileReader(fileName), 1024);
  }
  catch (FileNotFoundException e)
  {
    ...
  }
}

public String readLine()
{
  String s = null;

  try
  {
    s = myInFile.readLine();
  }
  catch (IOException e)
  {
    ...
  }
  ...
}
```

A beginner does not necessarily want to deal with different types of Java I/O classes or exceptions. `EasyReader` provides an adequate façade.

The Façade design pattern can also be used for encapsulating a process that involves several steps. Suppose we are designing an application for storage and automatic retrieval of scanned documents (e.g., parking tickets). A document has a number printed on it, and we want to use OCR (Optical Character Recognition) to read that number and use it as a key to the document. The OCR subsystem may include several components and classes: `ImageEditor`, `TextLocator`, `OCRReader`, and so on. For example:

```
...
Rectangle ocrArea = new Rectangle(200, 20, 120, 30);
ImageEditor imageEditor = new ImageEditor();
image = imageEditor.cut(image, ocrArea);
TextLocator locator = new TextLocator();
ocrArea = locator.findTextField(image);
String charSet = "0123456789";
OCRReader reader = new OCRReader(charSet);
String result = reader.ocr(image, ocrArea);
...
```

A client of the OCR subsystem does not need to know all the detailed steps — all it wants from the OCR subsystem is the result. The OCR subsystem should provide a simple façade class, something like this:

```
public class OCR
{
  public static String read(Image image, Rectangle ocrArea)
  {
    ImageEditor imageEditor = new ImageEditor();
    image = imageEditor.cut(image, ocrArea);
    ...
    return result;
  }
}
```

10.3 Strategy

The Strategy design pattern is simply common sense. If you expect that an object may eventually use different strategies for accomplishing a task, make the strategy module "pluggable" rather than hard-coded in the object. For example, in the design of our *Chomp* project, we neglected to make provisions for choosing different strategies for the ComputerPlayer. What if we need to support different levels of play or different board sizes? Do we change the ComputerPlayer class every time? And what if we need to choose a strategy at run time?

Obviously we need to change how strategy is handled in Chomp and the Strategy design pattern helps us to do it right. That's what we asked you to do in Question 7 for Chapter 1: to implement the Strategy design pattern.

The first step is to define an interface, Strategy, and have it implemented in different strategy classes. For example:

```
public interface Strategy
{
  Position findBestMove(ChompGame game);
  Position findRandomMove(ChompGame game);
}

public class Strategy3by7 implements Strategy
{
  ...
  public Position findBestMove(ChompGame game)
  {
    ...
  }
  ...
}
```

We then pass a `Strategy` object to the `ComputerPlayer`'s constructor and/or provide a method in `ComputerPlayer` that sets its strategy:

```
public class ComputerPlayer
    implements Player, ActionListener
{
  ...
  private Strategy strategy;
  ...

  public void setStrategy(Strategy s)
  {
    strategy = s;
  }
  ...
}
```

We can call `setStrategy` from `init` or `main` or from another higher-level class. We can even change the strategy in mid-game.

The Java Swing package follows the Strategy pattern for laying out components in a container. Different strategies are implemented as different types of `Layout` objects. A particular layout is chosen for a container by calling its `setLayout` method. For example:

```
JPanel panel = new JPanel();
GridBagLayout gbLayout = new GridBagLayout();
panel.setLayout(gbLayout);
```

❖　❖　❖

Our `Strategy` interface in *Chomp* could be even more general if we managed to exclude the references to `ChompGame` from its method calls. After all, there is only one game going on. There must be a way to make it accessible in all classes rather than passing it as a parameter. Maybe the Singleton pattern, described in the next section, can help.

10.4 Singleton

Suppose we want to have a "log" file in our program and we want to write messages to it from methods in different classes. We can create an EasyWriter object log in main. The problem is: How do we give all the other classes access to log? We only ever need <u>one</u> log file open at a time, and it is tedious to pass references to this file in various constructors and methods.

The first solution that comes to mind is to define a special LogFile class with a <u>static</u> EasyWriter field embedded in it. LogFile's methods are all static and they simply delegate their responsibilities to the corresponding EasyWriter methods. For example:

```
public class LogFile   // Does not follow Singleton pattern
{
  private static EasyWriter myLog;

  protected LogFile()  // Can't instantiate this class
  {
  }

  public static void createLogFile(String fileName)
  {
    if (myLog == null)
      myLog = new EasyWriter(fileName);
  }

  public static void println(String line)
  {
    if (myLog != null)
      myLog.println(line);
  }

  public static void closeLog()
  {
    if (myLog != null)
      myLog.close();
  }
}
```

Now main can call LogFile.createLogFile("log.txt"), and client classes can call LogFile.println(msg).

This solution works, but it has two flaws. First, `LogFile`'s methods are limited to those that we have specifically defined for it. We won't be able to use all `EasyWriter`'s methods unless we implement all of them in `LogFile`, too. Second, `LogFile` is a class, not an object, and we have no access to the instance of `EasyWriter` embedded in it. So we cannot do things with it that we usually do with an object, such as pass it to constructors or methods, add it to collections, or "decorate" it as explained in the next section.

The Singleton design pattern offers a better solution: rather than channeling method calls to the `EasyWriter` instance in the `LogFile` class, make that instance accessible to clients. Provide one static method in `LogFile` that initializes and returns the `EasyWriter` field embedded in `LogFile`, but make sure that that field is initialized only once and that the same reference is returned in all calls. For example:

```
public class LogFile
{
  private static EasyWriter myLog;

  protected LogFile()   // Can't instantiate this class
  {
  }

  public static EasyWriter getLogFile(String fileName)
  {
    if (myLog == null)
      myLog = new EasyWriter(fileName);
    return myLog;
  }

  public static void closeLog()
  {
    if (myLog != null)
      myLog.close();
  }
}
```

Now any method can get hold of the log file and use all `EasyWriter`'s methods. For example:

```
EasyWriter log = LogFile.getLogFile("log.txt");
log.print(lineNum);
log.print(' ');
log.println(msg);
```

This design is better, but not perfect. When the `get...` method takes an argument, as above, it gives the impression that we can construct different objects (e.g., log files with different names). In fact, the parameter has an effect only when the `get...` method is called <u>for the first time</u>. All the subsequent calls ignore the parameter. We could provide an overloaded no-args version of `get...` and call it after the log file is created.

In a slightly more sophisticated version, our `LogFile` class could keep track of the file names passed to its `getLogFile` method and report an error if they disagree. Or perhaps it could keep a set of all the different log files and return the file that matches the name. But then it wouldn't be a Singleton any more... Have we just discovered a new design pattern?

10.5 Decorator

Suppose you are designing a geometry package. You have started a little class hierarchy for triangles:

```
public abstract class Triangle
{
  ...
  public abstract void draw(Graphics g);
}

public class RightTriangle extends Triangle
{
  ...
  public void draw(Graphics g)
  {
    g.drawLine(x, y, x+a, y);
    g.drawLine(x, y, x, y-b);
    g.drawLine(x+a, y, x, y-b);
  }
}

public class IsoscelesTriangle extends Triangle
{
  ...
  public void draw(Graphics g)
  {
    g.drawLine(x, y, x-c/2, y+h);
    g.drawLine(x, y, x+c/2, y+h);
    g.drawLine(x-c/2, y+h, x+c/2, y+h);
  }
}
```

So far, so good. Now you want to add the letters *A, B, C* to denote vertices in your drawings. And sometimes to draw a median. Or a bisector. Or just a median but no letters. Or three medians. This is beginning to look like a nightmare. What do you do? Do you extend each of the classes to satisfy all these multiple demands? Like this:

```
public class RightTriangleWithMedian extends RightTriangle
{
  . . .
  public void draw(Graphics g)
  {
    super.draw(g);
    g.drawLine(x, y, x+a/2, y-b/2);
  }
}


public class IsoscelesTriangleWithMedian extends IsoscelesTriangle
{
  . . .
  public void draw(Graphics g)
  {
    super.draw(g);
    g.drawLine(x, y, x, y+h);
  }
}
```

And so on. And what if you want to construct a triangle object and sometimes show it with letters and sometimes without? Polymorphism won't allow you to show the same object in different ways.

The Decorator design pattern helps you solve these two problems: (1) the lack of multiple inheritance in Java for adding the same functionality to classes on diverging inheritance branches (e.g., adding letters to drawings of all kinds of triangles) and (2) the difficulty of changing or extending the behavior of an individual object at run time (e.g., drawing the same triangle object, sometimes with letters and other times without), as opposed to changing or extending the behavior of the whole class through inheritance.

The idea of the Decorator pattern is to define a specialized "decorator" class (also called a *wrapper* class) that modifies behavior or adds a feature to the objects of the "decorated" class. Decorator uses real inheritance only for inheriting the decorated object's data type. At the same time, decorator uses a kind of do-it-yourself "inheritance," actually modeled through embedding. It has a field of the decorated class type and redefines all the methods of the decorated class, delegating them to that embedded field. The decorator adds code to methods where necessary. The decorator's constructor initializes the embedded field to an object to be decorated.

This is how the code might look in our `Triangle` example:

```
public class TriangleWithABC extends Triangle
{
  private Triangle myTriangle;

  public TriangleWithABC(Triangle t)
  {
    myTriangle = t;
  }

  public void draw(Graphics g)
  {
    myTriangle.draw(g);
    drawABC(g);
  }

  ...

  private drawABC(Graphics g)
  {
    ...
  }
}
```

A more formal decorator diagram is shown in Figure 10-1.

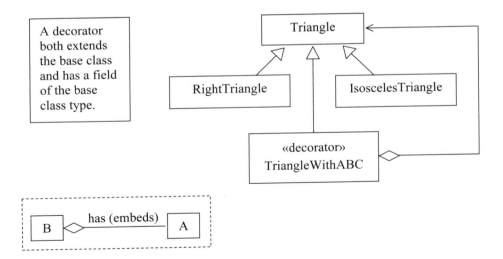

Figure 10-1. The Decorator design pattern

Now you can pass any type of triangle to your decorator. Polymorphism takes care of the rest. For example:

```
Triangle rightT = new RightTriangle(...);
Triangle isosT = new IsoscelesTriangle(...);
Triangle rightTwABC = new TriangleWithABC(rightT);
Triangle isosTwABC = new TriangleWithABC(isosT);
...
rightTwABC.draw(g);
isosTwABC.draw(g);
```

Or, for short:

```
Triangle rightTwABC =
      new TriangleWithABC(new RightTriangle(...));
Triangle isosTwABC =
      new TriangleWithABC(new IsoscelesTriangle(...));
rightTwABC.draw(g);
isosTwABC.draw(g);
```

This solves the first problem — adding the same functionality to classes on diverging inheritance branches.

You can also change the behavior of an object at run time by using its decorated stand-ins when necessary. For example:

```
Triangle rightT = new RightTriangle(...);
Triangle rightTwABC = new TriangleWithABC(rightT);
...
rightT.move(100, 50);        // moves both rightT and rightTwABC
...
rightT.draw(g);              // draw without A,B,C
...
rightTwABC.draw(g);          // draw THE SAME triangle with A,B,C
...
```

Since a decorated triangle is still a `Triangle`, we can pass it to another decorator. For example:

```
Triangle rightT = new RightTriangle(...);
Triangle rightTwABCwMedian =
    new TriangleWithMedian(new TriangleWithABC(rigthT));
```

Exactly the same structure would work if the base type to be decorated (e.g., `Triangle`) were an interface, rather than a class.

One problem with decorators is that we need to redefine all the methods of the base class (or define all the methods of the interface) in each decorator. This is repetitive and laborious. A better solution is to define a kind of abstract "decorator adapter" class, a generic decorator for a particular type of objects, and then derive all decorators from it. This structure is shown in Figure 10-2. The code may look as follows:

```
public abstract class DecoratedTriangle extends Triangle
{
  protected Triangle myTriangle;

  protected DecoratedTriangle(Triangle t)
  {
    myTriangle = t;
  }

  public void move(int x, int y)
  {
    myTriangle.move(x, y);
  }

  public void draw(Graphics g)
  {
    myTriangle.draw(g);
  }

  ...  // redefine ALL other methods of Triangle
}
```

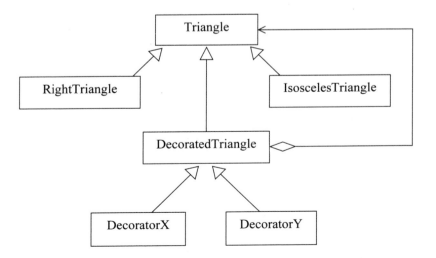

Figure 10-2. The Decorator design pattern with the intermediate abstract decorator class

Now you can derive a specific decorator from `DecoratedTriangle`, redefining only the necessary methods:

```
public class TriangleWithABC extends DecoratedTriangle
{
  public void TriangleWithABC(Triangle t)
  {
    super(t);
  }

  public void draw(Graphics g)
  {
    super.draw(g);
    drawABC(g);
  }

  private drawABC(Graphics g)
  {
    ...
  }
}
```

Decorators are a source of subtle bugs. An object of a decorator class possesses the same fields as the decorated object (because a wrapper class extends the wrapped class) but they are not used and may be not initialized. This may cause problems when a wrapped object is passed to a method that expects an unwrapped object and refers directly to its fields. That is why we should not really refer directly to fields of other objects passed to methods, even if they appear to be objects of the same type. Before you decorate a class, make sure it follows this convention.

In our own projects, we could have benefited from the Decorator pattern in Lab 2.7. In that project, we defined the `LinkedListFromFile` class, derived from `LinkedList`, with code to read a list from a file. A better way of doing this would be to implement the `java.util.List` interface in a `DecoratedList` class, then derive a `ListFromFile` decorator from it, so that we could decorate both `LinkedList` and `ArrayList`, adding methods or constructors to read a list from a file.

Decorators must be used with caution: too many decorative layers make code unreadable. The Java stream I/O package, for example, uses decorators extensively. As a result, we felt it was necessary to put a reasonable façade on it.

10.6 Composite

The Composite design pattern is a "recursive" pattern useful for nested structures. It applies when we want a list or a set of things of a certain type to also be a thing of that type.

Consider the example from Section 4.2 in the chapter on recursion. In it we discussed a list that can hold either strings or other lists of strings. We presented the following recursive code for printing out all the strings from all the lists and sublists:

```java
public void printAll(LinkedList list)
{
  Iterator iter = list.iterator();
  while (iter.hasNext())
  {
    Object obj = iter.next();
    String className = obj.getClass().getName();
    if ("java.lang.String".equals(className))
      System.out.println((String)obj);
    else // if ("java.util.LinkedList".equals(className))
      printAll((LinkedList)obj);
  }
}
```

Note the awkward `if-else` in this code — it is necessary because in the above setup a `String` and a `List` are different types of objects. The code would become more elegant if we used the Composite design pattern. Consider, for example the following two classes:

```java
public class Message
{
  private String myLine;

  public Message(String line)
  {
    myLine = line;
  }

  pubic void print()
  {
    System.out.println(myLine);
  }
}
```

```
public class Text extends Message
{
  private List myLines;     // contains Message type of objects

  public Text()
  {
    myLines = new LinkedList();
  }
  ...

  public void print()
  {
    Iterator iter = myLines.iterator();
    while (iter.hasNext())
      ((Message)iter.next()).print();
          // works polymorphically both for a simple Message
          //   object and for a composite Text object
  }
}
```

Note that a `Text` object both is a `Message` and contains a list of `Messages`. Therefore, we can add `Message` objects to a `Text` object without worrying whether they are simple "one-liners" or other "texts." For example:

```
Message fruits = new Text();
fruits.add("apples");
fruits.add("and");
fruits.add("bananas");
Message song = new Text();
song.add("I like to eat");
song.add(fruits);
song.print();
```

When we call `print` for a `Text` object, polymorphism makes sure that all the `Messages` in its internal list are printed properly.

The `java.awt` package uses the Composite pattern for handling GUI components: a `Container` is a `Component` and we can also add `Components` to it. Polymorphism makes sure that all components, both "simple" and "composite," are correctly displayed.

10.7 MVC (Model-View-Controller)

Suppose you are designing a 3-D geometry package. You want to demonstrate visually that the surface area of a sphere is proportional to its radius squared and that the volume is proportional to the radius cubed. When the user enters a new radius, your program displays a scaled picture of the sphere, the numbers for the surface area and volume, and perhaps a bar chart that compares them. The user can also stretch the model sphere with a mouse and the numbers change automatically (Figure 10-3).

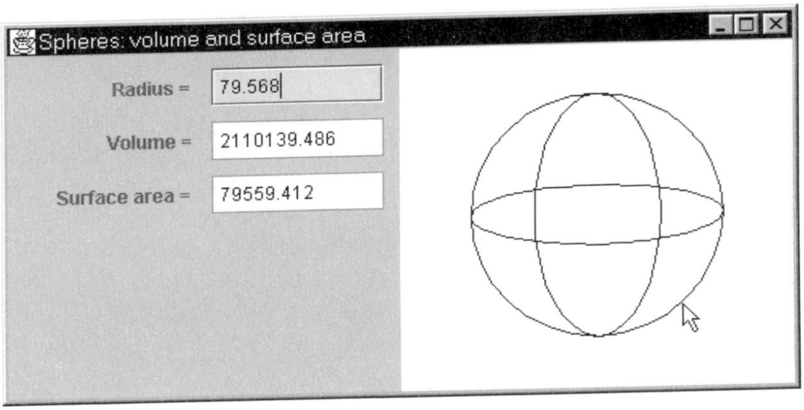

Figure 10-3. Sphere model with text and mouse input

As you know, the first rule in a program of this kind is to isolate the model part (representation of a sphere) and separate it from the GUI part (control and display functions). In this example, we can discern several different "views" of the model: the graphics view that shows a picture of the sphere, the text view that displays the numbers for the surface area and volume, and perhaps other views. It is reasonable to implement these different views as different classes.

There are also a couple of different "controllers": one lets the user type in the radius of the sphere, the other lets the user change the radius with the mouse. Again we may want to implement them as different classes. The problem is how to structure the interactions between all these classes. The MVC design pattern offers a flexible solution.

MVC applies to situations where you have a "model" class that represents a system, a situation, or a real-world or mathematical object. The model's fields describe the state of the model. The model class is isolated from the user interface, but there are one or several "views" of the model that reflect its state. When the state changes, all the views have to be updated.

You might be tempted to set up a "totalitarian system" in which one central controller updates the model and manages all the views. In this approach, the model is not aware that it is being watched and by whom. The controller changes the model by calling its modifier methods, gets information about its state by calling its accessor methods, and then passes this information to all the views (Figure 10-4). For example:

```
//  "Totalitarian system"

public class SphereController implements ActionListener
{
  private Sphere sphereModel;
  private TextView view1;
  private GraphicsView view2;
  ...

  public SphereController()
  {
    sphereModel = new Sphere(100);
    view1 = new TextView();
    view2 = new GraphicsView();
    ...
  }

  private void updateViews()
  {
    double r = sphereModel.getRadius();
    view1.update(r);
    view2.update(r);
  }

  public void actionPerformed(ActionEvent e)
  {
    String s = ((JTextField)e.getSource()).getText();
    double r = Double.parseDouble(s);
    sphereModel.setRadius(r);  // update the model
    updateViews();             // update the views
  }
  ...
}
```

This setup becomes problematic if requests to change the model come from many different sources: GUI components, keyboard and mouse event listeners, timers, even the model itself. All the different requests would have to go through the cumbersome central bureaucracy.

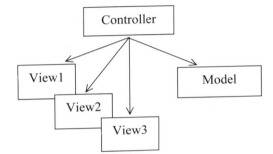

Figure 10-4. "Totalitarian" control of the model and the views

MVC offers a decentralized solution where the views are attached to the model itself. The model knows when its state changes and updates all the views when necessary (Figure 10-5). An MVC design can support several independent views and controllers and makes it easy to add more views and controllers.

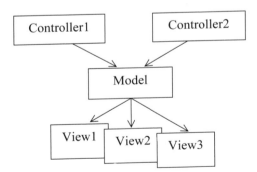

Figure 10-5. The MVC design pattern

In our example, the MVC code with one controller might look like this:

```java
public class SphereController implements ActionListener
{
  private Sphere sphereModel;
  private TextView view1;
  private GraphicsView view2;
  ...

  public SphereController()
  {
    sphereModel = new Sphere(100);
    sphereModel.addView(new TextView());
    sphereModel.addView(new GraphicsView());
    ...
  }

  public void actionPerformed(ActionEvent e)
  {
    String s = ((JTextField)e.getSource()).getText();
    double r = Double.parseDouble(s);
    sphereModel.setRadius(r);
  }
  ...
}

public class Sphere
{
  ...
  public setRadius(double r)
  {
    myRadius = r;
    updateAllViews();
  }
  ...
}
```

The model keeps all the views attached to it in some kind of a set or list.

❖   ❖   ❖

The Java library supports MVC designs by providing the Observable class and the Observer interface in its java.util package. If your "model" class extends Observable, it inherits a reference to the initially empty list of observers and the addObserver method for adding an observer to the list. Your class also inherits the setChanged method for raising the "model changed" flag and the notifyObservers method for notifying all the registered observers.

Each view registered with the model must implement the `Observer` interface and provide its one required public method:

```
void update(Observable model, Object arg);
```

The first argument is the observed model; the second argument is any object passed from the model to the view as a parameter.

Figure 10-6 shows how it all might look in our example.

```
public class SphereController implements ActionListener
{
  private Sphere sphereModel;
  ...

  public Controller()
  {
    sphereModel = new Sphere(100);
    sphereModel.addObserver(new TextView());
    sphereModel.addObserver(new GraphicsView());
    ...
  }

  public void actionPerformed(ActionEvent e)
  {
    String s = ((JTextField)e.getSource()).getText();
    double r = Double.parseDouble(s);
    sphereModel.setRadius(r);
  }
  ...
}

public class TextView
    implements java.util.Observer
{
  ...
  public void update(Observable model, Object arg)
  {
    Sphere sphere = (Sphere)model;
    ...
  }
}
```

Figure 10-6 continued

```
public class GraphicsView
    implements java.util.Observer
{
  ...
  public void update(Observable model, Object arg)
  {
    Sphere sphere = (Sphere)model;
    ...
  }
}


class Sphere extends java.util.Observable
{
  ...
  public void setRadius(double r)
  {
    myRadius = r;
    setChanged();            // Indicates that the model has changed
    notifyObservers();       // Or: notifyObservers(someObjectParameter)
  }
  ...
}
```

Figure 10-6. A sketch for the "Sphere" classes with `Observer/Observable`

The `notifyObservers` method in the model class calls `update` for each registered observer. If `notifyObservers` is called with some object as a parameter, that parameter is passed to `update` (as its second argument); if the model calls the overloaded no-args version of `notifyObservers`, then the parameter passed to `update` is `null`.

The complete code for our MVC sphere example with two controllers and two views is included on your student disk in the `Ch10\Mvc` folder 🖫.

❖ ❖ ❖

In our case studies and labs we tried to follow the MVC design pattern where possible. For example, in our *Chomp* case study (Figure 1-9 on page 23), the applet class and the players are controllers, the `ChompGame` class is the model, and the `ChompBoard` is the view. We did not use `Observer-Observable` there because the model had only one view and it was easier to handle it directly.

Java's Swing follows MVC in implementing GUI components. For example, the `JButton` class is actually a façade for the `DefaultButtonModel` (model), `BasicButtonUI` (view), and `ButtonUIListener` (controller) classes. This design makes it possible to implement "pluggable look and feel" by changing only the views.

MVC can be applied to more than just visual display: a "view" class can play sounds, update files, and so on. A "view" can also keep track of some global properties or statistics. For example, in our *SafeTrade* case study we can attach to each Stock object a "total volume" view that will keep track of (and possibly display) the total volume of all shares traded.

The MVC design pattern is not universal. While it is always a good idea to isolate the "model" from the user interface, the "view" and "controller" may sometimes be intertwined too closely for separation. When you are filling out a form on the screen, for example, the viewing and controlling functions go together. There is no need to stretch a design pattern to fit a situation where it really does not apply.

10.8 Summary

We have described half a dozen design patterns to give you an idea of what design patterns are about and to help you get started. Many more patterns have been published. Being generally aware of their existence brings the problem of sound OO design into focus. Following specific design patterns helps beginners avoid common mistakes. An OOP designer should gradually get familiar with the more famous patterns and learn how and when to apply them.

The Façade design pattern is used to shield clients from the complexities of a subsystem of classes by providing a simplified interface to them in one "façade" class. A façade may serve as a "black box" for a process or a function.

The Strategy design pattern deals with attaching strategies (algorithms, solutions, decisions) to objects. If you want your design to be flexible, isolate each strategy in its own class. Have a higher-level class or main choose a strategy and attach it to a client. Do not allow a client to create its own strategy, because that will make it harder to change that client's strategy.

The Singleton design pattern deals with situations where you need to have only one object of a certain class in your program and you want to make that object readily available in different classes. A "Singleton" class embeds that object as a static field and provides a static accessor to it. The accessor initializes the object on the first call but not on subsequent calls.

The <u>Decorator design pattern</u> solves the problem of adding the same functionality to classes on diverging inheritance branches without duplication of code. It also offers an elegant solution for modifying an object's behavior at run time. A decorator both extends the base class and embeds an instance of the base class as a field. The decorator's methods delegate their responsibilities to the embedded field's methods but can also enhance them. A decorator provides a constructor that takes an object of the base class (or any class derived from it) as an argument. That is why decorator classes are also called wrapper classes.

The <u>Composite design pattern</u> is used for implementing nested structures. A "composite" is a class that both inherits from a base class and contains a set or a list of objects of the base class type. This way a composite can hold both basic objects and other composites, nested to any level.

The <u>MVC design pattern</u> offers a flexible way to arrange interactions between a "model" object, one or more "controller" objects, and one or more "view" objects. The views are attached to the model, which updates all the views when its state changes. Java supports MVC design by providing the `Observable` class and the `Observer` interface in its `java.util` package. The "model" class extends `Observable`, which provides methods to add an observer to the model and to notify all observers when the model needs to update them. A view class implements the `Observable` interface and must provide the `update` method, which is called when observers are notified.

Design patterns offer general ideas but should not be followed slavishly. Don't try to stretch a pattern to fit a situation where it does not apply.

❖   ❖   ❖

OO design patterns and tools represent a bold attempt to turn the art of software design into something more precise, scientific, and teachable. But, behind all the technical terms and fancy diagrams, some art remains an essential ingredient. As we said in the prologue to the opening chapter, software structures are largely hidden from the world. Still, something — not only the need to finish a project on time — compels a designer to look for what Christopher Alexander called "the quality without a name": order, balance, economy, fit to the purpose, and, in Alexander's words, "a subtle kind of freedom from inner contradictions." Let us join this search — welcome, and good luck!

Exercises

1. Many people have found that the Java library classes `Calendar` and
    `GregorianCalendar`, which handle date and time, are hard to use.
    Sketchy documentation, a few unfortunate choices for method names, and
    the fact that the months are counted starting from 0 — all add to the
    confusion. The calendar classes are rather general, yet lack some useful
    methods that one would expect in a date class (e.g., methods that tell you the
    number of days between two dates and make dates `Comparable`).

    To get the current month (an integer from 1 to 12) and day you need to get a
    `GregorianCalendar` object first, then call its `get` method with the field ID
    parameter for the field you need:

    ```java
    import java.util.Calendar;
    import java.util.GregorianCalendar;
    ...
        Calendar calendar = new GregorianCalendar();
        int month = calendar.get(Calendar.MONTH) + 1;
        int day = calendar.get(Calendar.DATE);
    ```

    To find the number of days from one date to another date you need to get a
    calendar for each date, get the time difference in milliseconds, and convert it
    into the number of days. Something like this:

    ```java
    Calendar calendar1 =
        new GregorianCalendar(year1, month1 - 1, day1);
    Calendar calendar2 =
        new GregorianCalendar(year2, month2 - 1, day2);
    long ms = (calendar2.getTimeInMillis() -
            calendar1.getTimeInMillis());
    int days = ... // convert ms to days,
                // rounding to the nearest integer
    ```

Continued ➥

Write a simple "Façade" class `EasyDate` with fields for the month, day, and year. Make `EasyDate` objects immutable and `Comparable`. Supply a no-args constructor that creates an `EasyDate` with settings for the current date and another constructor that creates a date with a given month (1-12), day, and year. Provide three corresponding accessor methods, `getMonth`, `getDay`, and `getYear`. Add a `toString` method that returns a string for the date in the format `"mm/dd/yyyy"`, and a method

```
public int daysTo(EasyDate otherDate)
```

that returns the number of days from this date to `otherDate`.

2.■   The game of Goofenspiel is played by two players. Each player has the same set of cards, let's say 13 (one full suit), represented by values from 1 to 13. On each move the players simultaneously open one card. The bigger card wins and the player takes the trick (both cards). In case of a tie, neither player gets the trick and the cards are discarded. The player with most tricks wins.

In the computer version, the cards are open but the computer plays "honestly," not using the information about the opponent's move.

Devise a couple of different strategies for the computer and implement the game in accordance with the "Strategy" design pattern. Make the computer switch strategies if it loses two or three games in a row. ✓

3.   Test whether the `java.util.Calendar` class and its `getInstance` method follow the "Singleton" design pattern: that is, whether the same `Calendar` object is returned by all calls to `Calendar.getInstance`.

4. Write and test a "Singleton" class `FavoriteColor`, with methods

```
public static void set(Color c)
public static Color get()
```

The `set` method should throw an `IllegalArgumentException` if an attempt to reset the previously set favorite color is made.

5.▪ Define an abstract "decorator" class for `EasyDate` from Question 1. Write a decorator for `EasyDate` (extending the abstract decorator) that is aware of the English names for the months and whose `toString` method returns the date in the format `"<Month name> d, yyyy"` (e.g., `"May 10, 2005"`). Write another decorator class with methods

```
public int getDayOfWeek()
public String getDayOfWeekName()
```

`getDayOfWeek` returns this date's day of the week (e.g., 0 for Sunday, 1 for Monday, etc.) and `getDayOfWeekName` returns the name of this date's day of the week (e.g., `"Sunday"`). Hint: January 1, 1970 was a Thursday.

Test your two decorator classes in a small program that prints out the full dates (including month names) of Labor Day (the first Monday in September) and Thanksgiving (the fourth Thursday in November) for a given year.

6.   An "expression" is either a simple variable or the sum or product of two expressions (of any kind). Implement the `Expression` interface with one `int` method, `getValue`.

(a)   Write a class `Variable` that implements `Expression`. Provide the fields to hold the variable's name and its `int` value, appropriate constructors, and the `getValue` and `setValue` methods. Also provide the `toString` method that returns the variable's <u>name</u>.

(b)   Write the `SumExpression` and `ProductExpression` classes that implement `Expression` in accordance with the "Composite" design pattern. Provide a constructor for the `SumExpression` class that makes a sum expression out of two given expressions. Do the same for the `ProductExpression` class. For each of the classes, provide a method `toString` that converts this expression into the standard infix notation, adding parentheses around sums. Consider for example, the following code:

```
Variable a = new Variable("A");
Variable b = new Variable("B");


Expression aPlusB = new SumExpression(a, b);
Expression aPlusBsquared =
            new ProductExpression(aPlusB, aPlusB);

a.setValue(2);
b.setValue(3);

System.out.println(a + " = " + a.getValue());
System.out.println(b + " = " + b.getValue());
System.out.println(aPlusBsquared + " = " +
        aPlusBsquared.getValue());
```

Its output should be:

```
A = 2
B = 3
(A + B)  *  (A + B)  = 25
```

7.   Make sure the program for Goofenspiel from Question 2 complies with the MVC design pattern and revise it making use of `Observer/Observable`.

8.▪   `HanoiTowersPuzzle.java`, `HanoiTowersModel.java`, `HanoiTowersView.java`, and `HanoiTowersMove.java`, in the `Ch10\Exercises` 🖫 folder on your student disk make a simple GUI application that solves the *Towers of Hanoi* puzzle, described in Section 4.5. This implementation, however, is contrary to the MVC design pattern: the model is created and controlled by the "view." Modify this program to make it comply with MVC, using `Observer` and `Observable`.

9.♦   Explain why "MVC" and "Composite" (for the model) don't go together well. For example, the `SumExpression` or `ProductExpression` classes from Question 5 may fail as a model in MVC. Can you think of a way to make it work?

Appendix A: Interfaces and Classes in the AP Java Subset (AB)

java.lang:

class java.lang.**Object**

```
boolean equals(Object other)
String toString()
int hashCode()
```

interface java.lang.*Comparable*

```
int compareTo(Object other);
```

class java.lang.**Integer**
              implements java.lang.Comparable

```
Integer(int value)
int intValue()
boolean equals(Object other)
String toString()
int compareTo(Object other)
```

class java.lang.**Double**
              implements java.lang.Comparable

```
Double(double value)
double doubleValue()
boolean equals(Object other)
String toString()
int compareTo(Object other)
```

class `java.lang.`**String**
            `implements java.lang.Comparable`

```
int compareTo(Object other)
boolean equals(Object other)
int length()
String substring(int from, int to)
String substring(int from)
int indexOf(String s)
```

class `java.lang.`**Math**

```
static int abs(int n)
static double abs(double x)
static double pow(double base, double exp)
static double sqrt(double x)
```

`java.util.`Random

class `java.util.`**Random**

```
int nextInt()
double nextDouble()
```

`java.util`: Lists and Iterators

interface `java.util.`*List*

```
boolean add(Object obj)
int size()
Iterator iterator()
ListIterator listIterator()
```

class `java.util.`**ArrayList implements** `java.util.`**List**

```
// In addition to the List methods:
Object get(int index)
Object set(int index, Object obj)
void add(int index, Object obj)
Object remove(int index)
```

```
class java.util.LinkedList implements java.util.List

    // In addition to the List methods:
    void addFirst(Object obj)
    void addLast(Object obj)
    Object getFirst()
    Object getLast()
    Object removeFirst()
    Object removeLast()


interface java.util.Iterator

    boolean hasNext()
    Object next()
    void remove()


interface java.util.ListIterator extends java.util.Iterator

    // In addition to the Iterator methods:
    void add(Object obj)
    void set(Object obj)
```

java.util: Sets and Maps

```
interface java.util.Set

    boolean add(Object obj)
    boolean contains(Object obj)
    boolean remove(Object obj)
    int size()
    Iterator iterator()

class java.util.TreeSet implements java.util.Set
class java.util.HashSet implements java.util.Set


interface java.util.Map

    Object put(Object key, Object value)
    Object get(Object key)
    boolean containsKey(Object key)
    int size()
    Set keySet()

class java.util.TreeMap implements java.util.Map
class java.util.HashMap implements java.util.Map
```

AP: `Stack` and `Queue`

interface *Stack*

```
boolean isEmpty()
void push(Object obj)
Object pop()
Object peekTop()
```

class ArrayStack implements Stack
class ListStack implements Stack

interface *Queue*

```
boolean isEmpty()
void enqueue(Object obj)
Object dequeue()
Object peekFront()
```

class ListQueue implements Queue

AP: `PriorityQueue`

interface *PriorityQueue*

```
boolean isEmpty()
void add(Object obj)
Object removeMin()
Object peekMin()
```

AP: `ListNode` and `TreeNode`

```java
public class ListNode
{
  public ListNode (Object initValue, ListNode initNext)
    { value = initValue; next = initNext; }

  public Object getValue() { return value; }
  public ListNode getNext() { return next; }

  public void setValue(Object theNewValue) { value = theNewValue; }
  public void setNext(ListNode theNewNext) { next = theNewNext; }

  private Object value;
  private ListNode next;
}


public class TreeNode
{
  public TreeNode (Object initValue, TreeNode initLeft,
                                      TreeNode initRight)
    { value = initValue; left = initLeft; right = initRight; }

  public Object getValue() { return value; }
  public TreeNode getLeft() { return left; }
  public TreeNode getRight() { return right; }

  public void setValue(Object theNewValue) { value = theNewValue; }
  public void setLeft(TreeNode theNewLeft) { left = theNewLeft; }
  public void setRight(TreeNode theNewRight) { right = theNewRight; }

  private Object value;
  private TreeNode left;
  private TreeNode right;
}
```

Appendix B: Swing Examples Index

(In Addition to Java Methods)

EmptyBorder

```
Ch05\Messenger\Messenger.java
Ch06\Giggle\Giggle.java
Ch10\SafeTrade\GUILogin.java
Ch10\SafeTrade\TraderWindow.java
```

GridBagLayout

```
Ch10\SafeTrade\TraderWindow.java
```

JComboBox

```
Ch05\Messenger\MsgWindow.java
```

JFileChooser

```
Ch06\Cryptogram\Cryptogram.java
Ch06\Giggle\Giggle.java
```

JFrame

```
Ch05\Messenger\MsgWindow.java
Ch05\Morse\Telegraph.java
Ch10\SafeTrade\TraderWindow.java
```

JMenuBar

```
Ch06\Cryptogram\Cryptogram.java
Ch06\Giggle\Giggle.java
```

JOptionPane

```
Ch05\Messenger\Messenger.java
Ch06\Cryptogram\Cryptogram.java
Ch06\Giggle\Giggle.java
Ch10\SafeTrade\GUILogin.java
Ch10\SafeTrade\TraderWindow.java
```

JRadioButton

```
Ch10\SafeTrade\TraderWindow.java
```

JScrollBar

```
Ch03\Browser\BrowserView.java
```

JScrollPane

```
Ch06\Cryptogram\Cryptogram.java
Ch06\Giggle\Giggle.java
Ch05\Messenger\MsgWindow.java
Ch10\SafeTrade\TraderWindow.java
```

JTextArea

```
Ch05\Messenger\MsgWindow.java
Ch05\Morse\Telegraph.java
Ch06\Cryptogram\Cryptogram.java
Ch06\Giggle\Giggle.java
Ch10\SafeTrade\TraderWindow.java
```

Index